D1061030

Joseph Conrad

Joseph Conrad

Narrative Technique and Ideological Commitment

JEREMY HAWTHORN

Professor of Modern British Literature
University of Trondheim, Norway

Edward Arnold

A division of Hodder & Stoughton
LONDON   NEW YORK   MELBOURNE   AUCKLAND

ROBERT MANNING
ST. OZIER LIBRARY

OCT 29 1990

Tallahassee, Florida

PR
6005
.O4
Z7426
1990

ROBERT MANNING
STROZIER LIBRARY

OCT 30 1990

Tallahassee, Florida

For Bjørg

© 1990 Jeremy Hawthorn

First published in Great Britain 1990

Distributed in the USA by Routledge, Chapman and Hall, Inc.
29 West 35th Street, New York, NY 10001

British Library Cataloguing in Publication Data

Hawthorn, Jeremy *1942–*
 Joseph Conrad : Narrative technique and ideological
 commitment.
 1. Fiction in English. Conrad, Joseph, 1857–1924
 I. Title
 823'.912

 ISBN 0-340-52859-1

All rights reserved. No part of this publication may be reproduced or
transmitted in any form or by any means, electronically or
mechanically, including photocopying, recording or any information
storage or retrieval system, without either prior permission in writing
from the publisher or a licence permitting restricted copying. In the
United Kingdom such licences are issued by the Copyright Licensing
Agency: 33–34 Alfred Place, London WC1E 7DP.

Typeset by the author.
Printed and bound in Great Britain for Edward Arnold, the
educational, academic and medical publishing division of Hodder and
Stoughton Limited, Mill Road, Dunton Green, Sevenoaks, Kent
TN13 2YA by Biddles Ltd, Guildford and King's Lynn

Contents

Acknowledgements

Acknowledgements are due to Yale University Library, for permission to reproduce excerpts from the manuscript of Joseph Conrad's *Under Western Eyes* in the the Beinecke Rare Book and Manuscript Library, and to the British Library for permission to reproduce excerpts from 'The Rescuer', the manuscript of Joseph Conrad's *The Rescue*, Ashley Library 4787.

Two of the chapters in this book have been published previously in different versions. Chapter 9 was published as 'Bodily Communication in Joseph Conrad's *Under Western Eyes*' in *Anglo-American Studies* III(2), April 1983. Chapter 3 was published as 'The Incoherences of *The Nigger of the "Narcissus"*' in *The Conradian* II(2), November 1986.

I gratefully acknowledge a number of more personal debts incurred during the writing of this book. My largest debt is to Jakob Lothe of the University of Bergen, whose study *Conrad's Narrative Method* (Clarendon Press, 1989), I was privileged to be able to read before publication, and whose comments on my own work have always been penetrating. Josiane Paccaud of the University of Grenoble has read and commented very helpfully on my first chapter. Two anonymous readers read the complete typescript of the book and made a number of valuable comments and suggestions, and Gordon Williams provided helpful information about the Declaration of London. My considerable debt to these various readers should not obscure my own responsibility for any errors and inadequacies remaining in the book.

I am extremely grateful to Kirsti Rye Ramberg and Jarle Rønhovd for sharing their knowledge about computers and laser printers with me, and to my wife for putting up with all this for three years.

Publication of this book has been assisted by a grant from the Norwegian Research Council for Science and the Humanities. I am extremely grateful to the Council for its support.

Jeremy Hawthorn
University of Trondheim, Norway
November, 1989

A Note on References and Abbreviations

Conrad's work presents some problems to the literary critic wishing to quote from it. Conrad makes frequent use of ellipses, and it is frequently necessary to distinguish between his ellipses and those which represent the critic's omissions. In common with other recent studies of Conrad I use double-spaced ellipses to represent Conrad's own ellipses, and single-spaced ones to represent my own omissions from his text. All ellipses in quotations from writers other than Conrad represent my own abbreviation of the text unless otherwise indicated.

Conrad's 'Marlow' works also offer some additional difficulties. The standard Dent Collected Edition sets an opening inverted comma at the start of each paragraph 'spoken' by Marlow, but only at the end of full passages of narration. For the purpose of clarity, I have enclosed all quotations spoken by Marlow in opening and closing inverted commas. In common with current British practice I have used single inverted commas where the Dent Collected Edition uses double ones, and vice-versa.

All quotations from Conrad's works are from the Dent Collected Edition, and from the initial printing rather than from reset editions. The plates of this edition are photographically reproduced with some minor corrections in the recent World's Classics edition of some of Conrad's works published by OUP. Where such World's Classics editions exist I have checked quotations against them so as to include any minor corrections made to the text.

The following abbreviations have been used.

AF	*Almayer's Folly*
OI	*An Outcast of the Islands*
NOTN	*The Nigger of the 'Narcissus'*
TOU	*Tales of Unrest*
LJ	*Lord Jim*
HOD	*Heart of Darkness*
TEOTT	*The End of the Tether*
MOS	*The Mirror of the Sea*
SA	*The Secret Agent*
SSix	*A Set of Six*
UWE	*Under Western Eyes*

APR	*A Personal Record*
SL	*The Shadow-Line*
NLL	*Notes on Life and Letters*
TOH	*Tales of Hearsay*
LE	*Last Essays*
CLJC 1/2/3	Frederick R. Karl & Laurence Davies (eds.), *The Collected Letters of Joseph Conrad*, vol. 1 1861-1897, Cambridge, CUP, 1983; vol. 2 1898-1902, Cambridge, CUP, 1986; vol. 3 1903-1907, Cambridge, CUP, 1988.
JCLL 1 & 2	G. Jean-Aubry, *Joseph Conrad Life and Letters*, vols 1 & 2, London, Heinemann, 1927.
LCG	C. T. Watts (ed.), *Joseph Conrad's Letters to R. B. Cunninghame Graham*, London, CUP, 1969.

Introduction

> The value of creative work of any kind is in the *whole* of it. Till that is seen no judgment is possible. Questions of phrasing and such like - *technique* - may be discussed upon a fragmentary examination; but phrasing, expression - *technique* in short has importance only when the Conception of the whole has a significance of its own apart from the details that go to make it up . . .
>
> (CLJC 2, p. 332)

This comment - from a 1901 letter to Ford Madox Ford - provides ample confirmation of Joseph Conrad's understanding that technical skill and virtuosity were not alone sufficient to guarantee 'the value of creative work of any kind'. Conrad's development as a novelist involves the maturing and refinement of a variety of technical skills, but until and unless these are complemented and subtended by a larger vision and commitment - a 'conception of the whole' - they do not result in great art.

The present book is concerned with certain specific aspects of this interplay between technical accomplishment and artistic conception. Since the publication of my first book on Conrad in 1979, I have become increasingly engaged by the dialectic between the consummate control of narrative distance and perspective in Conrad's greatest fiction, and the moral and human commitment which this control serves. Put another way: I am fascinated by the productive interaction between an extreme flexibility and mobility of narrative on the one hand, and a rootedness of *moral and human* commitment on the other. This interests me partly because I see it as so central to Conrad's achievement, but also because it reminds us of what is perhaps *the* central problem of modernist fiction: how is the modern novelist to prevent a multi-perspectival view of the world (or even a view of 'the world' as inescapably constituted by and divided between multiple perspectives upon it) from degenerating into relativism, solipsism, and (very soon after) triviality? In my previous book on Conrad I argued that although recognizably modernist in many ways and prone to those solipsistic fears we associate with writers such as Pirandello, Joyce and Woolf, Conrad is essentially a materialist rather than an idealist, possessed of an unshakeable belief in the existence of a world independent of its perception by human beings.[1] I still believe this to be the case, and feel that it is one of the factors which determined that although Conrad was arguably the first great modernist novelist in the English language, his major fiction avoids many of the blind alleys of subsequent modernist (not to mention post-modernist) writing.

This is not all that original an observation. Ian Watt expressed a comparable opinion when, talking of the ways in which Conrad is both more contemporary and more old-fashioned than his modern peers, he explained

> Old-fashioned because Conrad's movement towards the ageless solidarities of human experience was much commoner among the Romantics and Victorians. But the first half of his life had forced Conrad to see that his problematic dependence on others was a necessary condition for the very existence of the individual self; and so during the second half of his life his imagination was impelled, in many different ways, to confront a more contemporary question, and one which was not to be of any particular concern to the other great figures of modern literature: 'Alienation, of course; but how do we get out of it?'[2]

The alienation with which Conrad engaged in his fiction forced certain techniques upon him. If he were fully to explore a world in which the experience of alienation was endemic, his fiction would have to be possessed of a maximal flexibility of narrative perspective. The isolated and hidden centres of consciousness, experience, and power of this world would have to be persuaded to give up their secrets to a narrative that could pass where no non-fictional consciousness could freely enter. But unless his narrative maintained some fixed reference points – moral, evaluative, human – this supreme narrative mobility would be to no avail, would have no justifying goal, would be lost in experiential space.

Now in one sense what I have said so far, although it clearly reflects very important advances in the theory of narrative that have been attained during the past decade or so, does not chime with a broadly based consensus amongst many of those theorists of narrative who have been influenced by Structuralist ideas. I talk of Conrad, rather than of his narrators, 'narrative voices', dominant ideologies, or whatever. Did not such theorists as Roland Barthes and Michel Foucault long ago announce the death of the author and conclude that the ceremony of the funeral was over?

Nevertheless, I start not just with Conrad's fiction, but with Conrad and (and in) his fiction. For what I have to say of technique and commitment in Conrad's works has a polemical relevance to developments in modern narrative theory. This theory has been of enormous value to our understanding of fiction through its painstaking and detailed isolation of productive technical distinctions. But in its tendency to limit itself to such work and, indeed, to deny the worth of more traditional moral approaches to literature which insist upon the human situation and responsibilities of reader and writer – including what Conrad calls 'the conception of the whole' (and he means the writer's conception) – it risks enslaving its undoubted insights to a variety of more or less trivial ends. This is not to suggest that I recognize no discontinuities between an author's everyday beliefs, attitudes and commitments, and those beliefs, attitudes and commitments which crystallize artistically in the creative moment; clearly there are such discontinuities – and not least so far as Conrad is concerned. But these discontinuities are not absolute. They involve processes of mediation, transformations of vision, which join the human being's and the writer's insights and ideologies. We should trust the tale rather than the teller, but narrative transformations of extra-literary visions serve as links between tale and teller.

No modern critic of the novel can fail to be radically indebted to the work of those modern narrative theorists who have established not just a detailed vocabulary for the isolation and investigation of significant narrative detail, but also that set of fundamental insights which lies behind this vocabulary. To this work I am happy to acknowledge a substantial debt. And yet the insights of which I speak have themselves, I believe, to be complemented by another 'conception of the whole'. In his essay, 'Structure and History in Narrative Perspective: The Problem of Point of View Reconsidered',[3] Robert Weimann insists that the question of the novelist's relationship with his or her work (and, by implication, with the world that the work engages with), and the narrator's relationship with the story told, cannot be divorced from each other. He concludes that

> In the act of telling his story, the teller of the tale is faced, not simply with a series of technical problems and not only with the rhetorical task of communication, but with a world full of struggle and change where the writer, in order to transmute his story into art, has constantly to reassess his relations to society as both a social and an aesthetic act. In the process of doing this, he will find that his own experience as an artist in history is so related to the social whole that the flexibility (which involves the precariousness) of this relationship itself is the basis on which representation and evaluation are integrated through point of view.[4]

It seems to me that at his greatest Conrad is always able, as Weimann puts it, to reassess his relations to society as both a social and an aesthetic act – and a key word here is *relations*. In his finest fiction, however impeccably skilled Conrad's manipulation of narrative perspective, he never forgets that a perspective is a relationship, *on* something or somebody *from* a particular human consciousness and situation. But not all of Conrad's fiction attains this level of achievement, and in subsequent chapters I will try to show how the loss of his moral or ideological anchorage is artistically disastrous to Conrad, however skilled his manipulation of narrative perspective may be. Weimann argues that although the modern novelist is unable to attain to the 'wholeness' available to earlier novelists, he or she can yet achieve an element of integrity through the linking of representation and evaluation. This seems to me to be one of the essential sources of Conrad's artistic and aesthetic integrity, and how it is achieved without unartistic intrusiveness is worthy of investigation.

Given the somewhat all-embracing nature of my comments so far, the topic of my first chapter might appear somewhat limited. To focus in on one particular element in Conrad's armoury of narrative techniques, and in such detail and at such great length, may on first sight appear perverse. But represented speech and thought is not just a technique of minor significance in Conrad's fiction (or in the novel in general); it is a crucially important means whereby narrative flexibility is not only enormously refined and extended, but also linked to the author's evaluative and moral commitments. By following Conrad's developing use of represented speech and thought from *Almayer's Folly* through to *Chance*, I hope to be able to illustrate the way in which a technique which is central to his artistic achievement is useless when detached from an intellectually active moral consciousness. I will argue, moreover, that essential technical decisions concerning the use of represented speech and thought have their moral and ideological side; to put it crudely, to determine what the narrative knows and in what ways it knows what it knows, the author has to engage with the question of what the narrative – and, thus, indirectly, the author – believes and is committed to.

In three chapters I suggest that artistic failure or, at least, incomplete success, in Conrad's fiction is typically related to a failure on precisely this point: a failure to determine what values the narrative espouses or underwrites. And although such failures are not *mechanically* related to problems in Conrad's own system of beliefs and moral commitments, as I argue in my second, third and fourth chapters (on Conrad and social class, *The Nigger of the 'Narcissus'*, and *Chance*) there certainly is a relationship between Conrad's own hesitations and uncertainties, and artistic flaws in his fiction.

Hesitations and uncertainties are common to us all, of course, and in the case of many of the greatest artists they fuel the creative act. In a famous comment in one of his letters Keats defined what he called *negative capability* – the quality he believed went to form 'a Man of Achievement' – as the capability of being in uncertainties, mysteries, doubts, without any irritable reaching after fact and reason. The writer who has no doubts is hardly worth reading. But the hesitations and uncertainties that I see harming some of Conrad's works of fiction are moral and intellectual hesitations and doubts that are disfiguring, and in the chapters in question I will attempt to show why this seems to me to be so. A couple of preliminary answers are possible. Firstly, that a writer's choice of subject presupposes some sort of commitment to certain human values. It is not that the writer has to know all the answers, but that he or she should have some commitment to why the question or questions are important. And secondly, that where legitimate doubts and hesitations exist, then the narrative has either to *dramatize* them as I argue they are dramatized in *Heart of Darkness* but not in *The Nigger of the 'Narcissus'*, or acknowledge their existence and incorporate them into the artistic vision of the work as Conrad does in *The Secret Agent* and *Under Western Eyes* but not in *The Rescue* or *Chance*. The discovery of Marlow clearly plays a crucial rôle here, but there are other factors to consider in addition. In *The Nigger of the 'Narcissus'*, *The Rescue* and *Chance*, Conrad's failures to resolve (among other things) political and moral problems relating to race, class and gender, are disabling because the problems concerned require either a commitment from the author, or an artistic acknowledgement and dramatization of his inability to attain such a commitment. In the absence of such a 'conception of the whole', technical flexibility in the manipulation of artistic perspective becomes less a virtue and more akin to moral or intellectual vacillation.

In the three great works concerned with imperialism the story is quite different. 'An Outpost of Progress', *Heart of Darkness* and *Nostromo* weld an assured human and moral commitment on to a mature flexibility of technical perspective. Indeed, the flexibility owes much to this commitment, for it is this which tells the narrative where to go, what to look for, and how to judge what is found.

Typhoon, as I suggest in my chapter on this work, again shows Conrad almost self-consciously manipulating his narrative so as to obtain maximal flexibility of perspective. His adaptation of epistolary techniques in this work is powerfully linked to an investigation into the rôle of the imagination as enabling and disabling force. The ability to manipulate narrative perspective is thus linked to the imaginative act itself, that act of putting ourselves into the position of another person which is at the root of all moral discrimination and decision.

My chapter on *Under Western Eyes* may seem to concern itself with a somewhat abstruse element within the work. But Conrad's portrayal of non-linguistic, non-intellectual forms of human expression and communication is such as to remind us that imaginative sympathy with others has more than one route that can be followed. There is a comment in William Faulkner's *Absalom, Absalom!* which is relevant to my interest in Conrad's concern with bodily communication in *Under Western Eyes*: 'let flesh touch with flesh, and watch the fall of all the eggshell shibboleth of caste and colour'. We recognize the humanity of others, and express aspects of ourselves for them, in bodily and physical as well as linguistic and intellectual ways. These are also ways of obtaining a perspective on people and events, familiar to us all but too often forgotten. Conrad is not so much concerned with shibboleths of caste and colour in *Under Western Eyes*, but he is concerned with political oppression, and the moral dilemmas which are attendant upon political action, especially in a society that imposes secrecy on its members.

The very title of this work – arguably Conrad's last novel to achieve full artistic greatness – focuses our attention on to the issue of perspective, both human and narrative. What we see is related to where we are looking from. And in its concern with the paradox that to escape from alienation we must make moral choices which require the sort of many-sided perspective on events which we can rarely achieve precisely because of our alienation, the novel forces us to see the relevance of Razumov's experiences to ourselves. Like Razumov, we live in a world in which other people are sometimes reduced to a collection of disembodied parts, and in which our own thoughts and opinions do not match our experience of the world. To escape from an intolerable situation we must have the imaginative flexibility to interpret a world in which important truths are given to us only in the form of incomplete clues. But it is not enough to learn techniques of interpretation unless we have an unalienated ideal to which these techniques are subservient – as Razumov discovers. We need 'a conception of the whole' which is moral rather than purely technical.

In *A Personal Record* Conrad admitted that

> [W]hat is interesting to a writer is the possession of an inward certitude that literary criticism will never die, for man (so variously defined) is, before everything else, a critical animal. (APR, p. 96)

Our critical impulse drives us, like Razumov, to perfect better and better techniques of interpretation. But unless we have learned to put these techniques at the disposal of a determining moral intelligence, we will never exploit their potential for human betterment. Razumov learns this in the course of *Under Western Eyes*, and his discovery reflects a comparable discovery made by his creator at the level of his artistic creativity.

In my chapter on 'The Tale' I see this relatively neglected work of Conrad's to be concerned with related issues, but with a difference. What are the moral implications of our discovery that our powers of imaginative penetration are (as they necessarily are) limited? What if the writer of fiction puts his or her reader into a situation where the limits of imaginative perception can be vicariously experienced? What moral and intellectual conclusions can be drawn? Whereas in *Under Western Eyes* the reader habitually observes Razumov from a position of privileged knowledge, in 'The Tale' the narrator's ignorance of certain key matters parallels our own. Decoding here is less delayed than permanently postponed, and this act of postponement leaves the reader in a position familiar to every human being. Thus although 'The Tale' is undoubtedly a minor work in the canon of Conrad's fiction, and one with shortcomings familiar in other of his works which are recognizably melodramatic to a greater or lesser extent, in the history of Conrad's artistic grappling with the aesthetic transformations of his own doubts, contradictions and ignorance, the work has a summarizing and concluding importance which, I hope, justifies its closer study.

---

1 Jeremy Hawthorn, *Joseph Conrad: Language and Fictional Self-consciousness*, London, Arnold, 1979, p. 15.
2 Ian Watt, *Conrad in the Nineteenth Century*, London, Chatto, 1980.
3 In Robert Weimann, *Structure and Society in Literary History*, Charlottesville, UP of Virginia, 1976.
4 Weimann, p. 237.

1
Seeing and Believing: Represented Speech and Thought in Conrad's Fiction

Introductory: what is represented speech and thought?

Tracing the development of Conrad's use of a particular narrative technique through his most productive years as a writer of fiction may seem a somewhat dull technical exercise. But a study of this particular narrative technique is unusually revealing. For in choosing how to represent the speech, thought, consciousness of his or her characters, a novelist simultaneously makes crucial choices regarding the attitude that the narrative takes to them. And at the same time, the novelist reveals something of his or her attitudes to the story told, something of his or her own values and commitments. All such choices, like the choices a film director makes concerning camera placing and angle, allow a novelist to include some things and to exclude others; they have a determining effect upon the mood and tone of the story in question, and they *situate* the reader in a particular way, not just with regard to technical perspective, but also with regard to moral and human viewpoint. A novelist's decision concerning what the reader knows and how he or she knows it inevitably has a bearing on a range of issues: the relationship between narrative and story,[1] the relationship between writer and reader, the relationship between writer and work, and the relationship between the writer and the world which inspires and receives his or her creative work.

But the technique I have referred to as represented speech and thought – more economically, Free Indirect Discourse[2] – is especially revelatory of an author's choices and commitments. It provides the writer of fiction with enormous narrative flexibility and mobility. With its help the narrative can not only move freely *to* any point of action or experience, but also *from* any one point in the work's implied value-system to another. Gérard Genette has familiarized us with the important distinction between perspective and voice, between 'who sees' and 'who speaks'. The distinction is not identical to that between technical and ideological perspective, but it has strong points of similarity. So that a study of an author's use of Free Indirect Discourse (henceforth FID) not only helps us to recognize what he or she is interested in revealing, but also from what standpoint – technical and evaluative – he or she wishes the reader to experience this revelation.

FID is found neither in drama nor in non-narrative poetry. Conrad could have learned its use from any one of a whole range of novelists he is known to have read, but given the technique's apparently independent appearance in a number of different literatures no direct influence needs to be posited; it seems that it is one which emerges naturally in prose narrative. Conrad's use of the technique varies in range and extent very considerably from work to work. *Heart of Darkness* has hardly any examples of its use, while *The End of the Tether* has repeated and extensive ones. But although examples can be found throughout Conrad's writing career, one can observe Conrad developing and perfecting his use of the technique as he matures as a writer.

Let us start with the following passage:

> 'Kaspar! Makan!'
> The well-known shrill voice startled Almayer from his dream of splendid future into the unpleasant realities of the present hour. An unpleasant voice too. He had heard it for many years, and with every year he liked it less. No matter; there would be an end to all this soon.
>
> (AF, p. 3)

The initial few lines of *Almayer's Folly*, Conrad's first published work, also represent the first published example in his fiction of FID. We can note that the opening lines of the novel move from Direct Speech, through what is clearly a statement from an extra-mimetic[3] narrative perspective, to sentences which give us Almayer's own thought processes, but in a rather special form. 'An unpleasant voice too. He had heard it for many years, and with every year he liked it less'. These two sentences *could* be read as continuing the detached statements of an extra-mimetic (or even omniscient) narrator. But the final sentence quoted above exhibits the classic features of FID, and reacts back on the two sentences preceding it, making it clear that they too belong to this characteristic form of narrative.

'No matter; there would be an end to all this soon'. Dorrit Cohn, in her book *Transparent Minds*, suggests that FID 'may be most succinctly defined as the technique for rendering a character's thought in their own idiom while maintaining the third-person reference and the basic tense of narration'.[4] We know that the above sentence does not come from the narrator – at least, we can be quite sure of this upon rereading the novel – because the narrator knows very well that there will *not* be an end to 'all this' soon; it is Almayer's mistaken assumption that this is the case. But even upon initial reading of the novel most readers will respond to certain signs that tell them that they are reading FID. What are these signs? Firstly, the truncated form of the sentence such as 'An unpleasant voice too', which we take as typical of spoken English and thus – by implication – of a character's mode of thinking. Such truncation is not normally associated with the expression of a narrator's opinion in extra-mimetic or omniscient narration. Secondly, the use of colloquialisms not normally utilized in Reported Speech without an explanatory comment assigning them to an originator, especially exclamations or ejaculations ('No matter' in the above extract, for example). Thirdly, FID gives the impression, as Shlomith Rimmon-Kenan has it in her book *Narrative Fiction*, of combining Direct Discourse with Indirect Discourse. Rimmon-Kenan sums up the differences between Direct Discourse [DD – what I call Direct Speech], Indirect Discourse [ID – what I call Reported Speech], and FID in the following example:

DD: He said, 'I love her'
ID: He said that he loved her
FID: He loved her[5]

We see that in FID we have a characteristic deletion of the reporting verb and of the conjunction 'that' associated with Reported Speech – thus introducing a similarity with Direct Speech – along with a use of the verb form associated with Reported Speech. The transposition of tenses in FID involves, as Rimmon-Kenan points out, the same characteristic 'shift-back' of tenses to be found in Reported Speech. From the opening sentences of *Almayer's Folly*, therefore, we can reconstruct a hypothetical Direct Speech original for Almayer's thoughts: 'I have heard it for many years and with every year I like it less. No matter; there will be an end to all this soon'. Furthermore, FID normally retains deictics used in Direct Speech but amended in Reported Speech. We can suggest the following illustrative table again:

Direct Speech: 'There will be an end to all this soon'.
Reported Speech: 'He said that there would be an end to all that shortly (or before long)'.
FID: 'There would be an end to all this soon'.

Thus both the word 'soon' and also the use of 'this' rather than 'that' indicate that Conrad's sentence is FID rather than Direct or Reported Speech. Finally, as I have suggested, on a rereading the presence of FID is betrayed by the actual content of the utterance: we know that the narrator would not make this statement, and we know that Almayer could. Very often content is the only firm clue that we are dealing with FID.

Brian McHale has suggested that grammatical approaches to the definition of FID have their limitations. He sees it as typical of 'derivational' approaches to FID (that is, approaches which work from a presumed 'original' Direct Speech utterance through to Reported Speech and FID versions) that they account for FID strictly grammatically. He suggests an alternative approach derived from the work of Paul Hernadi, based upon the traditional Platonic typology of modes of poetic discourse.

> Hernadi's innovation is to posit a third category midway between authorial presentation (diegesis) and *re*presentation/impersonation (mimesis), namely 'substitutionary narration.'[6]

As McHale notes, one advantage of this approach is that 'one is now free to take his three types as points on a continuum along which other types of representation may be located'.[7] For literary-critical purposes this has clear advantages, for it matches one's intuitive sense of the continuum-like nature of the phenomenon one is investigating (especially in Conrad's works, where we find an exceptional flexibility and mobility in the manipulation of narrative perspective), and obviates the need for a string of 'exceptions' to certain rigid grammatical rules defining three (or more) fixed grammatical categories.

The presence of FID so early in Conrad's work suggests that it formed a natural part of his armoury of narrative techniques (it is also to be found in the short story 'The Black Mate', for those inclined to believe Conrad's protestation that this was his first attempt at writing fiction). Much of Conrad's fiction relies very heavily on FID; we might even say that many characteristic Conradian features would have been impossible without it. A failure to be alert to Conrad's use of FID can lead to serious misreadings: typically, an attribution of statements and sentiments to Conrad's authorial narrator[8] instead of to the character whose consciousness the FID is actually presenting for the reader.

But something needs to be added to these technical comments. In the example I have quoted from *Almayer's Folly* it is clear, surely, that Conrad's use of FID contributes, crucially, to *the perspective on Almayer we are given*; it involves a decision as to how the reader is encouraged to see *and to judge* Almayer. Without its use, the way we perceive and respond to Almayer would be different from what it is. A study of the rôle of FID in Conrad's fiction leads us straight into the moral complexities of these works.

The early novels

Conrad's early work shows a generally assured if restricted reliance upon FID, using it to represent thought rather than speech, and verbal rather than non-verbal thought. In his first attempts at fiction, FID is often resorted to for the purpose of rhetorical effects such as irony. Take the following passage from early on in *Almayer's Folly*:

> Startled by the unexpected proposal [from Hudig that he marry the latter's adopted daughter], Almayer hesitated, and remained silent for a minute. He was gifted with a strong and active imagination, and in that short space of time he saw, as in a flash of dazzling light, great piles of

shining guilders, and realized all the possibilities of an opulent existence. The consideration, the indolent ease of life – for which he felt himself so well fitted – his ships, his warehouses, his merchandise (old Lingard would not live for ever), and, crowning all, in the far future gleamed like a fairy palace the big mansion in Amsterdam, that earthly paradise of his dreams, where made king amongst men by old Lingard's money, he would pass the evening of his days in inexpressible splendour. As to the other side of the picture – the companionship for life of a Malay girl, that legacy of a boatful of pirates – there was only within him a confused consciousness of shame that he a white man – Still, a convent education of four years – and then she may mercifully die. He was always lucky, and money is powerful! Go through it. Why not? He had a vague idea of shutting her up somewhere, anywhere, out of his gorgeous future. Easy enough to dispose of a Malay woman, a slave, after all, to his Eastern mind, convent or no convent, ceremony or no ceremony. (AF, p. 10)

This passage probably presents no practised reader of fiction with any problems, although the narrative shifts which it contains are extremely complex. This suggests that readers adapt as naturally to FID in narrative fiction as writers do to its use. Full FID seems to me to start in the above passage with the sentence, 'He was always lucky, and money is powerful!' This clearly represents Almayer's, rather than a narrative, belief because the sentiments expressed are quite at odds with the implications of narrative irony earlier in the passage and in the novel. From the sentence we can retrieve a form of words which might actually have been used by Almayer – 'I've always been lucky, and money is powerful!'[9]

Now immediately preceding this sentence we have had a sentence that seems to be Direct Speech, although it lacks inverted commas. Before this sentence we have a long passage which appears in the main to be authorial narrative comment.[10] Why should we get this movement through three different narrative forms? One obvious explanation is that in the passage in question Almayer moves from what are primarily mental *images* to words, from visions of luxury to internal verbal comments upon his situation. At this time in his writing career Conrad seems to reserve FID for unambiguously verbal (rather than visual or imagistic) thought. Thus in *Almayer's Folly*, the slave-girl Taminah's consciousness is never rendered through FID, and we must presume that the explanation of this is that she has no self-consciousness (p. 112), and 'in the extremity of her distress she could find no words to pray for relief' (p. 118).

If we accept that in general the reader is most conscious of the presence of the narrative voice in Reported Speech, least conscious in Direct Speech, and either conscious or unconscious in the case of FID, then we can see that movement between these three forms allows the author to make the reader more or less aware of a guiding narrative presence at will and without drawing the reader's attention to such shifts of perspective. The passage quoted is a good example: at times we experience and think with Almayer, at times we look at him from the perspective of a particular system of attitudes and values provided by the narrative.

We see a similar pattern of Reported Speech used for the depiction of imagistic thought blending into FID for the depiction of verbal thought in another passage from *Almayer's Folly*:

> He remembered well that time – the look, the accent, the words, the effect they produced on him, his very surroundings. He remembered the narrow slanting deck of the brig, the silent sleeping coast, the smooth black surface of the sea with a great bar of gold laid on it by the rising moon. He remembered it all, and he remembered his feelings of mad exultation at the thought of that fortune thrown into his hands. He was no fool then, and he was no fool now. Circumstances had been against him; the fortune was gone, but hope remained. (AF, p. 11)

The move into FID is clearly signalled both by the content of the last two sentences quoted (that Almayer is not a fool is his own rather than a narrative opinion), and by the deictic 'now'. It is worth pointing out that were the penultimate sentence in the quoted passage to have been omitted, the final sentence would read as Reported Speech; the penultimate sentence, as unambiguous FID, prompts the reader to read the final sentence also as FID.

An important rule or pattern can be abstracted from this simple point. The reader naturally assumes a constancy of narrative perspective until given a clear sign that there has been a change. Thus where a sentence or utterance is ambiguous – as in the final sentence of the above extract – the reader takes his or her cue from preceding and succeeding sentences, and more from the former. Retrospective redefinition of narrative perspective normally involves meta-commentary rather than a mere switch of perspective, and Conrad's early work has a number of such examples.

Thus we find the following explanatory tags following passages of FID in *Almayer's Folly*: 'Such were Almayer's thoughts as, standing on the verandah of his new but already decaying house' (p. 4); 'At this point in his meditation' (p. 14); 'she thought' (p. 22); 'and so thinking' (p. 43); 'Such were Babalatchi's thoughts as he skilfully handled his paddle' (p. 61).[11] These meta-commentaries suggest a certain nervousness on Conrad's part relating to his early use of FID, a nervousness that the reader may not realize that the statements given represent the character's rather than a narrating consciousness. Clearly such retrospective signalling of FID is rather unsatisfactory; it interrupts the flow of the narrative, and forces the reader to go back over what has been read. It is probably significant that all the above quoted examples involve thought or self-address rather than dramatic speech. It might be a little misleading to say that they are all examples of represented thought rather than represented speech, as in many cases it seems that the character is almost speaking to himself. Distinguishing between represented thought and represented speech is more complex than one might at first think because two separate issues are involved here: firstly, is the character thinking or speaking, and secondly, is the character using words or engaging in imagistic – or at any rate non-verbal – thought? Although the former question seems the more important when one first seeks to distinguish represented thought from represented speech, it seems to me that the second question gets at an equally profound and productive distinction.

Almayer's Folly contains only examples of FID which are designed to convey the verbal, silent thought of a character. In neither *Almayer's Folly* nor *An Outcast of the Islands* is FID ever used for speech or for non-verbal thought; its use is exclusively reserved for the silent, verbal thoughts of an individual character. Indeed, where a character moves from speech to thought in these early novels, Conrad seems almost automatically to switch from either Direct or Reported Speech to FID. A typical example occurs early on in *An Outcast of the Islands*:

> 'Oh no, my dear, no,' muttered absently Mr Vinck, with a vague gesture. The aspect of Willems as a wife-beater presented to him no interest. How women do misjudge! If Willems wanted to torture his wife he would have recourse to less primitive methods. (OI, p. 10)[12]

It would seem, then, that although skilled, Conrad's use of FID in his early fiction is limited in scope. It allows him to move in and out of characters' consciousnesses with minimal disruption, avoiding the problems of an over-intrusive narrator who seems to be telling the reader things all the time. This last point notwithstanding, Conrad's use of FID allows him, even at this point, to exploit the potential for irony brought with it by the technique, an irony that depends upon a contrast between outlook and point of view of the character and those of the narrator or narrative perspective. Here is a representative passage from early on in *An Outcast of the Islands*:

> Willems walked on homeward weaving the splendid web of his future. The road to greatness lay plainly before his eyes, straight and shining, without any obstacle that he could see. He had stepped off the path of honesty, as he understood it, but he would soon regain it, never to leave it any more! It was a very small matter. He would soon put it right again. Meantime his duty was not to be found out, and he trusted

in his skill, in his luck, in his well-established reputation that would disarm suspicion if anybody dared to suspect. (OI, p. 11)

We see here almost a weaving together of Reported Speech and FID; the comment about the path of honesty must come from within Willems's consciousness, as the unambiguous FID of the latter half of the quotation includes comment upon this. ('It was a very small matter' must be the view of Willems rather than of the narrator.) The narrator also knows that Willems never will regain the path of honesty, so that the sentence beginning 'He had stepped off' must be FID. However, 'as he understood it' seems certainly narrator comment woven into this initial sentence of FID, and 'that he could see' serves both as Willems's comment to himself and also as an ironic warning to the reader from an extra-mimetic narrative perspective. This juxtaposition of two perspectives for ironic effect by means of FID becomes more and more developed as Conrad matures as a writer. It also, of course, introduces greater possibilities of ambiguity, an ambiguity that can lead both to problems and to new expressive potentialities. I will look more at this issue later.

What I would like to stress here is that in *Almayer's Folly* Conrad's use of FID seems always to carry some evaluative force. From the passages I have analysed so far it should be clear that when Conrad shifts from Reported Speech to represented thought we become far more conscious of the narrator and his or her values (or, to put it more precisely, we become more aware of the judgemental aspect of the narrative without being made conscious of an intrusive narrator). We may predict, therefore, that any attempt to isolate the values underwritten by Conrad's narrative will need to pay careful attention to the use of FID.

This can be illustrated by reference to one particular aspect of his early use of the technique. Conrad's first two novels involve a number of examples of FID used to convey the thoughts of 'native' people, and these have some particular points of interest.

There was in her the dread of the unknown; but otherwise she accepted her position calmly, after the manner of her people, and even considered it quite natural; for was she not a daughter of warriors, conquered in battle, and did she not belong rightfully to the victorious Rajah?

(AF, p. 22)

The words 'for was she' clearly introduce a passage of FID, for they express sentiments foreign to the narrative perspective of the novel. They also seem to echo a 'native' way of talking, using a form of word-inversion to form the sort of rhetorical sentences which Conrad often ascribes to Malayan speakers of English, and referring to Lingard as 'Rajah', which the narrator never does. We see this same mimicking of 'native' speech habits in the following example:

> the statesman of Sambir [Babalatchi] asked himself with a sinking heart when and how would it be given him to return to that house. He had to deal with a man more dangerous than any wild beast of his experience: a proud man, a man wilful after the manner of princes, a man in love. And he was going forth to speak to that man words of cold and worldly wisdom. Could anything be more appalling? What if that man should take umbrage at some fancied slight to his honour or disregard of his affections and suddenly 'amok'? (AF, p. 132)

This passage is, I think, represented (verbal) thought in the main: Babalatchi is asking himself, 'When will it be given to me to return to that house &c &c'. What is, I think, interesting about it is that while on the one hand it contains some formulations meant to indicate Babalatchi's manner of speaking – 'a man wilful after the manner of princes', 'and he was going forth' – it also contains words that are probably not such as would have been spoken by Babalatchi – 'take umbrage', 'fancied slight'.[13] And this leads to my substantive point. Surely these passages show us that while Conrad tries to get closer to the consciousness and way of thinking of these characters, he actually succeeds in getting nearer to a stereotyped, paternalist-colonialist view of them. They become slightly ridiculous. We look down rather patronizingly on the limitations of their understanding, on the quaintness of their way of expressing themselves. What we are given is not the characters 'in themselves', but as they appear to a contemporary European who is not unsympathetic to them, but who cannot escape from his preconceptions.

FID and narrative ambiguity

This sort of blending is one of the reasons why some commentators on FID have insisted that it offers us a form of 'dual voice', a mixing of 'narrative' and 'character' perspectives and consciousnesses.[14] I will come back to this issue later on.

Another reason is that the ambiguity allowed for by the technique may provide the opportunity for double attribution of utterances – not simultaneous double attribution, but consecutive or alternating, as with a person who sees Wittgenstein's duck-rabbit in rapid succession as duck/rabbit/duck/rabbit and so on. Consider the following passage:

> The sunlight streamed on her, on him, on the mute land, on the murmuring river – the gentle brilliance of a serene morning that, to her, seemed traversed by ghastly flashes of uncertain darkness. Hate filled the world,

filled the space between them – the hate of race, the hate of hopeless
diversity, the hate of blood; the hate against the man born in the land of
lies and of evil from which nothing but misfortune comes to those who
are not white. (OI, p. 359)

The first quoted sentence seems clearly to be narrative comment; it is not
Aïssa who thinks of the sunlight streaming on 'the mute land' or 'the
murmuring river' – she sees the world 'traversed by flashes of ghastly
darkness'. But in the part of the last sentence beginning with 'the hate
against the man' we seem to be in the presence of FID, for it is Aïssa and
not the narrator who believes Willems to come from 'the land of lies and
of evil from which nothing but misfortune comes to those who are not
white',[15] although this view may receive some implied sympathy from the
narrator. In between these two points there is uncertainty. Is the narrator
telling us that 'Hate filled the world', or is this what Aïssa believes at this
point? On the one hand it seems unlikely that Aïssa would think in such
conceptual terms given what we have been told of her, but on the other
hand one of the conventions of FID is that the words used by the writer
should not be assumed to have been used by the character concerned, so
that the words could be being used to evoke a non-verbalized attitude of
Aïssa.

Conrad's first two novels contain remarkably few ambiguities of this
sort, and those there are are of little importance. Even this early in his
writing career Conrad is adept at giving clear if not always subtle signals
regarding his use of FID. Just how small a signal is needed can be illustrated from the manuscript of Conrad's novel *The Rescue*, which is generally known as 'The Rescuer' after its early title. Near the beginning of this
manuscript there is an interesting passage introducing the mate Shaw to
the reader, and giving the reader Shaw's view of the captain, Lingard. A
deleted version reads as follows, deleted words in square brackets. We are
told of Shaw that of Lingard

> he generally approved although he recognized with regret that [the man
> had some absurd fads – 'bottom-upwards notions' – as he expressed it in
> discreet whisper]

The final manuscript version reads as follows:

> he generally approved although he recognized with regret that this man,
> like most others, had some absurd fads. He defined them as 'bottom-
> upwards notions'. (p. 18)

That slight change from 'the man' to 'this man' seems to me to be crucial,
edging this statement over into what is clearly FID. 'The man' could be

the narrator speaking; 'this man' is surely Shaw. (The passage is interesting, too, as it seems to represent a recurrent, rather than a specific, view or attitude of Shaw's.)

The common reader, I suspect, moves through *Almayer's Folly* and *An Outcast of the Islands* without being at all puzzled by the shifts of perspective accomplished by means of FID. This point is very important, for it suggests that when such ambiguity *does* occur in Conrad's work it is unlikely to be the result of any *technical* incompetence. When the reader does not know to whom an utterance or belief is to be ascribed in Conrad's fiction, it is very often arguable that Conrad himself either does not know or does not wish us to know. This point is relevant to my later consideration of *The Nigger of the 'Narcissus'*.

'An Outpost of Progress'

With 'An Outpost of Progress' we move to what is perhaps Conrad's first masterpiece, a work which seems without flaws, and in which Conrad's control of tone and perspective exhibits an astonishing maturity of judgement. One aspect of this maturity of judgement is Conrad's ability to sustain an ironic perspective on the two white men and what they represent, while introducing subtle modulations of pity and resignation – we could say of distance – within this consistency of tone. The description of the director of the ironically-named Great Trading Company on the second page of the story could, in some respects, be applied to the narrator of 'An Outpost of Progress': 'The director was a man ruthless and efficient, who at times, but very imperceptibly, indulged in grim humour'. There is a seeming ruthlessness in the assured finality of the pessimistic outlook of the narrator in this short story, but this ruthlessness is undercut and questioned by almost imperceptible touches of grim humour which bespeak a despairing concern and a humanity seemingly absent from the surface of the narrative.

In 'An Outpost of Progress' Conrad's use of FID is more varied and more sophisticated than it has been before.

> Gobila's manner was paternal, and he seemed really to love all white men. They all appeared to him very young, indistinguishably alike (except for stature), and he knew that they were all brothers, and also immortal. The death of the artist, who was the first white man whom he knew intimately, did not disturb this belief, because he was firmly convinced that the white stranger had pretended to die and got himself buried for some mysterious purpose of his own, into which it was useless to inquire. Perhaps it was his way of going home to his own country? At any rate, these were his brothers, and he transferred his absurd affection to them. They returned it in a way. Carlier slapped him on the back, and recklessly

struck off matches for his amusement. Kayerts was always ready to let
him have a sniff at the ammonia bottle. In short, they behaved just like
that other white creature that had hidden itself in a hole in the ground.

(OP, pp. 95-6)

One representative aspect of this passage is the contrast detectable
between the sad, almost wearied, and pitying certainty of the omniscient
narrative voice on the one hand, and the extremely limited understanding
of the characters considered on the other. In a curious way this short story
reminds us of the Christian God witnessing, sadly but with unsurprised
resignation, the shortcomings of His creation. This contrast is highlighted
in part through Conrad's use of FID, for this use allows him to juxtapose
the omniscience of the narrator and the blinkered outlook and understanding of the characters to maximal effect. 'Perhaps it was his way of going
home to his own country'[16] contrasts sharply with the all-knowing
comments which have preceded it, and the contrast is the more telling
because we move directly from narrative viewpoint to character viewpoint
with no interrupting meta-commentary or explanatory tag. In the next
sentence the words 'his absurd affection' give a clear indication that we
are leaving Gobila's consciousness and returning to the narrator's viewpoint, although the phrase 'these were his brothers' might be read as a
fragment of Gobila's thought inserted in the narrative flow for ironical
effect.[17] However, with the sentence beginning 'In short', we are unambiguously back into FID. (It cannot be Direct Speech because we have
'behaved' not 'behave'; it cannot be authorial comment because of the
content of the second part of the sentence.) Of course, the first-time
reader is not in a position to appreciate this until he or she gets more or
less to the end of the sentence, and so will read this sentence first
attributing it to the narrator and then correcting this attribution. The initial
misattribution makes an important contribution to the ironic tone of the
story, as the words involved have a bitter and even savage power when
given authorial force, and the flavour of this bitterness lingers even after
the reader has realized that the sentence is not authorial comment.

In this story Conrad uses FID to represent spoken utterance for
what I believe to be the first time in his fiction. The passage after the first
two sentences quoted below could represent Gobila's unspoken thoughts,
but the context suggests to me that it represents the words Gobila uses to
dissuade his warriors from burning and killing.

[Gobila's] heart was heavy. Some warriors spoke about burning and
killing, but the cautious old savage dissuaded them. Who could foresee
the woe these mysterious creatures, if irritated, might bring? They should
be left alone. Perhaps in time they would disappear into the earth as the

first one had disappeared. His people must keep away from them, and hope for the best. (OP, p. 107)

We should perhaps note in passing that Gobila turns out to be quite correct about Carlier and Kayerts disappearing into the earth, and his prophecy serves as a recognition of the power for self-destruction contained in the culture represented by the two white men.

We have only to imagine the above passage rewritten with Gobila's sentiments represented in Direct Speech to see how crucial Conrad's use of FID is in terms of irony and distance. The use of FID reminds us of the presence of the narrator all the time that Gobila's views are being expounded; it is almost as if we can see the narrator smiling in mournful agreement as he hears Gobila's words. Direct Speech would deny us this sense of the narrator's presence. On the other hand, were Gobila's views to be given to us in Reported Speech the narrator's presence would be too dominating and the passage would not so dramatically enact that experience of Gobila's way of seeing things.

Earlier on in the same passage we can find a striking example of Conrad's assured manipulation of narrative perspective.

> No one from Gobila's villages came near the station that day. No one came the next day, and the next, nor for a whole week. Gobila's people might have been dead and buried for any sign of life they gave. But they were only mourning for those they had lost by the witchcraft of white men, who had brought wicked people into their country. The wicked people were gone, but fear remained. Fear always remains. (OP, p. 107)

The sentence beginning 'But they were only mourning' is, technically, an interesting case. It seems to be FID, a sentence that adopts the point of view of Gobila's people and presents this as represented thought, although it could start as authorial narrative comment, shifting after 'mourning' to FID. Whatever the case, the sentence is noteworthy for presenting a viewpoint without implying that any particular speaker has used a comparable form of words. We are put into the collective consciousness of Gobila's people without being led to assume that any one of them would have expressed their thoughts or feelings in these, or similar, words – or, indeed, at all. The theoretical point here is that, as Ann Banfield puts it,

> Represented speech and thought [For a note on problems of terminology, see note 2] is neither an interpretation of the reported speech or thought which implies an evaluating speaker, nor a direct imitation or presentation of the quoted speaker's voice. Instead, the speech or thought of the SELF represented retains all its expressivity without suggesting that its

grammatical form was that uttered by an original speaker, whether aloud
or silently.[18]

The fact that we are dealing with a collective rather than an individual
consciousness makes this point even more relevant. Read as FID, the
sentence in question allows us to attribute an attitude to Gobila's people
without any assumption that they expressed – or were even conscious of
– this attitude. At the same time, the reader gets the feeling that he or
she is not crudely being told something about Gobila's people by the
narrator; it is as if for a moment we enter their collective consciousness
and experience it for ourselves. To quote Ann Banfield further, 'Represented speech and thought is . . . characterizable as a representation of
expression without this in any way implying a representation of communication'.[19]

I should say that it is also possible to interpret this sentence in
another way, as a narrative statement which, for the purpose of heavy
irony, mimics the assumed attitudes and terminology of Gobila's people.
I find this less likely, particularly in view of the fact that the following
sentences are clearly authorial, and use the phrase 'wicked people' as if
quoting it from another source. This is a favoured technique of Conrad's,
very often used for the purpose of the ironic pointing up of a contrast
between professions and actuality. When Conrad refers to Kayerts and
Carlier as 'the two pioneers of trade and progress', which is how they like
to think of themselves but which is clearly not what they are, a similar
technique is in use. The 'quoting' of the phrase 'wicked people' is not
ironic however; at this point the authorial narrator seems to accept the
characterization given to the slave-traders by Gobila's people, suggesting
indirectly that the moral judgements of the latter are far more reliable
than are those of Kayerts and Carlier.

What is striking in this paragraph is the masterly manipulation of
narrative distance and perspective. While the narrative flows freely the
reader is carried from the panoramic perspective of the authorial narrator
down into the limited (but not, in this case, inaccurate) collective consciousness of Gobila's people, and then back into the omniscience of the
narrator's view. The large generalizations of the latter ('Fear always
remains') accumulate more force as a result of being supported by the
testimony of the evidence brought to the reader by means of FID.

The 'dual voice' controversy

One general issue can be broached at this point. Perhaps the key dispute
dividing recent studies of FID has been that between 'dual voice' and the
'single voice' theories. The title of Roy Pascal's book *The Dual Voice*

makes his position on this issue clear. Pascal suggests that 'the simplest description' of what he prefers to term Free Indirect Speech, 'would be that the narrator, though preserving the authorial mode throughout and evading the "dramatic" form of speech and dialogue, yet places himself, when reporting the words or thoughts of a character, directly into the experiential field of the character, and adopts the latter's perspective in regard to both time and place'.[20] He argues, further:

> Critics have . . . often maintained that the use of free indirect speech permits the reader to experience fully and exclusively in terms of, and from the perspective of, the character, the subject. But this is not the case. Mimicry itself, as Leo Spitzer wrote, implies a mimic as well as a person mimicked; and the effect (and the fun) of mimicry depends on our awareness of the difference between the imitation and the real thing, as well as the likeness. That is, the narrator is always effectively present in free indirect speech, even if only through the syntax of the passage, the shape and relationship of sentences, and the structure and design of a story . . .[21]

However, from the extract quoted from Ann Banfield earlier, it will be apparent that she does not accept that FID involves 'mimicking'; to requote part of the cited passage,

> Represented speech and thought is neither an interpretation of the reported speech or thought which implies an evaluating speaker, nor a direct imitation or presentation of the quoted speaker's voice.

Banfield therefore argues against the 'dual voice' theory. Her arguments are extremely detailed, and cannot be cited in full here, but she makes it clear that in her view represented *speech* (but not represented thought) can sever the relation of SPEAKER and SELF such that in represented speech, 'there is still only one SELF, who is however the represented speaker, and not the SPEAKER of the E[xpression]'.[22] This distinction between speaker and self allows Banfield to argue that represented speech can represent but one self.

This would seem to fly in the face of my previous argument that FID can be used for ironic purpose, but Banfield contests this. She counters that a sentence of FID may be intended to be *read* ironically, but that 'the evidence for such a reading must come from elsewhere in the text', or even from extra-textual factors such as the reader's knowledge that the author of a novel is female.

Stated thus, the views of Banfield and of Pascal do not seem so much at variance as may first have seemed the case. We can posit that a sentence of FID represents but one *self*, but that the use of FID may be such as to encourage the reader to set the expression of this self in a certain context - an ironic one, for example. We can agree with Pascal (and Spitzer) that mimicking involves a mimicker, but not necessarily as a presence within the mimicking, more as signs around the mimicking.

The dual voice argument is complicated by the possibility of ambiguity: *are* some of the quoted sentences examples of FID? If it is accepted that the sentence about 'the witchcraft of white men' could be either FID or a heavily ironic statement from the narrator - if, in other words, the sentiment expressed originates in the narrator's consciousness rather than in that of Gobila's people - then a different sort of duality can be posited. The reader can read the sentence in question *either* as FID representing a collective consciousness of Gobila's people, *or* as an ironic narrative comment, in which words such as 'witchcraft' are used highly ironically. (We presume, of course, that Gobila's people would not use the word 'witchcraft' at all ironically.) As I suggested earlier, what we would have in such a case would be something like Wittgenstein's duck-rabbit; dual, but never perceivable as other than single in any one act of perception.

Before I leave 'An Outpost of Progress' one other example of FID should be examined. It occurs at the end of the story, after the killing of Carlier but before the return of the ship carrying the Managing Director.

> He sat by the corpse thinking; thinking very actively, thinking very new thoughts. He seemed to have broken loose from himself altogether. His old thoughts, convictions, likes and dislikes, things he respected and things he abhorred, appeared in their true light at last! Appeared contemptible and childish, false and ridiculous. He revelled in his new wisdom while he sat by the man he had killed. He argued with himself about all things under heaven with that kind of wrong-headed lucidity which may be observed in some lunatics. Incidentally he reflected that the fellow dead there had been a noxious beast anyway; that men died every day in thousands; perhaps in hundreds of thousands - who could tell? - and that in the number, that one death could not possibly make any difference; couldn't have any importance, at least to a thinking creature. He, Kayerts, was a thinking creature. He had been all his life, till that moment, a believer in a lot of nonsense like the rest of mankind - who are fools; but now he thought! He knew! He was at peace; he was familiar with the highest wisdom! Then he tried to imagine himself dead, and Carlier sitting in his chair watching him; and his attempt met with such unexpected success, that in a very few moments he became not at all sure who was dead and who was alive. (OP, pp. 114-15)

We see here a fascinating manipulation of narrative perspective as we experience Kayerts's thoughts alternately from outside and from inside as the text oscillates between omniscient narrative comment and FID (which starts, I think, in the third quoted sentence). We can note that it is still specifically *verbal* thought which apparently encourages Conrad to shift into FID; we are told that 'he argued with himself', and such arguing characteristically takes the form of verbal utterances rather than images.[23] When his thoughts move away from words, as when he tries to imagine himself dead and Carlier watching him, then the narrative switches back to authorial comment (and is, incidentally, grimly funny).

Conrad's use of FID in this passage has a complex effect on the reader. In one sense it makes Kayerts's isolation and self-delusion stand out that much more sharply while it also introduces an almost pitying element into the narrative. But what strikes one most of all here is the *assurance* of Conrad's narrative, including the use of FID. One never doubts that Conrad knows what he believes, knows how he views and judges the characters and actions he depicts in 'An Outpost of Progress'. Thus we witness what I have argued is characteristic of Conrad's great fiction: a fusion of supreme technical expertise with a consistency of moral and ideological outlook. Conrad knew what he thought of what he had witnessed in the Congo. The next work of his which I wish to consider may lead us to doubt whether he was quite so sure about what he thought of that which he had witnessed in the British Merchant Marine.

The Nigger of the 'Narcissus'

I argue in another chapter in the present volume that *The Nigger of the 'Narcissus'* is Conrad's problem work,[24] and Conrad's use of FID is fully implicated in the work's problematic aspects. The first striking use of the technique in the novella comes soon after the entry of James Wait. After his explanation of his late arrival on the ship – given in Direct Speech – the text continues as follows:

> He stopped short. The folly around him was confounded. He was right as ever, and as ever ready to forgive. The disdainful tones had ceased, and, breathing heavily, he stood still, surrounded by all these white men.
> (NOTN, p. 18)

This passage clearly indicates a shift into Wait's consciousness by means of FID. Grammatically, the use of 'these' rather than 'those' is a reliable indication of FID, but the content is also revealing. The repeated words 'as ever' would make no sense were they to be attributed to the narrator, for at this point the narrator has told the reader nothing about Wait. Nor would the narrator accept that Wait was surrounded by folly. As is well known, there are problems and complexities surrounding the narrator(s) of this novella,[25] who is/are at times omniscient, and at times describes himself as a member of the crew of the 'Narcissus', modulating between 'us' and 'them' when referring to the crew and finally emerging as 'I' at the end of the story. But none of these variants of the narrator's identity or status would allow us to attribute the words in question to him. However, the words 'The disdainful tones had ceased' seem clearly *not* to be attributable to Wait; these *must* be attributed to a personified or non-personified narrator. Conrad, then, mixes authorial narrative with FID here, although not in such a way as to cause any confusion. The lines immediately following this passage are, however, highly problematic, ending with the disturbing words, 'a face pathetic and brutal: the tragic, the mysterious, the repulsive mask of a nigger's soul'. As I argue in more detail in the subsequent chapter on *The Nigger of the 'Narcissus'*, the problem is that Conrad cannot decide *who* is saying these words because he has not decided *what* his attitude to various things in the novella is.

Before I leave this particular example of FID I would like to make one additional, important point about it. In contrast to Conrad's earlier habits, it seems as if his use of FID at this point represents, at least in part, non-verbalized thoughts. It seems highly doubtful that the following *words* would pass through Wait's mind: 'The folly around me is confounded. I am right as ever, and as ever ready to forgive. I am surrounded by all these white men'. Conrad's words here are designed to give us Wait's thoughts, attitudes, mental processes without suggesting that these were necessarily verbalized. As Ann Banfield puts it,

> In represented speech and thought . . . more than content is reproduced. . . . We are given a representation of the form or 'manner' of a speech or thought. But, while the form of the representation is linguistic, in the case of represented thought, the form of *what* is represented is not.
> . . .
> the speech or thought of the SELF represented retains all its expressivity without suggesting that its grammatical form was that uttered by an original speaker, whether aloud or silently.[26]

It seems to me that FID *may* in fact suggest a grammatical/verbal form of an originating utterance, but I agree with Banfield that it does not necessarily do so. In the case of the example under discussion, it seems most likely that it is Wait's non-linguistic consciousness that is represented by means of FID. Conrad, in other words, is expanding the scope and sophistication of his use of the technique at this stage of his writing career.

> He was cheered by the rattling of blocks, reassured by the stir and murmur of the watch, soothed by the slow yawn of some sleepy and weary seaman settling himself deliberately for a snooze on the planks. Life seemed an indestructible thing. It went on in darkness, in sunshine, in sleep; tireless, it hovered affectionately round the imposture of his ready death. It was bright, like the twisted flare of lightning, and more

full of surprises than the dark night. It made him safe, and the calm of its overpowering darkness was as precious as its restless and dangerous light. (NOTN, pp. 104-5)

If this passage presents no fundamental problems of ambiguity, it nevertheless faces the reader with certain difficulties. The first-time reader at this stage in the work cannot have made his mind up as to whether or not Wait really is ill, or is merely shamming. Given this fact, the phrase 'the imposture of his ready death' cannot at this stage of a first reading of the novella be safely attributed to Wait. Such a reader is likely, therefore, to take all of this passage as comment from the authorial narrator. For the reader engaged in rereading the novella, things are different. If he or she agrees with the current (but not quite unanimous) critical consensus that Wait is pretending to himself to be shamming so as to avoid having to face up to his impending death, then the above passage will be taken as FID. It is Wait to whom life seems an indestructible thing, hovering affectionately around the imposture of his own ready death; it is Wait who thinks (not necessarily in words) that the calm of life's overpowering darkness is as precious as its restless and dangerous light. For the second-time reader, the passage conveys remarkably effectively the self-deceptive play of Wait's thoughts – but it cannot do this to one reading the work for the first time.

It is worth remarking that the representation of Wait's private thoughts seems least well done when the narrative presents these thoughts in something like Direct Speech.

> Jimmy reached out for the mug. Not a drop. He put it back gently with a faint sigh – and closed his eyes. He thought:- That lunatic Belfast will bring me some water if I ask. Fool. I am very thirsty.
>
> (NOTN, pp. 112-13)

The use of represented thought in 'Not a drop', with its ambiguity as to the precise form taken by Wait's thoughts is far more effective than the clearly verbal thought beginning, 'That lunatic Belfast'. The problem with the latter is that it just isn't believable that Wait would have addressed himself so verbally in such a situation, and so the narrative here strikes the reader as artificial. (In contrast, as I argue in a later chapter, Razumov's use of direct address to himself in his thoughts comes over as appropriate and convincing.)

Interestingly, many of the other examples of FID in *The Nigger of the 'Narcissus'* seem designed to express a collective rather than an individual consciousness, such as we saw FID doing already in 'An Outpost of Progress'.

> We remembered our danger, our toil – and conveniently forgot our horrible scare. We decried our officers – who had done nothing – and listened to the fascinating Donkin. His care for our rights, his disinterested concern for our dignity, were not discouraged by the invariable contumely of our words, by the disdain of our looks. Our contempt for him was unbounded – and we could not but listen with interest to that consummate artist. He told us we were good men – a '"bloomin" condemned lot of of good men.' Who thanked us? Who took any notice of our wrongs? Didn't we lead 'a dorg's loife for two poun' ten a month?' Did we think that miserable pay enough to compensate us for the risk to our lives and for the loss of our clothes? (NOTN, p. 100)

The quoted passage clearly ends with Donkin's words, presented successively by means of Reported Speech, Direct Speech and represented speech. One effect of this really quite complex succession of techniques to present a single speech (or set of speeches) of Donkin's, is to vary the distance between narrator and character. While the use of Reported Speech stresses the present moment of the narrative and the presence of the mature narrator, the use of Direct Speech implies a strong – even ironic – evaluation of Donkin's words by the narrator, and the use of represented speech forces the reader to concentrate on the dramatic effect Donkin's words must have had upon his auditors. We see this in the use of FID at the start of the quoted passage, where the technique is used to render a collective consciousness of the crew to which the narrator belonged but from which he has now distanced himself. It is clearly the crew – including the immature narrator – who believe the officers to have 'done nothing'. They it is, too, who find Donkin 'fascinating', although this word may suggest ironic comment on the part of the mature narrator. Inasmuch as the words 'who had done nothing' represent the crew's collective consciousness, these words cannot be said to represent one *particular* linguistic utterance, although Conrad's use of FID to convey this collective belief or attitude has, paradoxically, some of the force of a particular, dramatic utterance. It is also the case that the crew would never have expressed themselves as their attitudes are expressed in FID, for had they so expressed themselves the contradictions and absurdities involved in their attitudes would have been displayed to them. (And it is precisely in order so to display these contradictions and absurdities that Conrad expresses these attitudes in a way that their holders would not have done.)

I suggested that Conrad's use of the word 'fascinating' might involve ironic comment on the part of the narrator, and this suggestion is perhaps worth more detailed consideration as it impinges upon the 'dual voice' controversy. It seems to be the case that the reader is meant to assume that the crew believed or asserted that their officers had done nothing and also that they found Donkin fascinating. It appears, furthermore, that whereas the former belief or assertion was made consciously and verbally, the latter fact was (perhaps) not consciously perceived by them: they found Donkin fascinating without thinking of him as fascinating. 'Fascinating' is the mature narrator's later characterization of the manner in which Donkin was perceived by the crew. Does not this suggest a 'dual voice', a mixing of the perspectives of characters and narrator?

In this case, I think not. The sentence can, I think, be read in two ways. Firstly, as an authorial narrative statement with an interjected piece of FID: there are in this reading two voices within the sentence, but no one part of the sentence represents both voices. Secondly, as a sentence which starts as authorial narrative statement and then moves into FID from 'who had done' to the end of the sentence. In this reading, 'fascinating' may be read ironically as a result of being juxtaposed with authorial narrative statements, but it represents only one 'self', in Banfield's terms; it is not attributable to two separate consciousnesses.

Here is a more difficult example:

> In the pauses of his impassioned orations the wind sighed quietly aloft, the calm sea unheeded murmured in a warning whisper along the ship's side. We abominated the creature and could not deny the luminous truth of his contentions. It was all so obvious. We were indubitably good men; our deserts were great and our pay small. Through our exertions we had saved the ship and the skipper would get the credit of it. What had he done? we wanted to know. Donkin asked:- 'What 'ee could do without hus?' and we could not answer. (NOTN, pp. 101-2)

The quoted passage ends with an odd presentation of part of a passage of Reported Speech as Direct Speech - presumably so as to allow Conrad to suggest Donkin's cockney dialect through non-standard spelling. This apart, the first quoted sentence is unambiguously authorial narrative statement drawing attention to the fact that the crew is ignoring what the narrator (and Conrad) saw as the inescapable facts of life at sea; 'impassioned orations' is obviously an uncomplicated example of authorial narrative irony. From this point we must move into FID, as the sentiments expressed are those of the crew rather than those of the narrator. Now as Banfield has pointed out, the actual words used in FID do not necessarily represent the verbal form of the sentiments conveyed through the technique; we do not have to posit a crew whose members used phrases such as 'the luminous truth of his contentions' to represent their assessment of Donkin's arguments; phrases such as 'we were indubitably good men' could be read as scenic *representations* of Donkin's contentions.[27] It is hard, however, to avoid the conclusion that these words are deliberately chosen to indicate narrator-irony; thus it could be claimed that they simultaneously give us the substance of the crew's grievance *and* the narrator's judgement on this. This would appear to offer some support to the dual voice hypothesis.

As I have already suggested, new problems relating to Conrad's use of FID emerge in this work, and they are intimately bound up with some of the uncertainties relating to the novella's narrator. Take the following example:

> It was just what they had expected, and hated to hear, that idea of a stalking death, thrust at them many times a day like a boast and like a menace by this obnoxious nigger. (NOTN, p. 36)

It seems to me impossible to be sure to whom the words 'this obnoxious nigger' should be attributed. This could be represented speech, and could represent the attitude of the crew of the 'Narcissus'. But the phrase could equally well have a narrative force. The word 'this' rather than 'that' might suggest the former, but the narrator might use the word 'this' for emphasis. Now we have seen that in other works *grammatical* ambiguity has often been resolved by *content*, by our knowing to whom certain opinions or attitudes must be attributed. The opinions of Conrad's authorial narrators in *Almayer's Folly* and *An Outcast of the Islands* are not such as can easily be confused with the opinions of Almayer or Willems, or, indeed, of any of the other characters. To indicate that this is not the case in *The Nigger of the 'Narcissus'* is to say something revealing about this work.

The early Marlow narratives

What is striking when we turn to the first 'Marlow' stories is that Conrad's use of FID drops very dramatically indeed. This is all the more noticeable when these works are compared to 'The Return' and *The End of the Tether* – both works with extra-mimetic authorial narrators and both containing examples of FID on almost every page. An example of FID from *Heart of Darkness* may help to explain this striking variation. Marlow is reporting his conversation with the 'brickmaker', and oscillating between Direct Speech and FID. I pick the report up half-way through.

> 'He did not make bricks – why, there was a physical impossibility in the way – as I was well aware; and if he did secretarial work for the manager, it was because 'no sensible man rejects wantonly the confidence of his superiors.' Did I see it? I saw it. What more did I want? What I really wanted was rivets, by heaven! Rivets. To get on with the work – to stop the hole. Rivets I wanted. There were cases of them down at the coast – cases – piled up – burst – split! You kicked a loose rivet at every second step in that station yard on the hillside. Rivets had rolled into the grove of death.' (HOD, p. 83)

Conrad's problem here, I think, stems from three factors. The first is that Marlow is reporting a conversation in which he himself partook. What Marlow reports himself as having said has to be something that it is believable that he might have said to the brickmaker. Secondly, there is the oral nature of Marlow's narrative. What we read must also be something that Marlow might have said to his narratees. And, finally, the reader must be able to distinguish between what Marlow said to them, and what he said to the brickmaker. That contrast between Direct Speech and FID which is quite clear on the printed page in omniscient or extra-mimetic narrative is far from this in an ostensibly oral narrative.

Thus the reader can easily perceive that much of the above passage consists of an alternation between Direct Speech and represented speech. But it is more or less impossible for readers of *Heart of Darkness* to see where the break comes between represented speech (what Marlow said then to the brickmaker) and authorial narrative comment (what Marlow says now to his narratees). 'As I was well aware' could be represented speech: the brickmaker is saying, 'As you are well aware'; or it could be Marlow's narrative interpolation: 'I, Marlow, was aware that this was the case'.[28] We presume that Marlow would not have used the term 'the grove of death' to the brickmaker, which renders the sentence in which this reference takes place unambiguous. But generally speaking, the clues that render entrance into or exit from FID apparent are more difficult to place naturally in an ostensibly spoken narrative.

There is one other point to make. The very anonymity of an authorial narrator allows for easy passage into the consciousness of a character by means of FID. With the Marlow stories, the continued presence of a personified and intra-mimetic narrator who is *speaking* his story to a group of auditors makes such a movement more complicated. In general, FID can successfully be used under such circumstances only when mimicry or imitation would be natural in the narrating situation depicted. The problem the writer faces, of course, is that spoken mimicry depends heavily on intonational clues which are not available in writing. In the quoted example Marlow uses FID much as one would use imitation in ordinary life – to convey a more dramatic sense of his frustration about the rivets to those listening to his story – and those ambiguities which present themselves to us as readers would probably not have bothered someone listening to a spoken narrative account. Banfield points out that Conrad's Marlow stories resemble the Eastern European *skaz* genre, in which the whole tale (or, as in Conrad's case, a very large part of it) is deemed to take the form of an oral narrative. And *skaz* does not typically make use of FID.

The following passage illustrates perfectly why this is so.

'"Will they attack, do you think?" asked the manager, in a confidential tone.

'I did not think they would attack, for several obvious reasons. The thick fog was one. If they left the bank in their canoes they would get lost in it, as we would be if we attempted to move. Still, I had also judged the jungle of both banks quite inpenetrable – and yet eyes were in it, eyes that had seen us. The river-side bushes were certainly very thick; but the undergrowth behind was evidently penetrable. However, during the short lift I had seen no canoes anywhere in the reach – certainly not abreast of the steamer. But what made the idea of attack inconceivable to me was the nature of the noise – of the cries we had heard. They had not the fierce character boding of immediate hostile intention. Unexpected, wild, and violent as they had been, they had given me an irresistible impression of sorrow. The glimpse of the steamboat had for some reason filled those savages with unrestrained grief. The danger, if any, I expounded, was from our proximity to a great human passion let loose.' (HOD, pp. 106-7)

I believe that the average reader reads most of the above passage as a record of Marlow's *thoughts* in response to the manager's question, thoughts which he reports to his auditors on the *Nellie*. It is only the last sentence quoted which confirms that the passage reports on what Marlow actually *said* to the manager and the other pilgrims, conveyed to us by represented speech; and indeed the following paragraph provides us with the pilgrims' startled response to Marlow's 'regular lecture'. Were the passage quoted to have omitted the final sentence above, and had the following paragraph been deleted, then there would be no way of telling whether we were reading represented thought (Marlow thinking to himself), or represented speech (what Marlow said to the pilgrims at the time).

If we turn to *Lord Jim* the evidence seems to support what has been claimed above. The first part of the novel given to us by an omniscient authorial narrator contains many examples of FID, normally represented thought, used to depict the manner in which Jim indulges in processes of self-deception.

The tumult and the menace of wind and sea now appeared very contemptible to Jim, increasing the regret of his awe at their inefficient menace. Now he knew what to think of it. It seemed to him he cared nothing for the gale. He could affront greater perils. He would do so – better than anybody. Not a particle of fear was left. Nevertheless he brooded apart that evening .... (LJ, p. 8)

Jim deceives himself: he was afraid, he still is afraid, and his failure to admit and confront his fear will lead to his fatal jump. (Compare the comments of the French Lieutenant on fear.) There are many comparable examples of FID in the opening part of the novel. Once Marlow takes over the narrative, however, we find far fewer examples; Marlow has no way of representing Jim's secret thoughts.

> 'He went off into a far corner, and coming back, he, figuratively speaking, turned to rend me. I spoke like that because I – even I, who had been no end kind to him – even I remembered – remembered – against him – what – what had happened. And what about others – the – the – world? Where's the wonder he wanted to get out, meant to get out, meant to stay out – by heavens! And I talked about proper frames of mind!' (LJ, p. 236)

We can again note that the use of represented speech here fits naturally into Marlow's ostensibly spoken narrative; if we read the passage aloud we can imagine Marlow's saying the words as written, repeating words said to him by Jim.

Generally speaking, then, the early Marlow works are not rich with examples of FID, for the reasons I have suggested. And this reminds us that the introduction of Marlow forced a number of changes of technique on to Conrad. In particular, the ability to suggest and imply general and particular judgements and evaluations, rather than to state them directly, was significantly lessened. This seems to have forced Conrad to make Marlow's judgements more overt than those of the narrators of early works had been, a development that had its positive and its negative sides. On the positive side it helped Conrad to avoid some of the incoherences from which I believe *The Nigger of the 'Narcissus'* suffers; more negatively, it results in a certain evaluative explicitness on the part of the narrator. That powerful sense of moral suggestiveness that we find in narrative statements elsewhere in Conrad's fiction now has to be located somewhere else – in the tension between frame and framed narratives, for example.

Typhoon

Ostensibly spoken narrative, then, restricts Conrad in his use of FID. A comparison between *Falk* and *Typhoon* confirms the same pattern; the former work offers few if any examples, *Typhoon* many. This, incidentally, is one of the reasons why the reader at times assumes that the narrative of the teacher of languages in *Under Western Eyes* is a written one in spite of its colloquial and 'oral' qualities: it makes much fuller use of FID.

A number of critics have misread passages in *Typhoon* as a result of a failure to recognize the use of FID. Take the following example.

> With a temperament neither loquacious nor taciturn [MacWhirr] found very little occasion to talk. There were matters of duty, of course

– directions, orders, and so on; but the past being to his mind done with, and the future not there yet, the more general actualities of the day required no comment – because facts can speak for themselves with overwhelming precision. (*Typhoon*, p. 9)

It is MacWhirr rather than the authorial narrator who thinks that facts can speak for themselves with overwhelming precision; indeed, there is a strong case to be made for the view that by the end of the tale even MacWhirr has discovered that this is not the case: facts demand interpretation. (It is, actually, hard to say whether what we have here is represented speech or represented thought; indeed, it could be claimed that we have neither, and that the words are a form of 'represented consciousness, belief, or attitude'.)

On occasions in this work it is likely that Conrad deliberately encourages misreading for artistic effect. Take the following passage.

Never for a moment could she shake herself clear of the water; Jukes, rigid, perceived in her motion the ominous signs of haphazard floundering. She was no longer struggling intelligently. It was the beginning of the end; and the note of busy concern in Captain MacWhirr's voice sickened him like an exhibition of blind and pernicious folly. (*Typhoon*, p. 53)

On first reading these words are, surely, taken as authorial. The reader is thus led to share Jukes's resignation and to believe that it is 'the beginning of the end' and that the ship will sink. On second reading we are aware, of course, that what we have here is represented thought: this is what Jukes thinks, but he is wrong. The effect is similar to what Ian Watt has termed 'delayed decoding', an impressionist capturing of momentary beliefs or experiences detached from the illuminating light of subsequent knowledge. Conrad is using FID to manipulate the reader's responses, to dramatize a character's mental stages for a reader who re-experiences them him or herself.

The End of the Tether

I mentioned earlier that *The End of the Tether* makes very extensive use of FID. As is well known, the second part of the published version of this work was written by Conrad under extremely difficult circumstances, although his story about a lamp having exploded and set fire to his manuscript such that the whole of the second half of the work had to be rewritten under great pressure has now been questioned.[29] Whatever the truth, the use of FID seems relatively constant throughout the story – suggesting that Conrad found this technique easy to use even when working under extreme pressure. *The End of the Tether* shows Conrad using FID not just frequently, but also in the more varied ways that we have seen already in those works written subsequent to his first two novels. The work contains both represented speech and represented thought, it uses the former to convey both iterative as well as particular utterances, and the use of the latter also displays an interesting variety. The scene in which Captain Whalley meets and talks to Captain Eliott includes an impressive variety of narrative techniques, moving from Direct Speech through authorial narrative comment, represented speech and represented thought – all in the space of a couple of pages. A section of this conversation lasting over a page is given with Whalley's contribution in Direct Speech and Captain Eliott's in both Direct Speech and represented speech, with the bulk in the latter. A brief example will illustrate this.

> 'Come, now. Aren't you a bit tired by this time of the whole show?' muttered the other, sullenly.
> 'Are you?'
> Captain Eliott was. Infernally tired. He only hung on to his berth so long in order to get his pension on the highest scale before he went home. It would be no better than poverty, anyhow; still, it was the only thing between him and the workhouse. And he had a family. Three girls, as Whalley knew. He gave 'Harry, old boy,' to understand that these three girls were a source of the greatest anxiety and worry to him. Enough to drive a man distracted.
> 'Why? What have they been doing now?' asked Captain Whalley
> .... (TEOTT, p. 201)

It is worth asking what difference it would make were Captain Eliott's contributions to the conversation all to be given in Direct Speech, instead of being in both Direct and – in the main – represented speech. The reader can transpose the relevant passages him or herself to test his or her own responses; my own feeling is that the switch into represented speech leads the reader to see Eliott from Captain Whalley's perspective. It is as if we hear Captain Eliott droning on about matters to which, given Whalley's problems, Whalley can hardly pay detailed attention or grant his full sympathetic concern. The use of represented speech in this scene somehow conveys Eliott's rather bumptious self-importance and his lack of a full sympathetic concern for Whalley and his possible problems, along with Whalley's difficulty in keeping his mind upon what Eliott is saying. Now such interpretative readings must needs be tentative. But to my mind there is no doubt that Conrad's use of FID in *The End of the Tether* adds very considerably to the modulations and complexity of tone in this work. Were all thought and speech in the work to be given either in reported or in Direct Speech then something central to the work would disappear.[30]

(The same could not be said of, for example, *The Rescue*, which makes very heavy use of both represented speech and represented thought.)

Other examples from this same work are, I think, interesting in different ways, and I would now like to examine some of these.

> But a half smile of pride lingered on [Massy's] lips; outside the solitary lascar told off for night duty in harbour, perhaps a youth fresh from a forest village, would stand motionless in the shadows of the deck listening to the endless drunken gabble. His heart would be thumping with breathless awe of white men: the arbitrary and obstinate men who pursue inflexibly their incomprehensible purposes – beings with weird intonations in the voice, moved by unaccountable feelings, actuated by inscrutable motives. (TEOTT, p. 224)

What is interesting about this example is that it comes in the context of a passage describing not one particular occasion, but repeated occasions; the narrative is iterative rather than dramatic ('would stand'; 'would be thumping'). Yet Conrad is still able to move into represented thought to describe the typical thoughts of those Lascars who heard the second engineer's intoxicated ramblings.

As I remarked before when discussing 'An Outpost of Progress', Conrad often uses FID to convey the thought processes of non-Europeans; presumably the fact that the content of these thought processes gives an unambiguous indication of to whom they should be attributed means that other clues or marks of transition can be dispensed with. Consider the following example.

> The record of the visual world fell through his eyes upon his unspeculating mind as on a sensitized plate through the lens of a camera. His knowledge was absolute and precise; nevertheless, had he been asked his opinion, and especially if questioned in the downright, alarming manner of white men, he would have displayed the hesitation of ignorance. He was certain of his facts – but such a certitude counted for little against the doubt what answer would be pleasing. Fifty years ago, in a jungle village, and before he was a day old, his father (who died without ever seeing a white face) had had his nativity cast by a man of skill and wisdom in astrology, because in the arrangement of the stars may be read the last word of human destiny. (TEOTT, p. 228)

There are few grammatical clues to the presence of FID here (perhaps one is the use of the deictic 'ago' rather than 'before'). Nevertheless, there is no ambiguity regarding the attribution of the sentiments uttered, because we believe the Serang rather than the narrator to have a view of the manner of white men as alarming, and to believe that the last word of human destiny can be read in the arrangement of the stars.

Sometimes, though, the exact point of transition between authorial narrator comment and FID is impossible to give. Consider the following example. The seventh chapter of the work opens with a page that, after an introductory sentence, consists of a lengthy sequence of represented thought. The opening of this sequence is unambiguous; when we read 'Everybody on board was his inferior', we know that we are following the thoughts of Massy rather than being presented with an opinion of the authorial narrator. But the sequence ends as follows:

> He had to struggle and plan and scheme to keep the *Sofala* afloat – and what did he get for it? Not even enough respect. They could not have given him enough of that if all their thoughts and all their actions had been directed to that end. The vanity of possession, the vainglory of power, had passed away by this time, and there remained only the material embarrassments, the fear of losing that position which had turned out not worth having, and an anxiety of thought which no abject subservience of men could repay. (TEOTT, pp. 218-19)

It seems to me that the last quoted sentence is unambiguously authorial because it looks at Massy's position in a way of which Massy himself would have been incapable. But what of the preceding sentence? This *could* be Massy's impossibly self-important notion of the respect he deserved, or the narrator's omniscient comment to the effect that although Massy thought he deserved more respect, he would still have thought this had all the thoughts and actions of his crew been directed to this end.

Far from this ambiguity being a flaw, it seems to me that it acts as a perfect transition point. Whichever way we read it it makes good sense, and it is not so important to know which of the readings to accept. I suspect that on an ordinary reading both meanings are taken in. If so, then one can posit a rather different sort of 'dual voice'.

Before moving on from *The End of the Tether* I would like to look at two more passages possessed of a different sort of ambiguity, an ambiguity which follows Conrad's insertion of parenthetical comment within a passage of represented thought.

> Sterne was greatly chagrined, however, to notice that [Whalley] did not seem anyway near being past his work yet. Still, these old men go to pieces all at once sometimes. Then there was the owner-engineer close at hand to be impressed by his zeal and steadiness. Sterne never for a moment doubted the obvious nature of his own merits (he was really an excellent officer); only, nowadays, professional merit alone does not take a man along fast enough. (TEOTT, p. 240)

> Sterne wriggled his shoulders with disgust. What was it? Indolence or what?

> That old skipper must have been growing lazy for years. They all grew lazy out East here (Sterne was very conscious of his own unimpaired activity); they got slack all over. (TEOTT, p. 249)

I think – but am not sure – that in both these passages the comments enclosed in parentheses represent authorial narrative comment. Sterne really is an excellent officer; he is very conscious of his own unimpaired activity (and his activity really is unimpaired). My doubt comes from the fact that in both cases the sentiments seem rather uncharacteristic: Conrad does not normally suggest that a morally corrupt person is 'really' an excellent officer, nor that such a person is unaffected by the temptations to 'loafing' presented by the East. Both comments *could* be represented thought, and could stand as tokens of Sterne's lack of accurate self-knowledge.

Nostromo

From what I have said so far it might be predicted that both *Nostromo* and *The Secret Agent* would contain plentiful examples of FID, as both novels involve the use of an extra-mimetic – at times omniscient – narrative perspective. (There are significant variations in Conrad's narrative method in both works, it should be added; the shift into the first-person on the first page of chapter 8, Part First of *Nostromo*, for example.)

FID is a crucial and indispensable element in what is perhaps Conrad's greatest novel. We may in retrospect remember *Nostromo* as a novel characterized by its omniscient narrative perspective, a work distinguished by the distance – ironic, contemptuous, and at times even pitying – between narrator and characters or events. But when we turn to a closer consideration of the narrative of this work we find that it is, rather, characterized by extreme flexibility of perspective, indeed by continual subtle shifts of voice and perspective. In my opinion FID is by far the most important means whereby this flexibility is attained. The narrative is not so much God-like as ghost-like, less a detached and all-seeing perspective looking down on characters and events, and more a wandering presence drifting in and out of characters, backwards and forwards in time, altering in identity from personified to non-personified narrator. And it is by means of FID that this ghost-like penetration of barriers, this continued shift of perspective, is achieved.

I want later to comment upon this contrast between the reader's memory of the narrative of *Nostromo* as simple and consistent, and its actual extreme flexibility and mobility. But first let me provide a few illustrations.

Then the tension of old Giorgio's attitude relaxed, and a smile of contemptuous relief came upon his lips of an old fighter with a leonine face. These were not a people striving for justice, but thieves. Even to defend his life against them was a sort of degradation for a man who had been one of Garibaldi's immortal thousand in the conquest of Sicily. He had an immense scorn for this outbreak of scoundrels and leperos, who did not know the meaning of the word 'liberty.'

He grounded his old gun, and, turning his head, glanced at the coloured lithograph of Garibaldi in a black frame on the white wall; a thread of strong sunshine cut it perpendicularly. His eyes, accustomed to the luminous twilight, made out the high colouring of the face, the red of the shirt, the outlines of the square shoulders, the black patch of the Bersagliere hat with cock's feathers curling over the crown. An immortal hero! This was your liberty; it gave you not only life, but immortality as well!

For that one man his fanaticism had suffered no diminution.

(*Nostromo*, pp. 20-21)

The passage reads easily, and surely presents the average reader with no problems. And yet complicated things are going on here. In the first sentence the perspective is an external one: Viola is seen from the outside: it is not he who thinks that he is contemptuously relieved or that his face is leonine, but the narrator. But with the next sentence we move, I think, into Viola's consciousness by means of represented (verbal) thought: it is not the narrator who feels that it is a sort of degradation for Viola to defend his life against these 'thieves', this is what he himself is thinking and these are the words which constitute his thoughts. In the last sentence of the first paragraph quoted we may feel that the words 'He had an immense scorn' usher in a narrative comment on Viola, but the content of the second half of the sentence, with Viola's characteristic and habitual modes of thought and terminology, again make it clear that it is Viola's own consciousness to which we are being made privy.

With the beginning of the second paragraph quoted we are back with an external perspective, but in the last two sentences of this paragraph we appear to rejoin Viola's consciousness. I say 'appear' because there is a slight possibility of ambiguity here; these last two sentences could be read as the ironic commentary of a detached narrator, although I doubt that this is either what Conrad intended or how most readers read them. But with the start of the third quoted paragraph, we are unambiguously back outside of Viola's consciousness, for we know that Viola would not use a term such as 'fanaticism' about himself. (And although we may accept the argument that the words used in represented thought need not necessarily represent words utilized in the thought of the character concerned, we must I think recognize that even the concept of fanaticism is foreign to Viola's view of his political ideals and commitments. There is an important theoretical point which should not be allowed to escape here: sometimes one can only have a particular thought by means of a particular word. In such cases, a passage of represented thought can confirm that a particular word must have had an enabling function in a character's thought.)

I have said that FID is central to the narrative of *Nostromo*, but I should add that its use does vary according to narrative circumstance and from character to character. Perhaps not surprisingly it does not figure in Decoud's letter to his sister. For perhaps less immediately obvious reasons, although the speech or thought of Captain Mitchell is sometimes given to us by means of FID, it is more typically revealed by means of Direct or Reported Speech. With a character such as Viola, by contrast, FID is used far more frequently, almost every time that he appears. It is not hard to suggest explanations of why such variations in the use of FID should be found in *Nostromo*.

The absence of FID in Decoud's letter can be attributed to a number of factors. Firstly, such an absence makes a clear stylistic distinction between Decoud's letter and the rest of the narrative of *Nostromo*. Secondly, we may perhaps assume that Decoud's sister does not know the people about whom Decoud is writing well enough to be able easily to detect the use of FID by reference to the content of Decoud's pronouncements. Thirdly, Decoud's letter is more about larger political forces and events than individual characters. And, finally, Decoud's egocentricity makes it more difficult for him to slip out of his own persona and to assume the identity of another person.

If we ask why some characters should call forth the use of FID in the narrative far more than others, there are again various possible reasons. Viola's monomania, his imprisonment within the world of Garibaldi's struggle, makes it very easy to put the mark of his character on FID; there is seldom any significant ambiguity in the use of FID which is connected to Viola. Here is what seems to me to be a rare example.

> Old Giorgio contemplated his children thoughtfully. There was two years difference between them. They had been born to him late, years after the boy had died. Had he lived he would have been nearly as old as Gian' Battista – he whom the English called Nostromo; but as to his daughters, the severity of his temper, his advancing age, his absorption in his memories, had prevented his taking much notice of them. He loved his children, but girls belong more to the mother, and much of his affection had been expended in the worship and service of liberty.
>
> (*Nostromo*, pp. 28-9)

There is a relatively unimportant ambiguity in the second quoted sentence – it is not clear whether the narrator is telling us that there is two years difference between Viola's daughters' ages, or whether Viola is thinking this, although it is probably the former. A similar, unimportant ambiguity can be found in the next sentence, although it is likely that this is represented thought as the subsequent sentence carries on from it and this sentence is unambiguously represented thought: the use of the name 'Gian' Battista' makes it clear that we are within Viola's consciousness. (There is a certain clumsiness in the formulation, 'he whom the English called Nostromo'; surely Viola would never *think* this, although he might well *say* it. Such comments seem almost like musical motifs to introduce a particular character, and it may be that this is how they are read. The thought is made 'Viola-like' without its being intended to represent the precise verbal form of Viola's thought.)

Following this the comment about Viola's being prevented from taking much notice of his daughters by his absorption in his memories must be authorial – the very point being made is that Viola himself is not conscious of something, so he cannot be thinking this himself. It is the final sentence which seems to me to be more interestingly ambiguous: is it Viola, or the narrator, who believes that 'girls belong more to the mother'? It seems to me that the sentence can convincingly be read in both ways; 'service of liberty' is a phrase that Viola himself would use, but it may be being quoted ironically by the narrator, who is surely more likely than Viola himself to talk of Viola's *worship* of liberty. Would Viola himself believe that, 'much of his affection had been expended in the worship and service of liberty'? I am not sure. We should notice that this minor ambiguity can be attributed to our uncertainty about the narrator's opinions: we know that Viola himself would probably believe that girls belong more to the mother, but we are (or, at least I am) less sure whether this would be likely to be the opinion of the narrator.

This is a trivial example, but the point is a substantive one: there is a clear relationship between the reader's sense of a particular set of beliefs which are underwritten by the narrative, and the avoidance of unproductive ambiguity with regard to the use of FID.

Consider too the following example:

> Old Viola had risen. He followed with his eyes in the dark the sounds made by Nostromo. The light disclosed him standing without support, as if the mere presence of that man who was loyal, brave, incorruptible, who was all his son would have been, were enough for the support of his decaying strength. (*Nostromo*, p. 468)

Once again this seems very straightforward, but is actually extremely complex. Much of this must be authorial comment. We have an external description of Viola, such as no character – including Viola himself – would have given. The words 'as if' clearly signal an authorial perspective:

it is the narrator, and not Viola, who suggests that it is as if (but not actually because) Nostromo's qualities support him, that Viola can stand without support. But in the same sentence, 'who was all his son would have been' is equally clearly to be interpreted as a statement from Viola's perspective rather than from that of the authorial narrator. And it is Viola, of course, and not the authorial narrator who considers Nostromo to be incorruptible. Such a statement from the narrator would be inescapably ironic. But we should not necessarily assume that Viola is actually *thinking* these thoughts at this moment, and that is why I have used the term 'FID' rather than 'represented thought'. What they represent is, perhaps, what Viola would have thought had he been thinking about Nostromo, and how this man's presence enabled him to stand without support. The words thus represent an attitude which is potential rather than actual in Viola, a set of beliefs of which he is not at this moment fully conscious, but which can serve to characterize his behaviour and his personality. What this short passage demonstrates to perfection is the supreme flexibility that FID gives Conrad in *Nostromo*, such that in one sentence we can glide from an authorial narrative perspective into represented thought and back again – without the reader being made conscious of the transitions at all (although of course responding to them). The passage also shows how Conrad seems almost incapable of avoiding FID when dealing with Viola: this character's presence seems invariably to call out the technique.

With Captain Mitchell, Conrad seems concerned to indicate a different sort of mental limitation from that illustrated in the case of Viola. We are told of Mitchell that he had, 'a strange ignorance of the real forces around him' (p. 136), that he 'did some hard but not very extensive thinking' (p. 338), and that he was 'too pompously and innocently aware of his own existence to observe that of others' (p. 338). His thoughts are neither very interesting nor are they significantly different from what he actually says, and so his represented thought cannot give the reader all that much of value. On occasions, we have to be told what he is not thinking, what he is incapable of thinking – as in the passage in which we learn of his lack of fear for his personal safety:

> He did some hard but not very extensive thinking. It was not of a gloomy cast. The old sailor, with all his small weaknesses and absurdities, was constitutionally incapable of entertaining for any length of time a fear of his personal safety. It was not so much firmness of soul as the lack of a certain kind of imagination – the kind whose undue development caused intense suffering to Señor Hirsch; that sort of imagination which adds the blind terror of bodily suffering and of death, envisaged as an accident to the body alone, strictly – to all the other apprehensions on which the sense of one's existence is based. Unfortunately Captain Mitchell had not much penetration of any kind; characteristic, illuminating trifles of

expression, action, or movement, escaped him completely. He was too pompously and innocently aware of his own existence to observe that of others. (*Nostromo*, p. 338)

Note how in the following passage we are informed that Mitchell's thoughts are not really coherent enough to be verbalized:

> Captain Mitchell's heart was so heavy that he would have preferred for the time being a complete solitude to the best of company. But any company would have been preferable to the doctor's, at whom he had always looked askance as a sort of beachcomber of superior intelligence partly reclaimed from his abased state. That feeling led him to ask ....
> (*Nostromo*, p. 346)

Note the word 'feeling'; we are not to suppose that Captain Mitchell thought, 'I have always looked askance at that man as a sort of beachcomber &c &c'. This is the verbal form into which the narrative translates Mitchell's *feeling*, a feeling he himself lacks the intelligence or self-awareness to bring to verbal specificity. In such a situation it is the narrative which has to *provide* words which crystallize the feeling into a thought. The use of represented thought would run the risk here of making Mitchell seem too self-aware, more intelligent, and more articulate about his mental processes. (I should admit that the passage could be read as represented thought, that it represents in words thoughts of Mitchell's which did not have this verbal form. But I think that this is unlikely, and that while the narrator is *telling* us that Mitchell had always considered Dr Monygham a sort of beachcomber of superior intelligence, we are not here to assume that at this moment Mitchell is *thinking* that he has always considered Monygham in this way.)

So far as Mitchell's speech is concerned, Conrad seems so concerned to indicate the extent to which this misses the point, that his narrative purposes are better served by techniques which reveal more accurately the actual words used by Mitchell: Direct or Reported Speech. For even where Conrad does use Reported Speech to convey Captain Mitchell's speech, it is often very close to Direct Speech. And even when dealing with Mitchell's iterative narrative (it is characteristic of Mitchell that he delivers 'set speeches'), Conrad soon moves into Direct Speech. It is as if the ironic presentation of an absurd character such as Mitchell almost requires the use of a technique that draws attention to the actual words he uses.

> Then he would begin by describing the getting away of the silver, and his natural anxiety lest 'his fellow' in charge of the lighter should make some mistake. Apart from the loss of so much precious metal, the life of Señor Martin Decoud, an agreeable, wealthy, and well-informed young gentle-

man, would have been jeopardized through his falling into the hands of his political enemies. Captain Mitchell also admitted that in his solitary vigil on the wharf he had felt a measure of concern for the future of the whole country.

'A feeling, sir,' he explained .... (*Nostromo*, p. 324)

We can note how Conrad first signals his ironic use of Mitchell's own term by placing 'his fellow' in inverted commas; this is either the narrator mocking Mitchell's term 'my fellow'; or a represented speech transformation of 'my fellow' with the addition of inverted commas to indicate narrator irony. Whichever is the case, the reader is sensitized to the possibility of Mitchell's own speech being related, and is able easily to detect this speech in the represented speech of the following sentence. This movement allows for a heavy concentration of authorial irony in the sentence which starts, 'Captain Mitchell also . . .'.[31] It is in such sentences as this that the dual voice theory of FID seems to me to receive strongest support, although one needs to stress that these two voices are 'either–or' rather than simultaneous, and that they belong to entirely different narrative levels. In this sentence we are conscious both of Mitchell's utterance (and, indeed, of some of the words he probably used when making his point), and also of the narrator's distanced irony. From this point Conrad can move on into Direct Speech and can reap maximum effect from the contrast between what Mitchell says (and how he says it), and what the reader knows the situation actually to be.

The effects produced by such constant and subtle shifts of narrative perspective are central to the power and richness of *Nostromo*, its extraordinarily three-dimensional appearance to the reader. Characters and events are constantly seen from a variety of perspectives, perspectives which are set against and illuminate one another. Some of the shifts of perspective are extremely fleeting – but not the less effective for this. In the middle of a passage describing in Reported Speech Mrs Gould's thoughts after watching the troops depart, we find the following sentence: 'Something like a slight faintness came over her, and she looked blankly at Antonia's still face, wondering what would happen to Charley if that absurd man failed' (p. 166). The use of 'Charley' rather than 'Charles Gould' or 'Gould' precipitates us unambiguously into Mrs Gould's consciousness, from whence it is that Barrios appears an 'absurd man'. But in the next sentence we are back in Reported Speech, having been given an emotional jolt by means of this rapid shift into and out of the mind of Mrs Gould.

Such shifts can often be difficult to establish for certain. Take the following comment from an essay on *Nostromo* by Kiernan Ryan:

Thus, although the text reveals only too clearly why the Sulacan people suffer, and will continue to suffer, under the '*imperium in imperio*' of Gould and the whole social order he represents, Conrad can nevertheless conclude from the scene in which Gould observes a woman kneeling by the side of a dying *cargador*, mortally wounded while defending the interests of the mine: 'The cruel futility of things stood unveiled in the levity and sufferings of that incorrigible people; the cruel futility of lives and [of] deaths thrown away in the vain endeavour to attain an enduring solution of the problem'. (The quotation is from *Nostromo*, p. 364. The word in square brackets is omitted in Ryan's quotation)[32]

Let us look at the passage concerned. After an authorial description of Gould's witnessing of the dying *cargador*, it reads as follows.

> The cruel futility of things stood unveiled in the levity and sufferings of that incorrigible people; the cruel futility of lives and of deaths thrown away in the vain endeavour to attain an enduring solution of the problem. Unlike Decoud, Charles Gould could not play lightly a part in a tragic farce. It was tragic enough for him in all conscience, but he could see no farcical element. He suffered too much under a conviction of irremediable folly. He was too severely practical and too idealistic to look upon its terrible humours with amusement, as Martin Decoud, the imaginative materialist, was able to do in the dry light of his scepticism. To him, as to all of us, the compromises with his conscience appeared uglier than ever in the light of failure. His taciturnity, assumed with a purpose, had prevented him from tampering openly with his thoughts; but the Gould Concession had insidiously corrupted his judgment. He might have known, he said to himself, leaning over the balustrade of the corridor, that Ribierism could never come to anything. The mine had corrupted his judgment by making him sick of bribing and intriguing merely to have his work left alone from day to day. Like his father, he did not like to be robbed. It exasperated him. He had persuaded himself that, apart from higher considerations, the backing up of Don José's hopes of reform was good business. He had gone forth into the senseless fray as his poor uncle, whose sword hung on the wall of his study, had gone forth – in the defence of the commonest decencies of organized society.
>
> (*Nostromo*, pp. 364-5)

Now it is indeed possible that the words quoted from *Nostromo* by Ryan can properly be attributed to an authorial narrator (which is not quite the same as saying that they can be attributed to Conrad himself). But there are clues here which may lead us to believe that rather than being a passage of authorial narrative, what we have is actually represented thought, and that the sentiments contained therein are more properly attributed to Charles Gould. Certainly some parts of this long passage are unambiguously Gould's represented thought. The phrase 'his poor uncle' emanates, surely, from Gould's rather than an authorial consciousness. And this suggests that all that follows after the sentence which begins, 'He might have known, he said to himself', is represented thought. But if so one of the sentences in this sequence echoes part of one prior to it: 'The mine had corrupted his judgement'; 'the Gould Concession had insidiously corrupted his judgment'. Thus it seems possible that a large amount of the first part of this paragraph, including the words quoted by Ryan, could be the represented thought of Charles Gould.

Certainly the words 'That incorrigible people' seem more likely to be Gould's than the authorial narrator's here,[33] and attributing them to Gould allows the reader to savour the irony of the fact that Gould's own wife, later on in the novel, picks up Dr Monygham's use of the word 'incorrigible' and applies this same word to her husband.

> Incorrigible in his devotion to the great silver mine was the Señor Administrador! Incorrigible in his hard, determined service of the material interests to which he had pinned his faith in the triumph of order and justice. Poor boy! (*Nostromo*, p. 521)

With this reading, the irony is that Gould thinks the 'people' incorrigible from the assumed vantage point of *knowing* how to 'attain an enduring solution of the problem', but his wife sees him as just as incorrigible, just as entrapped in a 'vain endeavour' to attain this 'lasting solution'. And, compounding the irony, whereas Gould thinks of his 'poor uncle'; his wife thinks of Gould himself as a 'poor boy!'.

On occasions one may suspect that Conrad uses represented speech in order to provide a less abrupt transition between authorial narrative and Direct Speech. Consider the following passage, in which Mrs Gould informs Viola that his house has been spared from demolition as a result of her intercession (Viola has, ironically, to leave the house later as a result of Nostromo's machinations to protect the silver).

> She talked to him in Italian, of course, and he thanked her with calm dignity. An old Garibaldino was grateful to her from the bottom of his heart for keeping the roof over the heads of his wife and children. He was too old to wander any more.
> 'And is it for ever, signora?' he asked. (*Nostromo*, p. 124)

There seems no obvious reason why Viola's response to Mrs Gould is given half in represented speech and half in Direct Speech other than to provide a bridge between authorial narrative and Direct Speech, unless Conrad wishes to maintain a distance from Viola's presence up to the point when his direct question can be introduced with maximal dramatic effect. In general Conrad seems to use Direct Speech when he wishes to push our consciousness of the narrator into the background and to stress the dramatic nature of particular scenes.

> Don Martin's soft hands suffered cruelly, tugging at the thick handle of the enormous oar. He stuck to it manfully, setting his teeth. He, too, was in the toils of an imaginative existence, and that strange work of pulling a lighter seemed to belong naturally to the inception of a new state, acquired an ideal meaning from his love for Antonia. For all their efforts, the heavily laden lighter hardly moved. Nostromo could be heard swearing to himself between the regular splashes of the sweeps. 'We are making a crooked path,' he muttered to himself. 'I wish I could see the islands.' (*Nostromo*, pp. 265-6)

It seems likely here that so far as Decoud is concerned Conrad is more interested in his mental processes, and so uses (I think) represented thought in the third sentence quoted[34] to describe what is going on in his head, while with regard to Nostromo Conrad is more interested in what is happening, and so switches to Direct Speech. One could cite as a parallel the shift from represented thought to Direct Speech in the scene where Hirsch leaves the gathering at which he has had his unsuccessful meeting with Charles Gould (pp. 204-5). Hirsch's thoughts are given to us in represented thought up to the point at which he is suddenly struck by the oddness of what Gould has said about the dynamite – and at this crucial point a switch to Direct Speech arrests the reader and increases the dramatic effect of Hirsch's questions.[35]

If we turn to consider Conrad's use of represented thought in *Nostromo*, we find fewer examples than of represented speech, and most of these examples involve what is clearly verbal thought. I can cite no example of represented thought in which the thought represented is unambiguously non-verbal. I have already referred to an ambiguous passage involving Captain Mitchell; here is a paragraph involving Nostromo, at the point at which he is refusing to get a priest for Viola's wife:

> He was feeling uneasy at the impiety of this refusal. The Padrona believed in priests, and confessed herself to them. But all women did that. It could not be of much consequence. And yet his heart felt oppressed for a moment – at the thought what absolution would mean to her if she believed in it only ever so little. No matter. It was quite true that he had given her already the very last moment he could spare.
> (*Nostromo*, p. 255)

What strikes me here is that when Nostromo experiences non-verbal mental processes we move out of represented thought into Reported Speech ('He was feeling uneasy', 'And yet his heart felt oppressed for a moment'). We will see the same sort of shift in *Under Western Eyes*. Note too that the final sentence quoted above is ambiguous in a different way: it could be represented thought, giving us the words Nostromo reassures himself with - or it could be an interpolated authorial narrative statement.

Let me return, now, to the issue I raised at the beginning of this section. Why is it that our memory of the narrative perspective of *Nostromo* is of a regularity and consistency that is at odds with its actual fluidity and mobility? The answer, it seems to me, is that there is a consistency of *ideological perspective* in this novel that encourages the reader to remember its *technical perspective* as much less varied than actually it is. In *Nostromo* we move from consciousness to consciousness, from vantage point to vantage point, but the narrative's ideological, moral, and political perspective on people and events - on *history* - remains constant in all its complexities. The narrative assessment of characters in this novel is always clear and always constant, which is not the case so far as *The Nigger of the 'Narcissus'* is concerned.

The Secret Agent

In one of the more revealing (and reliable) comments upon his own work in the 'Author's Preface' to this novel, Conrad reports that 'Even the purely artistic purpose, that of applying an ironic method to a subject of that kind, was formulated with deliberation and in the earnest belief that ironic treatment alone would enable me to say all I felt I would have to say in scorn as well as in pity' (p. xxvii). Scorn and pity; in *The Secret Agent* the alternation between these two emotions requires a perpetual and subtle modification of authorial distance, and the use of FID is a vital aspect of Conrad's achievement of this modification.

> The lodging-house was to be given up. It seems it would not answer to carry it on. It would have been too much trouble for Mr Verloc. It would not have been convenient for his other business. What his business was he did not say; but after his engagement to Winnie he took the trouble to get up before noon, and descending the basement stairs, make himself pleasant to Winnie's mother in the breakfast-room downstairs where she had her motionless being. He stroked the cat, poked the fire, had his lunch served to him there. He left its slightly stuffy cosiness with evident reluctance, but, all the same, remained out till the night was far advanced. He never offered to take Winnie to theatres, as such a nice gentleman ought to have done. His evenings were occupied. (SA, p. 7)

We see here a very delicate and subtle modulation of distance. The narrative is now strongly scornful with unambiguous authorial irony about Verloc's 'taking the trouble' to get up before noon, now verging on pity as in the penultimate sentence, which, if read as represented speech or thought (both are possible), leads us into Winnie's mother's (quite mistaken) view of Verloc. To attribute this last sentence to Winnie's mother we need to be aware that two paragraphs previous to the one quoted we have been told that in her opinion 'Mr Verloc was a very nice gentleman'. Again, we can see why the dual voice theory of FID should have arisen. It is true that the penultimate sentence gives us Winnie's mother's consciousness if read as FID. But it can also be read as ironic authorial comment, with the words 'nice gentleman' quoted ironically from the already reported opinion of Winnie's mother.

Consider another example, again from early on in the novel.

> [Verloc] surveyed through the park railings the evidences of the town's opulence and luxury with an approving eye. All these people had to be protected. Protection is the first necessity of opulence and luxury. They had to be protected; and their horses, carriages, houses, servants had to be protected; and the source of their wealth had to be protected in the heart of the city and the heart of the country; the whole social order favourable to their hygienic idleness had to be protected against the shallow enviousness of unhygienic labour. It had to – and Mr Verloc would have rubbed his hands with satisfaction had he not been constitutionally averse from every superfluous exertion. (SA, p. 12)

Note that no *grammatical* clues reveal that the bulk of this passage apart from the sentence in the present tense[36] and the final interjection is represented thought; it is the content that clearly denotes it to be depictive of Verloc's thoughts rather than of the opinions of the authorial narrator. Even the first-time reader of the novel is likely to recognize the clues provided by an ostensibly positive view of such things as 'hygienic idleness', which we would not expect from an authorial narrative in a work of Conrad's. (An additional puzzle here is that Verloc would be unlikely to use a term such as this, and even if we are to presume that he thinks the thought without using this precise formulation, we can't help feeling that the precise formulation includes the judgement of an authorial narrator. Again, the dual voice hypothesis would seem to offer a convenient way out.) The grammatical ambiguity forces the reader to test each sentence for the possibility of its being an authorial pronouncement, such that simultaneous with the apprehension of Verloc's opinion the reader hears as if echoed the ghostly ironic commentary of the authorial narrator, a commentary that runs as a sort of sub-text through the whole passage.

Much the same sort of comment could be made concerning the following passage.

> That was the form of doubt he feared most. Impervious to fear! Often while walking abroad, when he happened also to come out of

himself, he had such moments of dreadful and sane mistrust of mankind. What if nothing could move them? Such moments come to all men whose ambition aims at a direct grasp upon humanity – to artists, politicians, thinkers, reformers, or saints. A despicable emotional state this, against which solitude fortifies a superior character; and with severe exultation the Professor thought of the refuge of his room, with its padlocked cupboard, lost in a wilderness of poor houses, the hermitage of the perfect anarchist. (SA, p. 82)

In the last-quoted sentence, the words 'the Professor thought' make it more or less certain that the first part of the sentence is meant to represent his own thoughts by means of Direct Speech unenclosed in inverted commas. Without these words we could be dealing with narrative comment, and because the previous sentence is clearly authorial the reader naturally first reads the initial part of the final quoted sentence as heavily ironic authorial comment. This reading has to be retrospectively revised once the final part of the sentence has been read, but the ironic after-taste of the discarded reading lingers. Charles Jones suggests that

> Much of the novel's strength and attractiveness lies in this shifting of the reader's viewpoint brought about by his constant uncertainty of the nature of the linguistic data confronting him – i.e. whether it represents the author's narration, a particular character's direct or reported utterance, or a mixture of all three.[37]

I agree with Jones up to a point, but I do believe that the ambiguities to which he refers can be resolved by the reader after some effort.

Another revealing remark to be found in Conrad's 'Author's Note' to the novel is that 'I have no doubt, however, that there had been moments during the writing of the book when I was an extreme revolutionist, I won't say more convinced than they but certainly cherishing a more concentrated purpose than any of them had ever done in the whole course of his life' (p. xxviii). In *The Secret Agent* the authorial narrator seems almost to adopt and experience the consciousnesses and identities of characters on some occasions, while on other occasions viewing them from a strictly objective and detached perspective. Such identification is not characteristic of *Nostromo*, and in *The Secret Agent* it seems both the product and the cause of Conrad's extensive use of FID.

> The Professor had turned into a street to the left, and walked along, with his head carried rigidly erect, in a crowd whose every individual almost overtopped his stunted stature. It was vain to pretend to himself that he was not disappointed. But that was mere feeling; the stoicism of his thought could not be disturbed by this or any other failure. Next time, or the time after next, a telling stroke would be delivered –

something really startling – a blow fit to open the first crack in the imposing front of the great edifice of legal conceptions sheltering the atrocious injustice of society. Of humble origin .... (SA, p. 80)

The easy movement into the Professor's consciousness that the use of represented thought enables and reflects does not remind us of a similar tendency on the part of the narrator of *Nostromo*. But the movement has a clear ironic purpose; at the same time as we think and experience with the Professor, we also inspect his beliefs with disdain and contempt. Thus although we move *into* the Professor's consciousness and thought processes, we remain as readers *distanced from* him. In spite of the difference between this novel and *Nostromo*, both novels combine extreme flexibility and mobility of perspective with consistency of moral, ideological, and political viewpoint. It is this which ensures that we are never confused by the shifts of the narrative as we are in *The Nigger of the 'Narcissus'*.

The Assistant Commissioner dwells upon the domestic nature of Verloc's crime in *The Secret Agent*, and the action and setting of the novel are appropriately described as 'domestic' for more than one reason. Such domesticity may have made it easier for Conrad to move into his characters' consciousnesses in this novel than in a work such as *Nostromo*, in which a very un-domestic scene is depicted panoramically. Also characteristic of *The Secret Agent* is Conrad's exploitation of the potentialities for dramatic irony provided by represented thought.

Let us consider some examples.

Her [Winnie's mother's] selection made, the disposal of the rest [of her furniture] became a perplexing question in a particular way. She was leaving it in Brett Street, of course. But she had two children. Winnie was provided for by her sensible union with that excellent husband, Mr Verloc. Stevie was destitute – and a little peculiar. (SA, pp. 154-5)

The words 'that excellent husband' occur in what is unambiguously represented thought: this is exactly how Winnie's mother sees Verloc; I have already noted that she thinks of him as a 'nice gentleman'. But of course by this stage in the novel the reader is well aware that Verloc is anything but an excellent husband – certainly not in the way that Winnie's mother believes him to be.

[Winnie] glanced all round the parlour, from the corner cupboard to the good fire in the grate. Esconced cosily behind the shop of doubtful wares, with the mysteriously dim window, and its door suspiciously ajar in the obscure and narrow street, it was in all essentials of domestic propriety and domestic comfort a respectable home. Her devoted affection

missed out of it her brother Stevie, now enjoying a damp villegiature in
the Kentish lanes under the care of Mr Michaelis. (SA, pp. 194-5)

The final part of the last-quoted sentence must be represented thought, as
both reader and narrator know that Stevie is not enjoying anything at all,
having been blown to bits at Greenwich. The reference to 'Mr Michaelis'
rather than just to 'Michaelis' confirms that we have moved into Winnie's
consciousness, and this move creates a strong sense of dramatic irony. At
the same time, can we really imagine Winnie's using a word such as 'villegiature'? As I have suggested earlier, Conrad's use of represented thought
can include the use of words such as the character in question would
never use - but which express admirably an aspect of the authorial
narrator's attitudes or beliefs. Here the contrast between this slightly
absurd word and Winnie's down-to-earth mind is productive of a sense of
mingled absurdity and pity. Not only will Stevie never enjoy this
villegiature: Winnie will never enjoy the sort of culture in which such a
word might have currency. Given the irony earlier evoked in the passage
by the words 'her sensible union', its emotional force is rich and complex.
  Another example.

He was tired. A man isn't made of stone. Hang everything! Mr Verloc
reposed characteristically, clad in his outdoor garments. One side of his
open overcoat was lying partly on the ground. Mr Verloc wallowed on his
back. But he longed for a more perfect rest - for sleep - for a few hours
of delicious forgetfulness. That would come later. Provisionally he rested.
(SA, p. 259)

'That would come later' is either represented thought: Verloc believes he
will be able to sleep later - or extremely ironic narrative commentary:
Verloc will soon be dead. Some readers, I suspect, will read it as the
former, and read as such it invokes a strong sense of dramatic irony, for
even the first-time reader may have picked up sufficient proleptic clues to
recognize that Winnie is shortly to kill Verloc. The sentence, 'A man isn't
made of stone' is also nicely judged. This might represent the precise
words Verloc utters to himself - a Direct Speech ejaculation lacking
quotation marks. Alternatively, it could be represented thought - this is
either what Verloc is thinking in words, or a non-verbal state of mind. (In
the latter case, we are forcibly reminded of the ironic presence of the
authorial narrator - especially as there is a dramatic irony present here
too: very soon Verloc will be stone dead.) Or, finally, it could be a
comment from the authorial narrator.
  Very often Conrad uses both represented speech and represented
thought for more conventionally ironic purposes in *The Secret Agent*. The
comments of Toodles to the Assistant Commissioner at the start of chapter

10 are given in alternating Direct Speech and represented speech, and the effect here is to suggest an urbane narrative contempt for what Toodles says, as if his comments have only to be presented independently from the illuminating conventions appropriate to the understanding of Direct Speech to reveal the paucity of their content. It is as if the narrator adopts an exaggeratedly 'neutral' way of reporting what has been said, so as to draw attention to its content rather than to the personality of its utterer or the manner of its delivery. It should be remembered that in normal spoken utterance a similar technique can be used for the purpose of ridicule. Imagine a conversation between two individuals about a third's decision to retire.

> 'He does not intend to waste his time in retirement like other people. Oh good gracious no; he will occupy his time sensibly in all sorts of ways'.

Banfield claims that the language of narration is always written, and Pascal quotes Charles Bally to the effect that *style indirecte libre* 'does not occur in common linguistic usage and is purely a product of writing'.[38] But the technique is surely closely related to certain techniques of parody and mockery to be found in everyday conversation, and Josiane Paccaud has pointed out to me in a private communication that William Labov's *Language in the Inner City* provides a wealth of examples from speech.

It is possible, however, that such an ironic use of represented *thought* is much more a specifically written phenomenon.

> Mr Verloc watched [his wife]. She disappeared up the stairs. He was disappointed. There was that within him which would have been more satisfied if she had been moved to throw herself upon his breast. But he was generous and indulgent. (SA, p. 252)

By his own lights, of course, Verloc *is* generous and indulgent, but there seems little doubt that most readers are aware of an ironic narrative presence when reading the last-quoted sentence as represented thought. This is perhaps partly because the final two sentences in the passages can be read not as represented thought but as narrative commentary, and so read the last sentence necessarily involves the presence of a highly ironic narrative voice.

Elsewhere in this novel FID and authorial narrative comment are intertwined in extremely complex ways.

> [Verloc's] first really confidential discourse to his wife was optimistic from conviction. He also thought it good policy to display all the assurance he could muster. It would put heart into the poor woman. On his liberation, which, harmonizing with the whole tenor of his life, would be secret, of

> course, they would vanish together without loss of time. As to covering
> up the tracks, he begged his wife to trust him for that. He knew how it
> was to be done so that the devil himself – (SA, p. 250)

The first two sentences quoted are clearly authorial narrative report. The
third must be represented thought, as the narrator knows very well that
Verloc's conviction will not put heart into Winnie. The penultimate sentence can be read either as authorial narrative comment or as represented
speech ('As to covering up the tracks, I beg you to trust me for that').
And the final sentence seems unambiguously to be represented speech. But
the third sentence from the end is a complicated hybrid. To preserve the
flow and sense of Verloc's speech to his wife we must presume that he
tells her that they will vanish together, so that the last part of this
sentence must be represented speech. But the earlier part of the sentence
must be authorial narrative comment, as Verloc himself would never refer
to the secrecy of his eventual liberation as 'harmonizing with the whole
tenor of his life'. It is not just that Verloc would not use these precise
words, but that he could hardly think this thought in any – or no – words
at all. And of course the words as used cannot but express narrative irony.
Such rapid movement between represented speech, represented thought,
and authorial narrative comment can give the impression of a dual voice,
especially when some sentences are ambiguous regarding to whom they
should be attributed, making equally good (but different) sense as FID or
authorial narrative comment. It should be stressed, however, that for the
average reader such passages are rich and suggestive rather than complex
or 'split'. They present the reader with no problems because a narrative
consistency is established at the ideological rather than the technical level;
the technical complexities thus *serve* a higher consistency.

　　The Secret Agent also contains one interesting example of represented
thought, interesting because it demonstrates quite clearly that by now
Conrad was able to use represented thought even when the thought being
represented was not verbal or linguistic in form.

> She remembered now what she had heard, and she remembered it pictori-
> ally. They had to gather him up with the shovel. Trembling all over with
> irrepressible shudders, she saw before her the very implement ....
>
> (SA, p. 260)

'They had to gather him up with the shovel' must be represented thought,
as the reference to 'him' is quite inconsequential if the sentence is taken
as authorial narrative comment. Yet we have just been informed that
Winnie remembers pictorially. One could not have better proof of the fact
that the language of represented thought does not necessarily imply a
similar – or any – linguistic form to that of the thought(s) represented.

By this stage in his writing career Conrad has developed his use of FID to what may be near to being the limits of the technique. In subsequent works he will put this skill to good use, but no later work shows any *technical* advance on the sophistication of his use of FID in *The Secret Agent*.

Under Western Eyes

Moving now to *Under Western Eyes* I wish to focus upon Conrad's use of FID to represent Razumov's mental processes in this work. This is not to suggest that the thought and speech of other characters in the novel is not conveyed to the reader by means of FID, it is; but it is with regard to Razumov's thought, rather than to his speech or to the speech or thought of other characters that the use of FID in *Under Western Eyes* is of especial interest, for it seems to be restricted to the depiction of verbal thought.

My basic thesis is that the nature of Razumov's mental processes changes radically as a result of changes in his circumstances, and that the narrative of the teacher of languages not only has to convey these changes, but - in order so to do - to adapt itself to them. When I use the term 'mental processes' I mean something more fundamental than that Razumov has different thoughts: I mean that he thinks in a fundamentally different manner, that his thoughts assume a different form: specifically verbal and self-interrogatory.

Razumov's circumstances change fundamentally twice in the course of *Under Western Eyes*: firstly on Haldin's involvement of him in his act of political terrorism, an involvement which culminates in Razumov's act of betrayal; and secondly when he confesses to Nathalie Haldin and to the emigré Russians in Geneva. Between these two points Razumov's situation is marked by a cluster of linked characteristics.

For a start, his isolation becomes more complete and more oppressive. Already conscious of his lack of a family and a 'name' and described by the teacher of languages as 'as lonely in the world as a man swimming in the deep sea' (p. 10), Razumov suddenly finds himself far more thoroughly cut off from his kind.

> 'I want to be understood.' The universal aspiration with all its profound and melancholy meaning assailed heavily Razumov, who, amongst eighty millions of his kith and kin, had no heart to which he could open himself. (UWE, p. 39)

As the teacher of languages remarks a few lines further on (sounding in this instance very much like Joseph Conrad), 'No human being could bear a steady view of moral solitude without going mad'. The word 'moral' is important. Razumov is not cut off from day-to-day intercourse with his kind, from casual contact with his fellows. But he has no 'heart to which he could *open* himself', no free and open communication such as dissipates moral solitude. As the teacher of languages points out, it is for this reason that Razumov welcomes contact even with Mikulin, going to meet him, 'with the eagerness of a pursued person welcoming any sort of shelter' (p. 304).

Razumov's isolation is compounded by fear, and productive of secrecy, and this 'isolation/fear/secrecy' complex is crucial to an understanding of the mental processes which the narrative of *Under Western Eyes* has to convey and represent. As Sophia Antonovna says to the teacher of languages at the end of the novel:

> 'There are evil moments in every life. A false suggestion enters one's brain, and then fear is born – fear of oneself, fear for oneself.'
> (UWE, p. 379)

We are told early on of Razumov that he 'was always accessible, and there was nothing secret or reserved in his life' (p. 7). But as a result of the all-embracing fear produced by Haldin's unsolicited visit, Razumov becomes a person with a secret self, a person with many reservations. And this fear engenders in him a peculiarly *verbal* mode of thought. In one of his long encounters with Sophia Antonovna, the following passage of represented thought occurs:

> It seemed to him he would have given anything to be sitting inside all alone. He was inexpressibly weary, weary in every fibre of his body, but he had a reason for not being the first to break off the conversation. At any instant, in the visionary and criminal babble of revolutionists, some momentous words might fall on his ear; from her lips, from anybody's lips. As long as he managed to preserve a clear mind and to keep down his irritability there was nothing to fear. The only condition of success and safety was indomitable will-power, he reminded himself. (UWE, p. 248)

Now it is possible that the first quoted sentence here is intended to represent non-verbal thought, and that the second sentence could be direct authorial comment. But the terminology used in the third sentence makes it quite clear that this is represented thought which mirrors the actual language used by Razumov in his thinking, and towards the end of the passage we learn why his thinking is so verbal in character: 'As long as he managed to preserve a clear mind and to keep down his irritability *there was nothing to fear*'. Because of his fear he has to keep enjoining himself to behave in certain ways, and such self-address *has* to be verbal. The imperative is a verbal mode: one cannot tell oneself to do something by means of a graphic image.

One of Conrad's striking insights in the novel is that when one is continually suppressing statements out of fear, one's mind starts to wander. Open and free conversation involves its own discipline; one's mind does not wander off. But if what one says is fenced off from what is really occupying or dominating one's mind, then what one says can become so uninteresting that one's mind wanders away from it. Razumov discovers this during his interviews with Mikulin. He is struck by Mikulin's glossy hair.

> 'Could it be a wig?' Razumov detected himself wondering with an unexpected detachment. His self-confidence was much shaken. He resolved to chatter no more. Reserve! Reserve! All he had to do was to keep the Ziemianitch episode secret with absolute determination, when the questions came. Keep Ziemianitch strictly out of all the answers.
> (UWE, p. 90)

Note the interesting contrast here: Razumov tries to restrict his output of spoken words ('chattering'), but enjoins himself in verbal imperatives. The last sentence quoted above could presumably be easily rendered in Direct Speech: it is what Razumov says to himself. The use of represented thought has the effect, however, of increasing the distance between the narrator and Razumov.

This connection between fear and verbalizing is insisted upon a few pages later, again with reference to Razumov's conversation with Sophia Antonovna.

> He waited, not very alert now, but with the grip of the ever-present danger giving him an air of attentive gravity. Who could have written about him in that letter from Petersburg? A fellow-student, surely – some imbecile victim of revolutionary propaganda, some foolish slave of foreign, subversive ideals. A long, famine-stricken red-nosed figure presented itself to his mental search. That must have been the fellow! (UWE, p. 258)

The danger forces Razumov to think carefully about his behaviour, and this thought takes the appropriate form of a verbal question to himself – appropriate, because this is how we do typically think when in a tight spot; we start talking silently to ourselves, asking ourselves questions, conducting an interior dialogue with ourselves. Interestingly, it appears to be a visual image that presents itself to Razumov's mind in response to his self-questioning, but his response to this image is again verbal. Most revealingly, Conrad has to move the narrative out of represented thought to convey the image of the red-nosed student presenting itself to Razumov (technically, this is a comment by the narrating teacher of languages). But we move back into represented thought for Razumov's (verbal) response to the vision of this figure.

This particular example is an important one, for it reveals that when a sequence of represented thought is being interpreted by the reader as a guide to the precise verbal content of the thought process displayed, then it is well-nigh impossible for the represented thought suddenly to start conveying thoughts which are visual or imagistic and non-verbal in nature. Imagine how the reader would have responded had the last two sentences of the previous quotation read as follows:

> The long, famine-stricken red-nosed figure of course! That must have been the fellow!

The reader might in such a case have assumed that an image of the red-nosed student *accompanied* Razumov's thought, but he or she would surely have assumed that Razumov's recollection of the student was achieved verbally, was part of a string of verbal thoughts. The example confirms again that the reader will assume a consistency in the form of the speech or thought depicted in FID unless there is a clear sign that some break has occurred, and it also confirms that FID can be presented in such a way as to convey the precise verbal nature of the speech or thought depicted – the actual words involved.

Razumov's interior dialogues resemble his dialogues with others in more ways than one. Consider the following passage from the start of Part Third, which describes Razumov's thoughts following his conversation with the teacher of languages, as he gazes alone into the water under the bridge.

> 'What is the meaning of all this?' he thought, staring downwards at the headlong flow so smooth and clean that only the passage of a faint air-bubble, or a thin vanishing streak of foam like a white hair, disclosed its vertiginous rapidity, its terrible force. 'Why has that meddlesome old Englishman blundered against me? And what is this silly tale of a crazy old woman?'
>
> He was trying to think brutally on purpose, but he avoided any mental reference to the young girl. (UWE, p. 198)

Razumov is '*trying* to think brutally on purpose', and this conscious effort leads him to think dialogically, to think in verbal utterances, in conversational questions to himself. But at this point he is no more open in his conversation with himself than he is in his public conversations with others: he avoids awkward subjects with himself just as he does with the teacher of languages or with Sophia Antonovna. A few lines further down we are told: 'And even in that privacy, his thought had some reservations of which he was vaguely conscious'. 'Trying to think brutally' does not exclude a measure of self-deception. And to *convey* this self-deception the narrative has to move out of represented thought and into authorial narrative comment.

My reference above to the apparently visual image of the red-nosed student which comes into Razumov's thoughts should make it clear that although his thought is depicted as being dominantly verbal and dialogic, it is by no means presented as exclusively so. Indeed, Conrad is able to portray in a marvellously subtle manner the way in which verbal and non-verbal forms of thought interact in Razumov's mind.

> 'The craze of an old woman – the fussy officiousness of a blundering elderly Englishman. What devil put him in the way? Haven't I treated him cavalierly enough? Haven't I just? That's the way to treat these meddlesome persons. Is it possible that he still stands behind my back, waiting?'
> Razumov felt a faint chill run down his spine. It was not fear. He was certain that it was not fear – not fear for himself – but it was, all the same, a sort of apprehension as if for another, for someone he knew without being able to put a name to the personality. (UWE, p. 199)

This seems to me a wonderful depiction of the way – familiar, surely, to all of us – in which a stream of inner verbal questions is interrupted by a nagging doubt or sense of apprehension which is not verbal and which cannot be recognized and identified until one has 'put a name' to it. The switch from Direct Speech to represented thought as Razumov tries to isolate and identify the 'faint chill' is strikingly effective in conveying a shift in the form of his thinking.

Putting one's thoughts into words is an essential part of understanding oneself, of bringing suppressed responses, thoughts, feelings – moral scruples or misgivings – into the light of conscious knowledge. If we bear in mind what Razumov has to be brought to understand in the course of *Under Western Eyes* it is not surprising that the narrative should time and time again insist upon the predominantly verbal nature of his mental processes. It is when we are *trying* to think, forcing our brains to grapple with *problems*, that we most consistently think in words rather than images or other non-verbal forms of thought. But again we note that to convey this process the narrative cannot restrict itself to represented thought.

It is not accidental – I would argue – that the depiction of Razumov's thought processes in *Under Western Eyes*, although it relies both on Direct Speech and on FID, involves an unusually high percentage of Direct Speech. Direct Speech allows the essentially verbal nature of his thought processes to be revealed absolutely unambiguously.

Nor is it accidental that one of the longest speeches Razumov makes to Haldin after he has betrayed him is concerned with secrecy, advancing the view that life is full of secret places. I have argued elsewhere that if a literate and educated individual is isolated, scared of other people to the extent that he or she must keep certain things secret from them, but forced continually to make decisions, to act in the world, then this is productive of a characteristic set of mental processes, of ways of thinking. Writing about *Jane Eyre* I argued that what such circumstances produce in such a person is a characteristically *verbal* and *dialogic* set of mental processes.[39] I took issue with the view that internal dialogue should be seen merely as a technically undeveloped and crude narrative *method*, a means whereby far more sophisticated mental processes could be displayed in simplified form for the reader, and argued that fully verbalized internal dialogue is actually the way in which an educated person thinks in given circumstances. One quotation I included in this article on *Jane Eyre* is, I think, worth giving again here.

It is from L. S. Vygotsky's pioneer work *Thought and Language*, and in it Vygotsky argues that the social acquisition of language structures the development of thought in the developing child, and that as the child's use of language is initially dialogic the dialogic form is crucial to the development of thought. Vygotsky's view is that *egocentric speech* – when the developing child talks to itself – is a stage transitional between the social use of language and its silent internalization into thought. Most relevant to the present inquiry is Vygotsky's argument that if a young child is faced with difficulties or problems to solve, the amount of egocentric speech increases dramatically.

> in these difficult situations the coefficient of egocentric speech almost doubled, in comparison with Piaget's normal figure for the same age and also in comparison with our figure for children not facing these problems. The child would try to grasp and to remedy the situation in talking to himself: 'Where's the pencil? I need a blue pencil. Never mind, I'll draw with the red one and wet it with water; it will become dark and look like blue.'[40]

Not only does problem-solving call forth egocentric speech, it calls forth *a question and answer* format here. Jane Eyre's internal dialogues are also characterized by such a format, apparently called forth by the need on the part of an educated, isolated and powerless person, to solve problems in a hostile environment. As Caryl Emerson has said in a commentary on Vygotsky's study of egocentric speech in the child, 'conversation with oneself' is 'the natural dynamic of problem solving'.[41]

If we return to *Under Western Eyes* we find that Razumov's thought processes subsequent to his betrayal of Haldin and prior to his confession are of two sorts. Firstly *visions*, of himself and of Haldin, and secondly highly *verbal* thoughts characterized by a dialogic structure which includes an unusually high percentage of *questions*. Surely Razumov asks himself more questions than any other Conradian character. Connected to this is what in the context of Conrad's fiction is surely an untypically high incidence of Direct Speech used to express and convey a character's thoughts. Although the verbal form of interior dialogue can be conveyed both by Direct Speech and by represented thought, the latter technique clearly runs a greater risk of ambiguities than does Direct Speech. With Direct Speech the reader *knows* that Razumov has used certain words to himself, whereas with represented thought the verbal nature of the thoughts may be less instantly perceived by the reader. Even so, where Direct Speech is replaced by represented thought it *is* recurrently clear that it is *verbal* thought that is being represented; examples of Razumov's represented thought in which it is unclear whether the thought represented is verbal or non-verbal or where it is apparent that the thought is non-verbal, are hard to find in this novel.

In the second paragraph of *Under Western Eyes* the teacher of languages tells the reader that 'Words, as is well known, are the great foes of reality', and yet it is words that Razumov consistently uses to deal with the demands of this reality. *Under Western Eyes* will explore this tension and will seek to reveal how helpful words are to Razumov in his hours of need. On the third page of the novel the teacher of languages comments upon the written record left by Razumov, remarking both that it is inconceivable that Razumov should have wished any human eye to see it,[42] and also that 'There must be a wonderful soothing power in mere words since so many men have used them for self-communion'. Razumov's written record thus parallels his silent thought processes, being a use of words for self-communion or interior dialogue.

Before Razumov has started to grapple with this new set of problems thrust upon him by Haldin, his thought is not so strikingly verbal in form.

> Razumov saw himself shut up in a fortress, worried, badgered, perhaps ill-used. He saw himself deported by an administrative order, his life broken, ruined, and robbed of all hope. He saw himself – at best – leading a miserable existence under police supervision, in some small, far-away provincial town ....
>
> He saw his youth pass away from him in misery and half starvation – his strength give way, his mind become an abject thing. (UWE, p. 21)

This graphic or imagistic grappling with his situation and his likely future soon gives way to an increasingly verbal response, and it does so at the point at which Razumov begins to try to decide what he should *do*. This response is conveyed to us via represented thought.

> He shuddered. Then the peace of bitter calmness came over him.
> It was best to keep this man out of the streets till he could be got rid of
> with some chance of escaping. That was the best that could be done.
>
> (UWE, p. 21)

Once Razumov is out in the street on his way to Ziemianitch he
indulges, according to the account of the teacher of languages which is
ostensibly based on Razumov's own record, in a 'tumult of thoughts' full
of 'exclamatory repetitions'. But after his abortive encounter with
Ziemianitch he again has to decide what to *do* and now his thoughts, given
to us in Direct Speech, are full of verbal questions to himself – and
answers to these questions.

> 'What are the luridly smoky lucubrations of that fellow to the clear
> grasp of my intellect?' he thought. 'Is this not my country? Have I not got
> forty million brothers?' he asked himself, unanswerably victorious in the
> silence of his breast. (UWE, p. 35)

That 'unanswerably victorious' should not be passed by too hurriedly.
Razumov's interior dialogue at this stage is seen clearly as a process of
self-deception, one which becomes even more apparent two paragraphs
later when he starts to talk in clichés of such an obvious form that they
draw attention to themselves. Conrad makes a characteristic use of ellipsis
to suggest an ironic distance between narrator and character here,[43] and
again characteristically he combines it with represented thought. The
thought is, however, again clearly verbal in origin, and indeed the passage
moves finally into Direct Speech.

> Of course he was far from being a moss-grown reactionary.
> Everything was not for the best. Despotic bureaucracy . . . abuses . . .
> corruption . . . and so on. Capable men were wanted. Enlightened
> intelligences. Devoted hearts. But absolute power should be preserved –
> the tool ready for the man – for the great autocrat of the future.
> Razumov believed in him. The logic of history made him unavoidable.
> The state of the people demanded him. 'What else?' he asked himself
> ardently, 'could move all that mass in one direction? Nothing could.
> Nothing but a single will.' (UWE, p. 35)

Razumov is engaged in interior dialogue here, and yet it is not like a real
dialogue. It is too one-sided: one point of view is hogging the conversation
and alternative beliefs are allowed no real sway. Note the subtle effect of
the sentence, 'Razumov believed in him'. This shifts us from represented
thought to authorial comment in such a way as to suggest an ironic but
pitying detachment on the part of the narrator – again, technically the
teacher of languages, but probably read by most readers as a more anony-

mous detached narrator. (The phrase could, it is true, be a clumsy example of represented thought, conveying that Razumov thought, 'I believe in him'. I think this unlikely.)

In this example Razumov is both hectoring persuader but also hectored listener. At the start of *Under Western Eyes* we are told that in discussion, 'he was easily swayed by argument and authority', and this seems to be as true of his inner arguments as of more public ones. After the betrayal Razumov has an 'argument' with himself while talking to Haldin, but this argument is neither honest nor open.

> 'H'm,' muttered Razumov, and biting his lower lip he continued to walk up and down and to carry on his strange argument.
> Yes, to a man in such a situation – of course it would be an act of kindness. The question, however, was not how to be kind, but how to be firm. He was a slippery customer . . . (UWE, p. 58)

Only as a result of an extraordinary process of self-deception is Razumov able to tell himself that it would be an act of kindness to murder Haldin, forgetting that this is so only because Razumov himself has just betrayed him. We should not assume that because one is arguing with oneself one must be telling the truth . . .

The following day Razumov goes to three lectures and attempts to work on his prize essay in the library, but:

> His new tranquillity was like a flimsy garment, and seemed to float at the mercy of a casual word. Betrayal! Why! the fellow had done all that was necessary to betray himself. Precious little had been needed to deceive him.
> 'I have said no word to him that was not strictly true. Not one word,' Razumov argued with himself.
> Once engaged on this line of thought there could be no question of doing useful work. The same ideas went on passing through his mind, and he pronounced mentally the same words over and over again.
> (UWE, p. 71)

A number of things are worth commenting upon here. Firstly, that it is a *word* that keeps coming back to torment Razumov and it is the same *words* he pronounces mentally again and again. Secondly, that Razumov's arguing with himself continues to be palpably Jesuitical; he attempts to defend himself against the moral reproaches implicit in the word 'betrayal' by means of a technical point – that no word he said to Haldin was not strictly true. And thirdly that although Razumov's thought processes are given to us partly by means of represented thought, it is clear that the words used in the narrative are directly parallel to the words which constituted these thought processes.

By the time of a much later conversation between Razumov and Sophia Antonovna, we are told of the former that

> He had argued himself into new beliefs; and he had made for himself a mental atmosphere of gloomy and sardonic reverie, a sort of murky medium through which the event appeared like a featureless shadow having vaguely the shape of a man; a shape extremely familiar, yet utterly inexpressive, except for its air of discreet waiting in the dusk. It was not alarming. (UWE, p. 246)

It is clear here that Razumov has argued himself into a lie, a view of Haldin's betrayal which refuses to recognize Haldin's humanity but transforms him into 'a featureless shadow'.

If one talks to oneself one does in some sense divide oneself. Just before he decides to betray Haldin, a 'voice seemed to cry within' Razumov (p. 33); it is as if the extreme pressure he is facing is splitting him in two. The doubling that we see in literal form in 'The Secret Sharer' – written, we should remember, during a break from the writing of *Under Western Eyes* – seems to be duplicated in the longer work in a more existential form. Both Razumov and the young captain in 'The Secret Sharer' have a certain amount in common – especially if we include the young captain's double, Leggatt. Razumov is described as 'as lonely in the world as a man swimming in the deep sea' (p. 10), which is how the young captain first witnesses Leggatt, and, leaving the drawing-room in which he has met Madame de S— and Peter Ivanovitch,

> [Razumov] felt, bizarre as it may seem, as though another self, an independent sharer of his mind, had been able to view his whole person very distinctly indeed. (UWE, p. 230)

The other person is surely a part of himself, an unacknowledged part – perhaps even the part which sees his own brain suffering on the rack (p. 88).

Both Razumov and the young captain in 'The Secret Sharer' keep written records, records which are intended for the eyes of their respective writers. Razumov's written account is described by the teacher of languages as his 'mental and psychological self-confession, self-analysis' (p. 308), and the same commentator argues that the record 'could not have been meant for any one's eyes but his own'.

> Mr Razumov looked at it [the record], I suppose, as a man looks at himself in a mirror, with wonder, perhaps with anguish, with anger or

despair. Yes, as a threatened man may look fearfully at his own face in the glass, formulating to himself reassuring excuses for his appearance marked by the taint of some insidious hereditary disease. (UWE, p. 214)

His writing, then, is an attempt to discover something in himself which is hidden to his own view, just as sight of his face in a mirror reveals something seemingly unexpected.

In his listless wanderings round about the table he caught sight of his own face in the looking-glass and that arrested him. The eyes which returned his stare were the most unhappy eyes he had ever seen.

(UWE, p. 69)

During Razumov's last meeting with Nathalie Haldin, the teacher of languages reports that Razumov, 'seemed to me to be watching himself inwardly, as though he were trying to count his own heart-beats' (p. 349).

I suggested, earlier on, that there is throughout *Under Western Eyes* a tension between the disillusioned view of language which is held by the teacher of languages, and Razumov's attempt to grapple with his problems by means of words. But while Razumov concentrates upon words, other forms of human communication work their effect on him. In a further chapter on *Under Western Eyes* in this book I attempt to show how important non-verbal communication is in this novel, a novel full of references to gestures, posture and expressions, and in which references to eyes and hands (the most communicative parts of the human body) are to be found in abundance. When Razumov finally confesses to Nathalie Haldin, he does so by means not of a word, but of a gesture – he points to his own breast. The dialectic of verbal and non-verbal communication in *Under Western Eyes* is extremely complex, and no simple conclusion can be drawn as to the greater moral force of the one or the other – it is their interaction and interdependence that is insisted upon. What we are led to see, however, is that words alone will not lead us to the truth.

Conrad's use of FID to portray Razumov's thought processes in *Under Western Eyes* is interestingly different from its use elsewhere in his works. The technique's ironic and 'dual voice' potentialities are made comparatively little use of, and where they are used it is typically with regard to characters other than Razumov: Kostia and Peter Ivanovitch, for example. What Conrad seems most concerned to display with regard to Razumov is the verbal nature of his thought processes, his use of words to argue with himself. In the depiction of these thought processes FID constitutes a variation from the use of Direct Speech and is used primarily as such.

One other rather different point should be made about Conrad's use of FID in *Under Western Eyes*. As several commentators have pointed out, just as the reader's awareness of Marlow's narrating presence in *Heart of Darkness* or *Lord Jim* can be encouraged or suppressed, so too the technical continuity of the teacher of languages' narrative covers a wide range of variations in the reader's awareness of this narrating presence. This is related to the use of FID in the work, for some passages of FID in the novel can be read as conventional omniscient or semi-omniscient extra-mimetic narratives. Let me give one example. When Haldin announces that it was he that killed de P–, Razumov's thoughts are given to the reader in a passage of Reported Speech which shifts into represented thought (p. 16). The next three paragraphs are of represented speech – giving the reader what Haldin said to Razumov. And yet they can be read quite comfortably as extra-mimetic authorial commentary. Take the last two of these paragraphs.

> After throwing his 'engine' he ran off and in a moment was overtaken by the panic-struck people flying away from the spot after the second explosion. They were wild with terror. He was jostled once or twice. He slowed down for the rush to pass him and then turned to the left into a narrow street. There he was alone.
>
> He marvelled at this immediate escape. The work was done. He could hardly believe it. He fought with an almost irresistible longing to lie down on the pavement and sleep. But this sort of faintness – a drowsy faintness – passed off quickly. He walked faster, making his way to one of the poorer parts of the town in order to look up Ziemianitch.
>
> (UWE, p. 17)

It seems to me that the reason why the reader is not bothered by some of the tensions in the narrative conventions of the novel is precisely that Conrad's use of FID allows the presence of the teacher of languages to become far more ghostly at times. Not only could these two paragraphs be read as conventional authorial narrative, the second paragraph could be seen as the displaying by such an omniscient narrator of the private emotions of a character under stress. Few readers surely remain fully conscious that what we actually have here is the teacher of languages' account of Haldin's speech to Razumov, drawn from Razumov's retrospective written account. And this is just as well – for the more aware the reader is of this complex narrative chain, the more he or she must be struck by several of its attendant implausibilities. In just the same way, the teacher of languages' long introductory account of Peter Ivanovitch, drawn from the latter's book, has to keep reminding the reader of the account's origin in the book, as the passage reads so easily as conventional authorial narrative. The potentiality of FID to 'lose the narrator' is useful to Conrad; it allows the narrative of *Under Western Eyes* to flow smoothly, with the reader being reminded of its technical origin or chain of delivery only when it suits the author.

In summary, then, two points must be stressed. First, that Conrad's use of FID in *Under Western Eyes* is perfectly adapted to the successive forms that Razumov's thoughts take as his life proceeds through a number of clearly distinguished stages. Second, that the technical implausibilities attendant upon Conrad's use of the narrating teacher of languages are artistically unimportant because there is a unifying narrative centre *behind* this ostensible source, a centre constituted by the ideological, moral and political coherence of the work's implied scheme of values.

Chance

It would be repetitive to go through *Chance* in the same detail. Many commentators have noted that Conrad's narrative technique in this work seems unnecessarily over-complex; Jocelyn Baines pointed out in 1960 that some passages in the novel relay events to the reader through no fewer than four consciousnesses, and this may explain why it is impossible in certain cases to say whether we are dealing with represented thought or represented speech. For example, when Marlow meets Flora de Barral outside the hotel in which Mr Fyne is talking to Roderick Anthony, Flora tells Marlow the story of her frustrated suicide attempt.

> 'She told me all this with simplicity. My voice had destroyed her poise – the suicide poise of her mind. Every act of ours, the most criminal, the most mad presupposes a balance of thought, feeling and will, like a correct attitude for an effective stroke in a game. And I had destroyed it. She was no longer in proper form for the act. She was not very much annoyed. Next day would do. She would have to slip away without attracting the notice of the dog. She thought of the necessity almost tenderly.' (*Chance*, p. 203)

The passage continues in like vein for a few lines more, then reverts to Direct Speech. Thus it seems likely that the concluding four sentences above are meant to be read as represented speech – the speech of Flora to Marlow. But they also read as if they could be represented thought – a representation of Flora's thoughts immediately subsequent to the aborted suicide attempt. The ambiguity is related to an unnecessarily complicated chain of narrative which is not notably fruitful or generative of any particularly valuable effect. At times in *Chance* the suspicion may arise that Conrad seems to use represented speech for no better reason than that of providing some narrative variety, some relief from Direct Speech.

'"But, papa," she cried, "I haven't been shut up like you." She didn't mind speaking of it because he was innocent. He hadn't been understood. It was a misfortune of the most cruel kind but no more disgraceful than an illness, a maiming accident or some other visitation of blind fate. "I wish I had been too. But I was alone out in the world ...."'

(*Chance*, p. 360)

The content makes it crystal clear that the sentences in-between those of Direct Speech are represented speech, and represent Flora's uninterrupted speech. The only reason why Conrad switches from Direct to represented speech and back again seems to be that this gives a little variety, although it is possible that another intention is to remind us of the presence of Marlow, the narrator who is able to narrate Flora's speech for us.

Conrad certainly uses represented speech for the purpose of achieving distance in *Chance*. When we are given a conversation between Mr Powell and Mr Franklin, a switch from Direct to represented speech at a crucial moment has an important distancing effect.

'I don't understand why you are so hard on the captain, Mr Franklin. I thought you were a great friend of his."
'Mr Franklin exclaimed at this. He was not hard on the captain. Nothing was further from his thoughts. Friend! Of course he was a good friend and a faithful servant. He begged Powell to understand that if Captain Anthony chose to strike a bargain with Old Nick to-morrow, and Old Nick were good to the captain, he (Franklin) would find it in his heart to love Old Nick for the captain's sake. That was so. On the other hand, if a saint, an angel with white wings came along and – " (*Chance*, pp. 301-2. The Dent house style results in a rather confusing use of inverted commas here, and one suspects that the complex chain of narrative may have been too much for the compositor.)

The switch to represented speech distances us from Mr Franklin, encourages us to see the encounter more from Powell's than from Franklin's point of view. There is perhaps even a slight hint of irony generated by such distancing: it is well known that colloquial speech can be made to sound absurd if put into Reported Speech ('He said that he would be damned if &c &c'), and the same is true of represented speech. One slight clumsiness can be pointed out here: Conrad has to include the name 'Franklin' in brackets after a use of 'he' which might be puzzling to the reader without the explanation.

Of all the Marlow narratives, *Chance* contains by far the highest percentage use of FID. We can explain this, I suspect, by a comparison with *Under Western Eyes*. In both novels, the presence of the *speaking* narrator is frequently lost (to the reader and, one suspects, to Conrad too). But in *Chance* the ideological confusions that I discuss in a later chapter compound the problems raised by too heavy a reliance upon FID in a spoken narrative. Far too often in this novel we don't know where we are. Who is speaking or thinking? Who is judging or witholding judgement? What is the scale of values that is appealed to? The case of *Chance* shows that ideological vacillation and complexity of narrative perspective together create confusion for the reader.

Conclusion

In his *Marxism and the Philosophy of Language*, V. N. Vološinov, in concluding comments on what he terms 'Quasi-Direct Discourse' (FID), sees the emergence of this mode as part and parcel of 'the victory of extreme forms of the picturesque style' and as representative of 'the *general, far-reaching subjectivization of the ideological word utterance*'.[44] But as we have seen in Conrad's work, to utilize more and more of the resources of FID is not necessarily to abandon oneself to subjecti*vism*. It is true that this technique provides the writer with the most technically advanced means to shift the narrative from consciousness to consciousness without drawing the reader's attention to such shifts, but such a technical resource alone does not make for subjectivism.

Indeed, where this technical resource is backed up by ideological clarity, penetration, and commitment, then what we have is very far from subjectivism. In some of Conrad's greatest works of fiction we get, rather, a sense of a social and physical world which is not dependent upon or created by the individual consciousness, but which includes and can be influenced by it. This sense comes from Conrad's ability to combine the narrative flexibility given him by techniques such as FID with an ideological, moral, and political penetration and commitment which can direct and organize his technical resources. To see well you need both good eyes, and a brain that tells you what to look for and how to interpret what you see.

---

1   I say 'narrative' rather than 'narrator', as it is frequently misleading to suggest that a work of fiction has a narrator, even if it is narrated. Nevertheless, all works of narrative give the reader a more or less coherent sense of a determining force regulating the telling, and this sense of a determining force (which is not *mechanically* to be associated with the real-life author) inevitably leads the reader to associate the telling with a set of values, a view of the world.

2 Problems of terminology abound in this field in English. In French and German the terms *style indirect libre* and *erlebte Rede* are relatively straightforward. In English a bewildering range of terms can be found to apply to the same phenomenon: Free Indirect Speech (or Discourse); Represented Speech and Thought, Narrated Speech and Thought, and narrated monologue. After years of doggedly sticking to the term Free Indirect Speech on the grounds that it fits in well with the cognate terms Direct Speech and Reported (or Indirect) Speech, I have now to admit that represented speech and represented thought are terms which are more precise, which identify the technique with narrative, and which make an important distinction between the representation of speech and that of thought. In the interests of brevity, however, I shall often refer generally to Free Indirect Discourse when I do not wish to distinguish between the representation of speech and thought, and represented speech or represented thought when I do. It should be noted that not all Free Indirect Discourse represents either speech or thought; it can represent unexpressed attitudes, ideological assumptions, and so on. In accordance with current conventions I shall not capitalize the latter terms, but will continue to capitalize Free Indirect Discourse (FID), Direct Speech, and Reported Speech.

3 Extra-mimetic – outside the created world of the fictional text. The narrative voice in *Almayer's Folly* comes from a different level of reality from that in which the characters live – something that is not true of all novels, or of all novels written by Conrad. (It is often not true of those novels with a personified narrator.)

4 Dorrit Cohn, *Transparent Minds: Narrating Modes for Presenting Consciousness in Fiction*, Princeton, Princeton UP, 1978, p. 100.

5 Shlomith Rimmon-Kenan, *Narrative Fiction: Contemporary Poetics*, London, Methuen, 1983, p. 111.

6 Brian McHale, 'FID: A Survey of Recent Accounts', *Poetics and Theory of Literature* 3 (1978), pp. 257-8.

7 McHale, p. 258.

8 The term 'authorial narrator' should not be taken to imply that Conrad is speaking in his own voice, merely that the point of view is that of a narrator who has an existence 'outside the story being told'.

9 The use of FID often encourages the reader to attempt to 'recover' a Direct Speech original, but unless we are clearly dealing with represented *speech* this can be something of a wild goose chase. And even with represented speech a search for the 'original' utterance can be on a par with asking how many children Lady Macbeth had.

10 I have said that the opening part of the passage I have quoted 'appears in the main to be authorial narrative comment'. There are some slight ambiguities relating to the originating consciousness in this part of the passage to which attention should perhaps be drawn. Take the following words: 'The consideration, the indolent ease of life – for which he felt himself so well fitted – his ships, his warehouses, his merchandise (old

Lingard would not live for ever)'. Is it the narrator who tells us that as a general truth Almayer felt himself well fitted for consideration and indolent ease of life, or do the words 'for which he felt himself so well fitted' indicate that as he is fantasizing about consideration and indolent ease of life Almayer thinks that he is well fitted for such things? And is the parenthetical comment about old Lingard the narrator's explanation of why Almayer thinks 'his ships, his warehouses, his merchandise', or Almayer's own comment to himself? It seems to me that these questions are very difficult to answer; so far as the latter one is concerned, Conrad does very often use parentheses to indicate a change of originating consciousness in his narratives, but they do not invariably have this function. The last sentence in the passage quoted also displays some interesting ambiguities. The content of this sentence makes it clear enough that it is Almayer's consciousness that we are following, but Almayer would surely not think of himself as being possessed of an Eastern mind, and so 'to his Eastern mind' is probably a narrative interjection.

11 This statement actually follows Direct Speech unenclosed in inverted commas, but this Direct Speech has followed FID.

12 I should note that there are certain ambiguities about this passage. I think that everything after the first sentence is narrated thought, but the second sentence could be an interpolated comment from the authorial narrator, and the last two sentences could be Direct Speech lacking inverted commas, and representing either Vinck's thoughts or his speech to his wife.

13 The inverted commas around 'amok' are interesting; presumably they serve as a sign from the narrator to the reader that this word has a special significance for Babalatchi. They are thus extra-mimetic: Babalatchi does not 'speak' them, and they are thus outside the represented speech.

14 See Roy Pascal, *The Dual Voice: Free Indirect Speech and its Functioning in the Nineteenth-Century European Novel*, Manchester, Manchester UP, 1977; and for a counter-view, Ann Banfield, *Unspeakable Sentences: Narration and Representation in the Language of Fiction*, London, Routledge, 1982.

15 FID can, as I have said, stand for something other than a *particular* act of thought or speech. It can represent an attitude that exists *in potentia*, an ideological position, a frame of mind.

16 This could be Direct Speech lacking quotation marks, but this seems very unlikely given the surrounding context.

17 I am grateful to Josiane Paccaud for this suggestion.

18 Banfield, p. 108. Banfield's approach is distinguished by its reliance upon a transformational-generative (TG) theoretical foundation, which is not uncontroversial. See McHale's criticism of an earlier article of Banfield's in his already-cited article. Where Banfield uses 'neither' and 'nor', I would prefer to use 'not necessarily . . . nor'.

19 Banfield, p. 111.

20 Pascal, p. 9.

21 Pascal, p. 137.

22 Banfield, p. 123.

23 See the discussion below concerning Razumov's interior dialogue and his arguing with himself in *Under Western Eyes*.

24 See the chapter on *The Nigger of the 'Narcissus'* in the present volume.

25 See the chapter on *The Nigger of the 'Narcissus'* in the present volume.

26 Banfield, pp. 80, 108.

27 I am grateful to Josiane Paccaud for this suggestion.

28 Ann Banfield comments on a part of this passage in *Unspeakable Sentences*, p. 122.

29 The editors of *The Collected Letters of Joseph Conrad*, commenting upon one of the letters in which Conrad described the disaster, note that it may have been only the second of three instalments that was destroyed, but was probably the entire second half. CLJC 2, p. 428n.

30 We find a comparable passage on pp. 93-4 of *Typhoon*, in which Captain MacWhirr's letter to his wife about the typhoon is quoted directly, while her thoughts are given in represented thought. The effect is to suggest her lack of interest in what is written.

31 Josiane Paccaud has pointed out to me that this sentence could either be represented speech, with a Direct Speech original of Mitchell's something like 'I admit that . . .', or it could be Reported Speech, the content of which follows 'admitted that'.

32 Kiernan Ryan, 'Revelation and Repression in Conrad's *Nostromo*'. In Douglas Jefferson and Graham Martin (eds.), *The Uses of Fiction: Essays on the Modern Novel in Honour of Arnold Kettle*, Milton Keynes, Open University Press, 1982, pp. 80-81. I should add that Ryan raises some very challenging and important problems concerning *Nostromo* in his article.

33 My argument here should acknowledge the fact that the word 'incorrigible' is applied to other characters in *Nostromo*. Decoud is described as 'incorrigible in his scepticism' by the authorial narrator (*Nostromo*, p. 300); Pedrito Montero is, this narrator tells us, 'incorrigibly lazy and slovenly' (*Nostromo*, p. 387), and Dr Monygham, referring to Father Corbelàn and Antonia, ejaculates 'Incorrigible!' to Mrs Gould (*Nostromo*, p. 510). It need not necessarily, therefore, be Charles Gould who considers the Costaguanians to be incorrigible; it might well be the authorial narrator. My feeling is, however, that on balance the former seems to be the more likely of these alternatives in this instance. It is perhaps worth noting that Stein, in *Lord Jim*, is also associated with this same word:

> 'Stein was the man who knew more about Patusan than anybody else. More than was known in the government circles I suspect. I have no doubt he had been there, either in his butterfly-hunting days or later on, when he tried in his incorrigible way to season with a pinch of romance the fattening dishes of his commercial kitchen.' (p. 219)

34 It could be authorial comment.

35 Compare Charles Jones's detailed analysis of the presentation of the speech of Verloc and Winnie in *The Secret Agent*. Before the death of Stevie, Winnie's speech is presented almost entirely in Direct Speech, and where Reported Statements are made they 'have all strong hints of the *direct* throughout'. Verloc's speech at this time is, in contrast, 'revealed mainly by means of the *indirect* or the narrated'. With the death of Stevie these characteristics are reversed. Finally, subsequent to the murder of Verloc, 'no less than 95% of Winnie's speech is represented by type (iv) *direct*'. (That is, speech enclosed in inverted commas without the inclusion of Subject or Predicate). (Charles Jones, 'Varieties of Speech Presentation in Conrad's *The Secret Agent*', *Lingua* 20, 1968, pp. 174-5.)

36 My attention was drawn to the significance of the sentence in the present tense by Gudrun Kauhl, in discussion of her paper 'Narrating Positions: Narrative in *The Secret Agent*', at the Joseph Conrad conference held in Copenhagen and Lund, September 1988. Her suggestion was that such sentences represented fragments of ideology held up for scrutiny in the text of the novel. One is reminded of Marlow's reference in *Heart of Darkness* to 'this narrative that seemed to shape itself without human lips' (HOD, p. 83).

37 Charles Jones, p. 163.

38 Banfield, pp. 241, 250; Pascal, p. 13.

39 Jeremy Hawthorn, 'Formal and Social Issues in the Study of Interior Dialogue: the Case of *Jane Eyre*'. In Jeremy Hawthorn (ed.), *Narrative: From Malory to Motion Pictures*, Stratford-upon-Avon Studies Second Series, London, Edward Arnold, 1985, pp. 86-99.

40 L. S. Vygotsky, *Thought and Language*, ed. & trans. Eugenia Hanfmann & Gertrude Vakar, Cambridge, Mass., MIT Press, 1962, p. 16.

41 Caryl Emerson, 'The Outer Word and Inner Speech: Bakhtin, Vygotsky, and the Internalization of Language', *Critical Inquiry* 10(2), December 1983, p. 253.

42 Either this was written before Conrad had decided to have Razumov give Nathalie his record, or the teacher of languages must be assumed to mean that at the time he wrote his record Razumov could not have wished any other eye to see it.

43 Conrad's use of ellipsis is a very interesting topic, and covers a range of functions. Its use for the purpose of ridiculing cliché-ridden speech occurs on a number of occasions. Another representative example in *Under Western Eyes* comes on page 59 of the work, and Mikulin's speeches to Razumov are packed with ellipses. It would seem that these speeches accord so well with Razumov's mode of thinking at this time that they help to persuade Razumov to do the work Mikulin suggests. Elsewhere in the Conrad canon there are other examples – early on in 'An Outpost of Progress', for instance, when Kayerts is talking to the director of the Great Trading Company. See my chapter on this work in the present volume.

44 V. N. Vološinov, *Marxism and the Philosophy of Language*, trans. Ladislav Matejka and I. R. Titunik, London, Harvard UP, 1973, p. 158.

I
Narrative and Ideology

2
Class and Society in *The Nigger of the 'Narcissus', The Secret Agent* and *The Rescue*

Ideology and art

I have already suggested that the connection between the opinions of Conrad the man and the artistic insight of Conrad the artist are neither one and the same nor are they totally distinct from each other. Much of Conrad's fiction is overtly concerned with social and political issues: novels such as *The Rescue, The Secret Agent* and *Under Western Eyes* are often and justifiably described as political novels; *The Nigger of the 'Narcissus'* is a work which includes many judgements of a social and a political nature; and no-one would dispute that *Chance* is obsessively concerned with the issue of feminism and women's rights. This list of works, however, includes two of Conrad's finest novels, two works generally considered to be failures or, at the least only very partial successes, and *The Nigger of the 'Narcissus'*, a work which I find impressive but flawed. I believe that the variation of Conrad's artistic achievement in these works is related (but not limited) to strengths and weaknesses in his creative vision at an ideological level.

In the next three chapters, therefore, I want to argue that Conrad's art is not untouched by the strength and weakness of his political and social ideas and understanding. One must of course distinguish between those ideas held consciously by Conrad and overtly expressed by him in extra-literary contexts, and the vision and understanding manifested in his works in covert and implicit forms. Nevertheless there are times when such overtly expressed extra-literary views are traceable in the works, and these times are in my opinion frequently at points of artistic failure.

In this chapter I want to examine some overt or implied analyses of society in certain of Conrad's works of fiction, concentrating in partic-ular on the issues of social structure and social class. Let me start with what seems to me to be a clear example of the imposition of an overt political opinion of Conrad's on to a literary work. As a young man Conrad availed himself of what it seems fair to describe as clichéd and intemperate socio-political formulations in commenting upon the issue of social class. In a letter to Spiridion Kliszczewski written 19 December

1885, he indulged in an outburst in response to the result of the recent General Election in Britain:

> By this time, you, I and the rest of the 'right thinking' have been grievously disappointed by the result of the General Election. The newly enfranchised idiots have satisfied the yearnings of Mr Chamberlain's herd by cooking the national goose according to his recipe. The next culinary operation will be a pretty kettle of fish of an international character. Joy reigns in St. Petersburg, no doubt, and profound disgust in Berlin: the International Socialist Association are triumphant, and every disreputable ragamuffin in Europe feels that the day of universal brotherhood, despoliation and disorder is coming apace, and nurses day-dreams of well-plenished pockets amongst the ruin of all that is respectable, venerable and holy.
>
> ....
>
> Where's the man to stop the rush of social-democratic ideas? The opportunity and the day have come and are gone! Believe me: gone for ever! For the sun is set and the last barrier removed. England was the only barrier to the pressure of infernal doctrines born in continental backslums. (CLJC 1, pp 15-16)

As I argue in my chapter on *The Nigger of the 'Narcissus'* in the present volume, sentiments comparable to those expressed in this letter can be seen to be behind the portrayal of Donkin in Conrad's early novella. This work is, among other things, a social parable, a projection on to the 'Narcissus' of what the reader is led to see as the social structure of England. And as I suggest, by providing Donkin as the representative of the class-conscious trade-union agitator, Conrad's depiction of the social and political contours of contemporary England becomes a highly tendentious, partial and (arguably) inaccurate one. Moreover, as I also argue, the work is split between what I have called a conservative-paternalist view of the working class and a conservative-reactionary one, oscillating between a sentimental glorification of his 'old chums' and a far more negative view of them as children in need of stern and powerful control.

The Nigger of the 'Narcissus' is saved from being nothing but a tediously reactionary social tract partly by its inner divisions, by the fact that Conrad's aesthetic instinct seems to have rebelled against the imposition of such a crude socio-political allegory on the work, and partly by its textural as against its structural richness. The sentiments in Conrad's letter help us to pick out a thread in the novella, but the novella is significantly more complex and more worthy of study than is the argument of the letter. It is as if Conrad tests sentiments similar to those to be found in the letter, in the novella of a decade later.

From this point in his writing career onwards, Conrad's treatment of social class in his fiction never gives such stereotypical elements or such simple reactionary prejudice as can be found in *The Nigger of the 'Narcissus'* implied or overt narrative approval. But this is not to say that problems of an ideological or political nature do not interfere with Conrad's art. The point is that where they do, it is more as a result of ideological confusion or contradiction than of the assertion of previously established beliefs. It is almost as if works such as *The Rescue* and *Chance* serve as screens on to which Conrad's views on social class or on feminism are projected so as to reveal their flaws and contradictions, while a work such as *The Secret Agent* serves as a means of escaping from his own prejudices and coming to a far more telling social analysis.

Idle individuals and idle classes

In a letter to Elbridge L. Adams of 20 November 1922, written, like Conrad's 1885 comments quoted earlier, after a British General Election, Conrad remarks:

> The Labour Party has attained by its numbers to the dignity of being the official Opposition, which, of course, is a very significant fact and not a little interesting. I don't know that the advent of class-parties into politics is abstractly good in itself. Class for me is by definition a hateful thing. The only class really worth consideration is the class of honest and able men to whatever sphere of human activity they may belong – that is, the class of workers throughout the nation. There may be idle men; but such a thing as an idle class is not thinkable; it does not and cannot exist. But if class-parties are to come into being (the very idea seems absurd), well then, I am glad that this one had a considerable success at the elections. It will give Englishmen who call themselves by that name (and amongst whom there is no lack of intelligence, ability and honesty) that experience of the rudiments of statesmanship which will enable them to use their undeniable gifts to the best practical effect. For the same reason I am glad that they have not got the majority. (JCLL 2, p. 285).

Conrad's comments here are by no means simple. Quite apart from the far more moderate tone to be witnessed in this letter than in the letter of 1885 (Conrad is now two years away from his death, rather than two years away from his thirtieth birthday), the pronouncements of the second letter are more subtle and less clichéd than are those of the earlier one. Conrad's comment that class for him is by definition 'a hateful thing' should not be taken to indicate that he never uses the yardstick of social class to define characters, nor that he does not recognize the existence of social classes. The quotation given above would seem to suggest that people may 'call themselves' members of one class or another, but that such labels are imposed upon rather than reflective of reality. However in both his fictional and non-fictional writing Conrad does place both individuals and groups by reference to social class. This is often ironic, as in his comment (following the *Titanic* disaster) that 'people, even of the third class (excuse my plain speaking), are not cattle',[1] and in his treatment of the lower-middle-class relatives of Miss de Barral in *Chance*. It is normally in his non-fictional writing that class labels are used as if they were unproblematic, however, as with his description of the husband of Madame Delestang in *A Personal Record* as a member of 'the *haute bourgeoisie* only' (p. 125).

In expressing the view that an idle class is unthinkable Conrad seems to be arguing that to count as a class, a group of human beings cannot be purely idle. If it is, then these human beings should be seen as a group of idle individuals rather than as a social class: activity is thus seen as a necessary constituent of classhood. But can we use this letter as a way into the understanding of Conrad's fictional treatment of social class?

In Conrad's short story 'The Informer' the anarchist Mr X, referring to the thousands of copies of his works that have been purchased by the 'well-fed bourgeois', challenges the narrator of the story:

> 'Don't you know yet,' he said, 'that an idle and selfish class loves to see mischief being made, even if it is made at its own expense? Its own life being all a matter of pose and gesture, it is unable to realize the power and the danger of a real movement and of words that have no sham meaning (SSix, p. 78).

At the end of this 'ironic tale', Mr X describes the anarchistic young lady's retreat into a convent as 'Gestures! Gestures! Mere gestures of her class'.

It is of course one of Conrad's characters rather than Conrad himself who makes reference to an idle class here, but the comment may still have some authorial force, even though the ending of the tale leaves open the possibility that Mr X's narrative has been a joke at the expense of the tale's narrator. Moreover, the sentiments expressed by Mr X seem to find an echo at various points in *The Secret Agent*, especially in the long scene depicting the gathering at the drawing room of the lady patroness of Michaelis. Her firm belief that the annihilation of all capital and resultant universal ruin will leave social values (and her own position) untouched, is on a par with the naïvety of the young woman in 'The Informer'. Conrad could have been told nothing about present-day radical chic that would have surprised him.

An idle class, one assumes, is constituted by a group of people for whom idleness is structurally prescribed by society. As we have seen from his letter to Adams, Conrad seems to have found such an idea very threatening. And indeed, in the early *The Nigger of the 'Narcissus'*, the social structure represented by the 'Narcissus' leaves no room for such an idle class. Donkin is idle – among other things – but his portrayal is not generally such as to suggest that he represents a whole social class, rather that he is the representative of a particular type of person.

It could of course be claimed that he represented the lumpen-proletariat, but not only would Conrad not have used this term, he seems not to have had a conception of this group as forming a class. Moreover, Donkin's portrayal as the malcontent continually implies that he is the outcast of a particular class – that class to which the mass of his fellow seamen belong. For similar reasons, it would be distinctly odd to argue that James Wait represented a social class; in different ways he is also portrayed as interloper or outsider (although as I argue, there is evidence to suggest that attitudes to the Negro in nineteenth-century Britain mirrored those towards the industrial working class, and there is a complex link between Donkin and Wait in the work).[2]

Idleness in *The Nigger of the 'Narcissus'*, then, is the prerogative of individuals rather than of one or more classes. It is outside the pattern of responsibilities and characteristics bequeathed to social groups by the society to which they belong. Captain, officers, men: all have their prescribed duties and responsibilities. To neglect these duties or to decline to carry out these responsibilities is possible as an act of individual dereliction, but it is not in the scheme of the world of *The Nigger of the 'Narcissus'* for a whole social class to be without duties or responsibilities – to be an idle class.

This, I think, represents a new version of a very old argument, the best-known version of which relies upon a comparison of social groups or classes to parts of the body (a famous, but by no means first, example of which can be found in Shakespeare's *Coriolanus*). The argument is heavily ideological precisely because the representation claimed is a partial and tendentious one. All the parts of the body do have a function (bits such as the appendix are not usually included in the reckoning), but Conrad must have been aware of the point of view that held that not all social classes were functional or necessary – the evidence of the two letters quoted makes this apparent. Idleness in *The Nigger of the 'Narcissus'*, however, is attributed only to maverick members of the lower orders, or to interlopers such as James Wait: it finds no place within the essential structure of normal society. Moreover, the attribution of idleness to Donkin turns contemporary socialist arguments on their head: far from the socialists being right that an idle class of property owners exists, it is those who spout socialist ideas who are themselves the real idlers according to the ideology of *The Nigger of the 'Narcissus'*.

In works written in the decade following *The Nigger of the 'Narcissus'*, however, the possibility of there existing such a thing as an idle class enters Conrad's work on several important occasions. Conrad's extra-literary opinion seems to have held fast that such a thing was an impossibility, but artistically this 'impossibility' returns very much as such repressed truths tend to do.

An important question that arises concerns the extent to which Conrad's investigation into the existence of an idle class in society – by which I mean a typical European society – makes contact with his consideration of the idleness to which Europeans living in colonial settings can succumb.[3] Part of the greatness of both *Heart of Darkness* and 'An Outpost of Progress' lies in their suggestion that the lack of restraint enjoyed by Europeans in Africa brings aspects of *European* civilization to the surface, reveals truths about the home culture. Is Conrad's investigation into 'an idle class' in works such as 'The Informer', *The Secret Agent* and *The Rescue*, made to connect with the idleness of Europeans in the Colonies? I shall return to this question, particularly with reference to *The Rescue*.

Overt placings of characters by means of social class are rarely definitive and final in Conrad's fiction. The somewhat insistent references to the lower-middle-class respectability of the relatives who look after Flora subsequent to her father's imprisonment in *Chance*, can be seen as an almost Dickensian reduction of a set of peripheral characters to a set of externally defined characteristics. This suggestion of near-parody is also present in Ossipon's 'popular quasi-medical study (in the form of a pamphlet seized promptly by the police) entitled "The Corroding Vices of the Middle Classes"'. The comments that I have already quoted from 'The Informer' are those of a character rather than those of an authorial narrator, and, moreover, a character whose 'extreme' political views may be such as to debar the reader from assenting to his social classifications. Comparable reservations apply to Mr Jones's comments on the lower classes in *Victory*, when he discovers that Ricardo is with Lena.

Similarly, the sustained irony observable in the following passage from *The Secret Agent* may be taken to colour the use of the word 'class', suggesting that its implied reductiveness fits in well with the somewhat stereotyped and clichéd opinions being expressed.

> Confident of the power of her charms, Winnie did not expect from her husband in the daily intercourse of their married life a ceremonious amenity of address and courtliness of manner; vain and antiquated forms at best, probably never very exactly observed, discarded nowadays even in the highest spheres, and always foreign to the standards of her class.
> (SA, p. 190)

Contrast, however, a far richer and more suggestive passage from early on in *The Secret Agent* which does not actually involve a use of the word 'class'.

[Mr Verloc] surveyed through the park railings the evidences of the town's opulence and luxury with an approving eye. All these people had to be protected. Protection is the first necessity of opulence and luxury. They had to be protected; and their horses, carriages, houses, servants had to be protected; and the source of their wealth had to be protected in the heart of the city and the heart of the country; the whole social order favourable to their hygienic idleness had to be protected against the shallow enviousness of unhygienic labour. It had to – and Mr Verloc would have rubbed his hands with satisfaction had he not been constitutionally averse from every superfluous exertion. His idleness was not hygienic, but it suited him very well. He was in a manner devoted to it with a sort of inert fanaticism, or perhaps rather with a fanatical inertness. Born of industrious parents for a life of toil, he had embraced indolence from an impulse as profound as inexplicable and as imperious as the impulse which directs a man's preference for one particular woman in a given thousand. He was too lazy even for a mere demagogue, for a workman orator, for a leader of labour. It was too much trouble.

(SA, p. 12)

There is a dim echo of the sentiments associated with the portrayal of Donkin in *The Nigger of the 'Narcissus'* in the last few lines of this passage, but its main emphasis is elsewhere. There is a clear identification of the embassy spy and the idle rich, a relationship which is structural, ideological and temperamental. Verloc's work to protect opulence and luxury is an alliance of the idle rich and the idle poor.

The phrase 'an idle class' does not figure in this passage. Is it therefore illegitimate to read it in such a way as to identify those who enjoy opulence and luxury with a particular social class? Should they not rather be seen as parasites on the fringes of a class, with Verloc's identification with them serving to strengthen such a reading? It seems to me that such a reading would be very strained. The passage implies very strongly that idleness is built into the structure of society rather than being parasitic upon it as in the world of *The Nigger of the 'Narcissus'*.

When Conrad does not actually use the word 'class', therefore, it is as if his art registers truths about contemporary European society which he is unable to see (or to accept) when he operates extra-artistically and makes use of the vocabulary of contemporary politics. And it is this insight that helps to make *The Secret Agent* such an extremely powerful novel, for the reader feels that in this work Conrad has escaped from those of his common beliefs and prejudices which were most damaging to his artistic penetration and understanding. It is almost as if what Conrad's own eyes cannot see, Conrad can see when looking through the eyes of Adolf Verloc.

The words 'protection' and 'hygienic' in the above passage merit close attention, as they reverberate through *The Secret Agent*, amassing layers of rich connotation in the process. In addition to writing his pamphlet on the corroding vices of the middle classes, we are told of Ossipon that he lectured on the socialistic aspects of hygiene; 'protective' and 'hygiene goods' are common euphemisms for contraceptives. The small cardboard box in Verloc's shop with 'apparently nothing inside' (p. 5) is labelled 'superfine India Rubber' in the serial version of the novel. Implied references to contraception abound in the novel, and seem to me to be especially associated with these two key words.

Now the larger importance of this pattern of associations seems to me to be that sterile self-enclosedness is seen to be a *structural* characteristic of the world of this novel, recurring on different levels of its world. In an interesting article on *The Secret Agent* Christine W. Sizemore has pointed out that there are innumerable 'boxes' in the novel: Verloc's shop, the boxes in it, the cash-box, the cab in which Winnie's mother is taken to her self-imposed exile, and many others.[4] I do not agree with all of Sizemore's conclusions (she assumes that Conrad implied a change in the contents of the box from contraceptive to pornography from serial to book version of the work), but her exposure of the chain of associations in the work seems to me to be very much to the point. The world portrayed in *The Secret Agent* is one in which secrecy, self-enclosedness, and sterility are the cells composing its fabric.

The view that labour is 'unhygienic', then, is seen to be that of a group of the idle rich whose sterile self-enclosedness enjoys a *typicality* in the world of the novel. These are no longer mavericks like Donkin, but representative units in a society in which idleness is legitimized at many different levels.

The opulence and luxury of these people cuts them off from an appreciation of the sources of their wealth. There is a Dickensian power in the vision that links these enjoyers of affluence and luxury with the embassy spy Verloc; it is comparable to the masterly way in which Dickens exposes a disregarded link between rich and poor through the disease imagery of *Bleak House* or the prison imagery of *Great Expectations* or *Little Dorrit*. This early passage from *The Secret Agent* makes of the social world of *The Secret Agent* quite a different thing from that of *The Nigger of the 'Narcissus'*. Idleness in *The Nigger of the 'Narcissus'* is an aberration, the result of a moral flaw or weakness in an individual who is thus defined as an outcast. Idleness in *The Secret Agent* is structural, it is built into the very fabric of society. In *The Nigger of the 'Narcissus'* idleness is a cancer; in *The Secret Agent* it is coded into the very genes of society and visible in different forms and at many different levels, from the 'domestic' to the public, from the lowest to the highest social classes. It is doubtless for this reason that the most negative impulse portrayed in *The Nigger of the 'Narcissus'* is that to abandon or cripple the ship by cutting the mast. Given the significance that the ship comes to enjoy in this work such an impulse is tantamount to destroying society. In contrast, the Professor's desire to destroy existing society in *The Secret Agent*, although finally seen as negative and evil, is not without positive associations in the work. The society to which we are made witness in *The Secret Agent* is so full of corruption that the impulse to begin again from scratch, to destroy all in one fell swoop, cannot be regarded in a wholly negative light.

The contrast between *The Nigger of the 'Narcissus'* and *The Secret Agent*, then, is the contrast between one work in which Conrad airs his political prejudices, and another in which he escapes from and scrutinizes them.

In an essay entitled 'Anarchism and Fiction', Graham Holderness has looked at the fictional treatment of anarchism in novels by a range of late nineteenth- and early twentieth-century writers, the best-known of whom are Zola, Conrad and Henry James. Holderness suggests that

> Conrad's comprehensive vision of a corrupt society, involving the institutions of marriage and private property, police and parliament, city and state, comes strikingly close to the vision of the anarchist.[5]

He continues, however, that as Conrad denies his Marxists and anarchists any genuine theory or political belief,

> the only kind of imaginative commitment he can make is to the Professor's dream of total annihilation. What can be done with a world like this, once it has been created; a world devoid of internal possibilities for redemption or improvement? There is only one final solution: destruction. The only people who can dream of destroying a world are the anarchist and the artist: the novelist who can unmake the world he has made at will.[6]

Holderness goes on to quote from Conrad's famous letter to Cunninghame Graham:

> L'homme est un animal méchant. Sa mechanceté doit être organisée. Le crime est une condition nécéssaire de l'existence organisée. La société est essentielment criminelle – ou elle n'existerait pas. C'est l'égoisme qui sauve tout – absolument tout – tout ce que nous abhorrons tout ce que nous aimons. Et tout ce tient. Voilà pourquoi je respecte les êxtremes anarchistes. – 'Je souhaite l'extermination generale' – Très bien. C'est juste et ce qui est plus c'est clair. On fait des compromis avec des paroles. Ça n'en finit plus. (LCG, p. 117. I have quoted at greater length than does Holderness. The errors in the French are Conrad's.)

In both *The Secret Agent* and 'The Informer' Conrad makes use of anarchist characters to survey the whole of established society from a highly
critical point of view. Conrad's own comments on *The Secret Agent*, written
the year of its book publication, are more revealing than is normally the
case with Conrad.

> But I don't think that I've been satirizing the revolutionary world.
> All these people are not revolutionaries – they are shams. And as regards
> the Professor I did not intend to make him despicable. He is incorrupt-
> ible at any rate. In making him say 'madness and despair – give me that
> for a lever and I will move the world' I wanted to give him a note of
> perfect sincerity. At the worst he is a megalomaniac of an extreme type.
> And every extremist is respectable.
>
> I am extremely flattered to have secured your commendation for
> my Secretary of State and for the revolutionary Toddles [*sic*]. It was very
> easy there (for me) to go utterly wrong.
>
> By Jove! If I had the necessary talent I would like to go for the
> true anarchist – which is the millionaire. Then you would see the venom
> flow. But it's too big a job. (CLJC 3, p. 491)

We need to remember that the letter from which this extract is taken
was written to Cunninghame Graham; Conrad habitually played down his
more conservative political beliefs when writing to this correspondent, and
his disclaimers may not be wholly sincere. Nonetheless, the implied linking
of the 'revolutionary world' with the 'revolutionary Toddles', and the overt
linking of this same world with 'the true anarchist – which is the million-
aire', are most thought-provoking. Such links help to strengthen the feeling
that idleness in *The Secret Agent* is determined structurally rather than
individually; the great man has his idle parasite Toddles, who thinks of
himself as a revolutionary, just as society at large has the pseudo-
revolutionary 'anarchists' and the benefactors of destructive anarchists
amongst the idle rich. The feeling that idleness in this novel is seen to be
embedded in the very structure of society is, on occasions, encouraged by
remarks emanating from the authorial narrator:

> a man must identify himself with something more tangible than his own
> personality, and establish his pride somewhere, either in his social
> position, or in the quality of the work he is obliged to do, or simply in
> the superiority of the idleness he may be fortunate enough to enjoy.
> (SA, pp. 116-17)[7]

Position, work, idleness: these are the different things which society
provides for various of its members to identify with, and even the work is
work that certain citizens are 'obliged to do'. This seems a far cry from the
vision of *The Nigger of the 'Narcissus'*, in the world of which all have their

allotted tasks, and those who are idle are so because they fail to honour their moral and social responsibilities. It is also a far cry from the view of work as the means whereby one discovers one's own reality, a view that we find in *Heart of Darkness*. Most important, this comment qualifies other suggestions in *The Secret Agent* that idleness is spread equally through society; without using the phrase 'an idle class' it certainly suggests that society is structured in such a way as to provide some with work and some with idleness.

Probably the central passage in any discussion of the social and political vision of *The Secret Agent* is that containing the discussion between Stevie and Winnie concerning the rôle of the police. Confronted with the brute fact that the cabman must either beat his decrepit horse or condemn his children to starvation, Stevie stammers out his conclusion: 'Bad world for poor people' (p. 171). Not only that, but as Winnie informs Stevie, this is no accident but the result of the way society is constructed.

> Guiltless of all irony, [Winnie] answered yet in a form which was not perhaps unnatural in the wife of Mr Verloc, Delegate of the Central Red Committee, personal friend of certain anarchists, and a votary of social revolution.
>   'Don't you know what the police are for, Stevie? They are there so that them as have nothing shouldn't take anything from them who have.'
> (SA, p. 173)

There is, as the text implies, a fine irony in the fact that it is the non-political Winnie, who does not believe in looking beneath the surface of things and who has no time for her husband's political friends, who states sincerely a belief which is the cornerstone of the political philosophy held by these same friends. But the perceptiveness of Winnie's gaze in this novel is perhaps, again ironically, mirrored by that of her creator.

'The gospel of the beastly bourgeois'

In any consideration of Conrad's attitudes towards social class, and of the manner in which a concern with social class entered into and affected his writing, *The Rescue* is a key document. In his pioneer article, '"The Rescuer" Manuscript: A Key to Conrad's Development and Decline', Thomas Moser[8] rightly argues that the survival of the manuscript which covers the first two-thirds of the final published work provides scholars wishing to investigate the 'great difference in quality between Joseph Conrad's early and later work, and a study of the sources and characteristics of this decline' with a unique opportunity.[9] Moser notes that this manuscript, which he entitles 'The Rescuer' to distinguish it from the published novel, covers almost the whole of Conrad's writing life. It was started by Conrad during his honeymoon in Brittany in March 1896.

> He worked on it intensively, but sporadically, for the next three years, writing at the same time, for relief, *Tales of Unrest* and the three great, short novels, *The Nigger of the 'Narcissus'*, 'Youth,' and 'Heart of Darkness,' as well as the first few pages of *Lord Jim*. Some time in 1899 he abandoned 'The Rescuer' completely in order to finish *Lord Jim*. . . . [H]e seems not to have touched the manuscript [again] until 1916, when he did do some work on it. He then laid it aside in order to write *The Arrow of Gold* (September 1917 to June 1918). In October 1918, Conrad, having by then had several typescripts taken, sold the manuscript to T. J. Wise, and finished the work by dictation on 25 May 1919.[10]

Moser suggests that Conrad gave up 'The Rescuer' in 1899 'at a point in the story between the time when Edith Travers moved to Lingard's brig, and the time when she and Lingard sailed together to the mainland'.[11] The remainder of the extant manuscript, therefore, is likely to date from 1916.

Moser's argument, developed with reference to Conrad's career as a whole in his subsequent book, is that Conrad gave up 'The Rescuer'

> because the subject was uncongenial, because he could not write the love story of Lingard and Edith, just as he could not even begin the love story between Stephen and Rita in *The Sisters*. There is something about the theme of love that elicits only bad writing from Conrad, something that frustrates his most strenuous efforts to create.[12]

My own position is that a study of the manuscript of 'The Rescuer', to the extent that it *does* reveal the reasons for Conrad's problems with the work and his abandonment of it, gives us a more complex picture than that suggested by Moser. If one wanted to simplify, however, it seems to me that there is as good a case to be made that Conrad's problems were as much involved with his difficulties in depicting and exploring certain aspects of social class as they were with the treatment of love.

The evidence of textual alterations is strong here. Changes made by Conrad either within the manuscript, or between the manuscript and the published *The Rescue*, seem recurrently to have something to do with social class, with a difficulty in finding the right word to convey something about the element of class in the identity of and the relationships between characters. Let me list some of these. Introducing Lingard to his readers in *The Rescue*, Conrad writes that he, 'like most of his class was dead to the subtle voices, and blind to the mysterious aspects of the world' (*The Rescue* p. 11). In 'The Rescuer' (p. 15) we can note that Conrad had first of all written 'class' and then replaced this by 'kind': only to revert to 'class' in the published version. In his first meeting with Carter, *The Rescue* has Lingard telling the former that 'I won't let inoffensive people – and a woman, too – come to harm if I can help it' (p. 39). Conrad's manuscript, however, reads not 'woman' but 'lady', as if even before Lingard had met Edith Travers Conrad was very much concerned with the fact of her social position. (In both the manuscript and in *The Rescue* we see a revealing movement from 'woman' to 'lady' on Lingard's first sight of 'the yacht people'; p. 55 in *The Rescue*.) In contrast, when Lingard ventures on board the yacht in *The Rescue* we are told that 'On the other side of the deck, a lady, in a long chair, had a passive attitude' (p. 122), while in 'The Rescuer' this lady is only a 'woman'. Later on, when Lingard is attempting to get Mrs Travers to persuade her party to come aboard the brig, in 'The Rescuer' (p. 306) he tells her that the cuddy is fit for a king, while in *The Rescue* (p. 159) it becomes fit for 'a lady'. There are also some interesting shifts from 'Edith' in the manuscript to 'Mrs Travers' in *The Rescue*,[13] the purpose of which seems to be both to modify the degree of intimacy apparent between the two and also to act as a reminder of the social gulf between Lingard and Mrs Travers.

If Conrad seems extremely conscious of the matter of social class in dealing with Lingard's perception of Mrs Travers, her perception of him seems to present similar problems. When Lingard tells his story to Mrs Travers, in 'The Rescuer' we can read: 'What if the narrator was only a common seaman .... ?' (p. 314). In *The Rescue* this becomes, 'What of it that the narrator was only a roving seaman' (p. 162), an alteration which has the effect of neutralizing a sharp placing of Lingard in class terms.

But it is not just Edith Travers who faces Conrad with the problem of how directly to refer to the matter of social class. When Lingard first sees her husband at relatively close quarters, we are told in *The Rescue* that 'The master of the brig looked upward into the face of a gentleman, with long whiskers and a shaved chin' (p. 59), whereas in 'The Rescuer' the passage reads 'He lifted his head and saw a man with long whiskers and a shaved chin' (p. 102). Readers of *The Rescue* will find a rather cutting description of Mr Travers which ends: 'He had a full, pale face; and his complexion was perfectly colourless, yet amazingly fresh, as if he had been reared in the shade' (p. 127). In Conrad's earlier manuscript the sentence continues further: 'shade, as though he had lived for years in a cellar, as though he had been kept all the time rolled up in damp cloths' (p. 241). The deletion removes what can legitimately be interpreted as a vein of class-contempt. And while in 'The Rescuer' Mr Travers is most concerned with 'the moral aspect' of what he sees as Lingard's disgraceful behaviour (p. 282), in *The Rescue* this becomes 'the social aspect' (p. 147). Moreover, in 'The Rescuer' the end of this last speech of Mr Travers's, we are told, 'came with a certain vehemence escaping partly through the nose'

(p. 282) – a touch that fixes a stereotyped upper-class characteristic upon Travers's way of talking. Not long after this, the reader of 'The Rescuer' is told that Lingard thinks of Mr Travers as a 'stuck-up fool' (p. 329).

Such textual evidence is only part of the story. Thomas Moser argues (correctly, I think) that 'the yacht people were the rock upon which "The Rescuer" foundered'.[14] Moser quotes Conrad's letter to Garnett in which he commented, 'You see, I must justify – give a motive – to my yacht people'. And yet this seems distinctly odd, for the problem of *motive* is surely not one that the yacht people raise. The problem is in portraying them accurately and convincingly from the outside and the inside, and of resolving the moral problems that their appearance raises for Lingard. It is here that 'The Rescuer' gives evidence to suggest that Conrad had enormous difficulties, difficulties which seem to have been greater with *Mr* Travers than they were with his wife. When the manuscript moves to a concern with Mr Travers the number of deletions multiplies rapidly within the manuscript, and much that is undeleted in the manuscript disappears in *The Rescue*. Neither Lingard nor Mrs Travers seem to engender the same level of manuscript deletion. We cannot explain these apparent difficulties by reference to a supposed inability of Conrad's to deal with the theme of love.

The Rescue and 'The Return' share a common interest in the sterility of a particular sort of bourgeois marriage, and the marital discussions of Mr and Mrs Travers bear striking similarities to those of Alvan Hervey and his wife. (Peter Keating has argued interestingly that 'The Return' owes much to the influence on Conrad of Ibsen's *A Doll's House*[15].) Both husbands are portrayed as stupid and spiteful men who cannot think beyond the narrow conventionalities of their class, who are incapable of questioning a clichéd belief in the duties associated with their position.

Writing to Edward Garnett on 29 September 1897, in response to Garnett's comments about 'The Return', Conrad expressed the frustration they engendered in him:

> I am hoist with my own petard. My dear fellow what I aimed at was just to produce the effect of cold water in every one of my man's speeches. I swear to you that was my intention. I wanted to produce the effect of insincerity, or artificiality. Yes! I wanted the reader to *see him think* and then to hear *him speak* – and shudder. The whole point of the joke is there. I wanted the truth to be first dimly seen through the fabulous untruth of that man's convictions – of his idea of life – and then to make its way out with a rush at the end. But if I have to explain that to you – to You! – then I've egregiously failed. (CLJC 1, p. 387)

More recent readers of 'The Return' have objected not that Conrad's intentions are unclear, but rather that they are far too clear: what Conrad calls 'the joke' of the story is too crudely and mechanically spelled out, so much so that Hervey becomes a puppet rather than a character, and the scenes involving him and his wife are melodramatic in the extreme. Similar objections could also be made to the long scene in *The Rescue* in which Mr and Mrs Travers engage in discussion, and in both 'The Rescuer' and *The Rescue* there is far more 'telling' than 'showing' so far as Mr Travers is concerned.

The issue of Conrad's relationship to the melodramatic is a complex one. Those of his works which have traditionally attracted the description 'melodramatic' are *The Rescue*, 'The Return' and *Victory*. (One might also include 'The Tale', although this has attracted much less comment from critics.) These are not, generally, works which have been accorded the highest praise within the Conrad canon, although debate concerning the merits of *Victory* still flourishes. What is striking is that these three works are the works in which Conrad tries most *overtly* to address the issue of social class. Such an intention, when linked to a desire to expose the shortcomings of the philistine bourgeois, seems typically to have propelled Conrad into the realms of melodrama. (The depiction of the lower classes does not seem to lead Conrad in the same direction.) M. H. Abrams's comments on melodrama seem painfully apt when applied to the three Conrad works I have mentioned:

> The protagonists are flat types; the hero and heroine are pure as the driven snow and the villain is a monster of malignity . . . The plot revolves around malevolent intrigue and violent action, while credibility both of character and plot is sacrificed for violent effect and emotional opportunism.[16]

Appropriately, the active villains of the three works I have mentioned are all men, while the female characters are passive, long-suffering and noble. It is true that Mr Jones in *Victory* is the only really stereotyped melodramatic villain, and the inclusion of the working-class Lena in *Victory* serves to increase this novel's conformity to melodramatic norms. But even in *The Rescue* and 'The Return' we have sensitive women suffering for breaches of conventional morality at the hands of insensitive and inflexible men – the very stuff of the melodrama. Moreover, the highly artificial conversations of the two married couples gives an unmistakably melodramatic feel to certain scenes in the two works. Consider the following:

> 'You deceived me – now you make a fool of him . . . It's awful! Why?'
> 'I deceived myself!' she exclaimed.
> 'Oh! Nonsense!' he said, impatiently.

'I am ready to go if you wish it,' she went on, quickly. 'It was due to you – to be told – to know. No! I could not!' she cried, and stood still wringing her hands stealthily.

'I am glad you repented before it was too late,' he said in a dull tone and looking at his boots. (TOU, p. 151)

The static theatricality of this exchange is worse than anything in *The Rescue*, but there is much in the scene that it comes from which reminds us of the scene in which Mr Travers confronts his wife with her supposed lapses from correct behaviour. In both scenes a stupid and self-important man who is in thrall to the surface conventions of his class criticizes his wife for lapses from these standards, without understanding that her perspective is so much wider that she no longer respects these conventions. Compare the following passages:

'For it is self-evident,' he went on with anxious vivacity, 'it is self-evident that, on the highest ground we haven't the right – no, we haven't the right to intrude our miseries upon those who – who naturally expect better things from us. Every one wishes his own life and the life around him to be beautiful and pure. Now, a scandal amongst people of our position is disastrous for the morality – a fatal influence – don't you see – upon the general tone of the class – very important – the most important, I verily believe, in – in the community. I feel this – profoundly.' (TOU, p. 164)

'As a matter of fact, as a matter of experience, I can't credit you with the possession of feelings appropriate to your origin, social position, and the ideas of the class to which you belong. It was the heaviest disappointment of my life. I had made up my mind not to mention it as long as I lived. This, however, seems an occasion which you have provoked yourself. It isn't at all a solemn occasion. I don't look upon it as solemn at all. It's very disagreeable and humiliating. But it has presented itself. You have never taken a serious interest in the activities of my life which of course are its distinction and its value. And why you should be carried away suddenly by a feeling toward the mere man I don't understand.'

(*The Rescue*, pp. 267-8)

The second passage is representative in that the conversation is less obviously theatrical and somewhat more credible than that to be found in 'The Return'. But even here Conrad's points are hammered home in too crude and unsubtle a manner. (It is noteworthy that in both passages the respective characters make overt mention of class.) In the final sentence above the reader is surely meant to register Travers's comment about 'the mere man' with disapproval: there is no doubt that for Conrad 'the mere man' (or 'woman', for that matter) is fundamental, while the 'origin, social position, and the ideas of the class to which you belong' are matters of the surface and thus clearly secondary. But it is hardly believable that such a person as Travers would actually make this sort of a comment. One suspects that a number of things are involved in these failures. Firstly, that Conrad is just not used to hearing people like Alvan Hervey or Travers talking, so that his attempt to give these characters speech has to rely upon secondary sources, sources which seem to owe much to melodrama. Secondly, that Conrad is writing too tendentiously: starting off with a thesis and using his characters to illustrate it. Thirdly, that Conrad is not clear in his own mind (or in his artistic sense) to what extent class characteristics *are* incorporated in 'the mere man'. And fourthly – as perhaps the letter to Garnett suggests – that Conrad's lack of faith in his readers' ability to see what he is doing leads him to exaggerations which are fatal.

Elsewhere Conrad found means to overcome this lack of faith in his readers. In *Heart of Darkness*, most notably, he actually dramatizes it in Marlow's expressions of his own lack of confidence in the discriminatory powers of his listeners. In *Under Western Eyes* the limited narrator has his limitations highlighted by other characters, and as these are the sort of limitations Conrad had good reason to fear in his readers these latter are encouraged to view themselves and their assumptions more critically. In *The Secret Agent* and *Nostromo* more complex narrative techniques are used to draw readers out of the prison house of their socially determined assumptions.

Finishing *The Rescue* in 1918-19 Conrad seems to have been aware of the theatricality of some of its scenes. Consider the following comment, describing Mrs Travers's perception of Lingard.

> she was worn out with watching the passionate conflict within the man who was both so desperately reckless and so rigidly restrained in the very ardour of his heart and the greatness of his soul. It was a spectacle that made her forget the actual questions at issue. This was no stage play; and yet she had caught herself looking at him with bated breath as at a great actor on a darkened stage in some simple and tremendous drama.
>
> (*The Rescue*, p. 282)

More specifically, Conrad actually used the word 'melodrama' to describe the nature of his failure with 'The Return'. Writing again to Edward Garnett a month after his previous cited letter, on 11 October 1897, Conrad explained

> You see I wanted to give out the gospel of the beastly bourgeois – and wasn't clever enough to do it in a more natural way. Hence the logic which resembles the logic of a melodrama. The childishness of mind coming to the surface. All this I feel. I don't see; because if I did see it

> I would also see the other way the mature way – the way of art. I would work from conviction to conviction – through inevitable moments to the final situation. Instead of which I went on creating the moments for the illustration of the idea. Am I right in that view? If so the story is bad art. It is built on the same falsehood as a melodrama. (CLJC 1, p. 393)

Conrad's self-criticism is impressively accurate.

One could cite, in contrast, Conrad's far more successful reference to (rather than use of) what is surely the melodramatic, in *The Secret Agent*.

> [Winnie] lamented aloud her love of life, that life without grace or charm, and almost without decency, but of an exalted faithfulness of purpose, even unto murder. And, as so often happens in the lament of poor humanity rich in suffering but indigent in words, the truth – the very cry of truth – was found in a worn and artificial shape picked up somewhere among the phrases of sham sentiment.
>
> 'How could I be so afraid of death! Tom, I tried. But I am afraid. I tried to do away with myself. And I couldn't. Am I hard? I suppose the cup of horrors was not full enough for such as me.' (SA, p. 298)

Commenting upon the melodramatic element in nineteenth-century working-class fiction, Martha Vicinus suggests that

> melodrama itself seemed like a psychologically accurate reflection of working-class life. Melodrama's character typing, with the clear struggle between good and evil, was attractive at a time when traditional values were being undermined; moreover, it provided a vehicle for the full expression of sentiment and emotion, without concern for character motivation or development. Melodrama appeals to those who feel that they have no control over their lives, but are prey to larger social forces; tragedy appeals to those who feel, however erroneously, that they can control their own lives.[17]

Given Conrad's uncertainty about the capacity of human beings to control their own lives, his occasional oscillation between melodrama and tragedy would not, on Vicinus's account, be too hard to account for. And it has to be said that the lower-class Winnie's situation seems more suitable for melodramatic treatment than do those of the upper-class characters of *The Rescue*, 'The Return' and 'The Tale'.

Conrad's gentlemen (and ladies)

It is instructive to compare Conrad's failure successfully to 'give out the gospel of the beastly bourgeoisie' in *The Rescue* and 'The Return', with his far greater success in exploring what we can term class characteristics by exploring the semantics of a word such as 'gentleman'. It is perhaps odd that whereas Conrad writes far more perceptively about social class when he does not actually use the word 'class', a concern with the semantics of a word such as 'gentleman' leads him into some extremely subtle analyses. In an excellent article on Conrad's *Victory*, 'Joseph Conrad and the Last Gentleman',[18] Tony Tanner points out that in *Victory* Conrad uses the word 'gentleman' more than sixty times, and he argues that

> As a word, a concept, a referent, a signal in social discourse, a recognizable hierarchical marker, it is completely destabilized; blurred by multiple recontextualization; and semantically depleted, if not emptied, by repeated and vague usage.[19]

If there is 'vague usage', I would argue, it is more to be attributed to Conrad's characters than to Conrad himself, for surely the usage is more multiple than vague; different characters mean different things by the word 'gentleman', but it is normally very clear what it is that they do have in mind in using the term.

Both *Victory* and *The Rescue* approach the issue of social class more in the context of an enquiry into the way social *relationships* are implicated in individual *identity*. For Ricardo in the former novel, following a gentleman is the alternative to being a wage slave (his own term): for him the issue of who or what he is cannot be separated from the sort of relationship he has to his superior(s). In like manner Mr Jones assumes that being a gentleman requires that he treat others in a certain way, and that he can require a certain treatment of them. In *The Rescue* the issue of social class is consistently bound up with characters' expectations of others, and with their view of their own responsibility to others. We see this in a parodic form in Mr Travers's response to what he sees as Lingard's incorrect behaviour.

> 'I won't admit the possibility of any violence being offered to people of our position. It is the social aspect of such an incident I am desirous of criticizing.' (*The Rescue*, p. 147)

Tanner opens his article with a quotation from *The Nigger of the 'Narcissus'*, that in which a group of seamen from the 'Narcissus' discuss – rather ludicrously – the characteristics of a gentlemen. Tanner does not comment upon this passage, but the implication of his using it at the head of his article is that the word 'gentleman' is already seen by Conrad to be problematic and of uncertain reference at the time of writing *The Nigger of the 'Narcissus'* – eighteen years before *Victory*. This point could, however, be made far more forcibly. The word 'gentleman' recurs regularly in Conrad's work, and very rarely in such a way as to allow one to assume that its meaning and reference are unproblematic. In striking contrast, the word 'lady', although it has a clear class significance in Conrad's work, seems rarely to be problematized in quite this manner. It is used in a quite neutral manner in 'The Informer', and when Mrs Travers gives some indication of its conventional associations in *The Rescue*, these are by no means as problematic as are the reverberations of the word 'gentleman'.

> 'And pray don't look upon me as a conventional "weak woman" person, the delicate lady of your own conception,' [Mrs Travers] said, facing Lingard, with her arm extended to the rail. 'Make that effort please against your own conception of what a woman like me should be. I am perhaps as strong as you are, Captain Lingard. I mean it literally. In my body.' (*The Rescue*, p. 254. The passage continues with Mrs Travers insisting too on her own courage.)

Conrad's use of the word 'gentleman' throughout his writing career is far less straightforward than this. In *Almayer's Folly*, his first published novel, an early conversation between Almayer and his daughter gives Almayer the occasion for the following comment.

> 'It is bad to have to trust a Malay,' he said, 'but I must own that this Dain is a perfect gentleman – a perfect gentleman,' he repeated.
>
> (AF, p. 18)

Almayer's confident use of the word undercuts the reader's confidence in its meaning and reference. Almayer's own moral corruption renders him unreliable in the use of a word which (as Tanner points out) carries a range of moral implications, and the assumption of racial superiority in Almayer's comments (made, we should remember, to a daughter whose mother was a child of Sulu pirates), indicates worryingly that a commitment to the values of a gentleman does not necessarily imply commitment to racial equality. And this is not to read *Almayer's Folly* in the light of inappropriately present-day values, as a glance at Conrad's impressive Author's Note to the novel will show. It is important to register that the 'gentleman' Travers has set out on his voyage in *The Rescue* in order to expose the Dutch colonial system, but it soon becomes apparent that he is filled with crude racial prejudices: he says to d'Alcacer and Mrs Travers of the situation in the region he is investigating, 'And if the inferior race must perish, it is a gain, a step toward the perfecting of society which is the aim of progress' (p. 148). The ironies resident in that final word are not unrelated to those which we can find in 'An Outpost of Progress'. Much later in Conrad's *oeuvre*, in *Victory*, the 'gentleman' Mr Jones asks Heyst: 'Do you believe in racial superiority, Mr Heyst?' And he answers his own question: 'I do, firmly' (p. 382). There seems good reason to suppose that one of the early experiences which caused Conrad to find the term 'gentleman' problematic was that of seeing it applied to or claimed by those who thought that gentlemanly responsibilities did not extend to dealings with other races. The contrast with Mrs Travers's lack of racial prejudice is insisted upon at various points in *The Rescue*. Consider an example to which I have already referred:

> 'The brig is small but the cuddy is fit for a lady,' went on Lingard
> with animation.
> 'Has it not already sheltered a princess?' she commented, coolly.
> (*The Rescue*, p. 159)

Both here and in 'The Rescuer', where we have 'king' instead of 'lady', Mrs Travers's response to Lingard has the effect of revealing an element of racial distinction in his use of language. Clearly when Lingard says 'lady' he thinks not just of class but of race; Mrs Travers's implied criticism of this assumption is worthy of note.

A 'perfect gentleman' in Almayer's usage, we realize, can be dedicated to a secret mission the purpose of which is so to enrich himself that he can live a life of ease and luxury in Europe. Ironically, of course, Dain *is* far more of a gentleman than is Almayer – that is, he is possessed of many more of the positive qualities traditionally attributed to the gentleman than is Almayer himself. But presumably the word is not one which Dain would use – of himself or of anyone else.

The passage in *Almayer's Folly* is worth comparing with ones from elsewhere in Conrad's fiction. In the short story 'Karain: A Memory', which was published only two years after *Almayer's Folly*, the seaman Hollis is talking to his fellows about the troubled Karain, who has sought their help.

> 'Ah! You are without guile,' said Hollis, sadly. 'You will learn . . .
> Meantime this Malay has been our friend . . .'
> He repeated several times thoughtfully, 'Friend . . . Malay. Friend,
> Malay,' as though weighing the words against one another, then went on
> more briskly –
> 'A good fellow – a gentleman in his way. We can't, so to speak,
> turn our backs on his confidence and belief in us.' (TOU, p. 47)

This passage is in sharp contrast to the one quoted from *Almayer's Folly*. Whereas in the earlier passage a morally unreliable character uses a word confidently, but has his confidence undercut by his lack of sensitivity towards the issues raised by his assumptions concerning race, in the above passage a morally subtle character is shown subjecting familiar words to a close scrutiny which involves exposing them to his (and others') assumptions about race. *Is* that seemingly unproblematic word 'friend' usable about a Malay? *Shouldn't* one be able to call a Malay a gentleman? Hollis clearly wants to do this, and yet he realizes that such an attribution cannot be made without complications, which is why he ends by describing Karain as a gentleman 'in his way'. The effect of this passage is certainly in part to expose some limitations in Hollis, but by doing this it exposes more serious ones in conventional attitudes encapsulated in the pragmatic conditions governing the use of the word 'gentleman'.

In 'The Rescuer' there is an interestingly similar passage, in which Lingard comments upon his friend the Prince Hassim:

> 'And he's a somebody, too; you can see that directly; a gentleman in their way.' ('The Rescuer', p. 125)

Although similar, there is a world of difference between Hollis's 'a gentleman in his way' and Lingard's 'a gentleman in their way'. The passage from 'The Rescuer' is one of many which do not appear in *The Rescue* and which set Lingard in a rather critical light. 'In their way' suggests that the standards of Malays cannot be put on the same scale as those of Europeans; 'in his way' suggests that there is one scale by which people can be measured, albeit in culturally distinct ways.

In these early examples, it is important to note, Conrad uses cultural clashes and contrasts to subject the term 'gentleman' to pressure and scrutiny. This is a technique which is central to Conrad's work: the movement between different cultures in his fiction is analogous in some ways to the scientist's technique of isolating that which has to be analysed by abstracting it from its normal context and setting it against a background which shows it in an unexpected or unusual light. In a more domestic context the fundamental values of a gentleman might be concealed by, or confused with, the adventitious surface appearance or transitory conventions attaching to the word. In the England of 1897 it might be easy to assume that a gentleman is a person who abides by certain forms of dress, speech and behaviour. But faced with a man from a completely different culture to whom such conventions are unknown, use of the word 'gentleman' forces one to consider whether or not there are deeper values and qualities which are gentlemanly, values and qualities which have only a conventional association with forms of dress, speech and behaviour.

Something of this is apparent in the introduction of Gentleman Brown in *Lord Jim*, although an altogether cruder form of critique is involved here. Brown is so clearly not a gentleman in any way, that his name acts more as an indication of his transparent cheek than as a means of subjecting the word 'gentleman' to scrutiny. The cultural and racial context in which Brown exercises his cheek is, however, important. His title – like that of 'Lord' Jim – is one that could, and would, hardly be laid claim to in Britain. Paradoxically, however, Brown's ability to make this false claim to gentility in a colonial land reveals to Conrad's readers that false claims to gentility may be made, and may depend upon surface adherence to a set of conventions rather than any deeper commitment to more fundamental values and qualities.

Leaving *Victory* aside, I suspect that most readers of Conrad remember *The Secret Agent* as the novel in which the word 'gentleman' is subjected to most telling pressure. In this novel, so far as I can see, there is no unambiguously positive or unproblematic use of the term 'gentleman'. Indeed, by its closing pages the reader has been made aware of a range of sinister and negative associations possessed by the term, associations very similar to those the same term gathers about itself in the course of *Victory* even though it is used far fewer times in the earlier novel.

> Mr Verloc, thinking of Mr Vladimir, did not hesitate in the choice of words.
> 'A Hyperborean swine,' he hissed, forcibly. 'A what you might call a – a gentleman.'
> The Chief Inspector, steady-eyed, nodded briefly his comprehension, and opened the door. (SA, p. 212)

In this passage Conrad manages to unlock the dark side of the semantic force of the word 'gentleman', a dark side that has perhaps always been the shadowy partner of its more positive usages. Mr Vladimir, Gentleman Brown, Mr Jones – all described as gentlemen, and all characterized by evil self-interest disguised (more or less successfully) in the surface conventions of gentlemanly behaviour. Verloc's belief that the most power-fully damning word he can use of Vladimir is 'gentleman', can perhaps be attributed to Vladimir's combination of a surface urbanity and an inner savagery; dormant in our understanding of the word 'gentleman' and part of that 'dark side' of which I have spoken, is the image of a man who uses conventions of appearance, speech and behaviour to *conceal* vicious or unworthy aims or qualities. This interpretation receives some support from a later use of the same word in *The Secret Agent*.

> With her eyes staring on the floor, her nostrils quivering with anguish and shame, she [Winnie] imagined herself all alone amongst a lot of strange gentlemen in silk hats who were calmly proceeding about the business of hanging her by the neck. (SA, p. 268)

Elsewhere in *The Secret Agent*, the positive connotations of the word are undercut as a result of the way it is used by naïve or morally suspect characters. In the opening pages of the novel we learn that 'In Winnie's mother's opinion Mr Verloc was a very nice gentleman' (p. 7). Mrs Neal attacks poor Stevie by announcing to him that, 'It's all very well for you, kept doing nothing like a gentleman' (p. 184). In a novel that is fierce in its contempt of 'hygienic idleness' the implications of the comment are of importance. A comparable use of the term can be found in the opening pages of *Youth*.

> '[The captain] said to me, "You know, in this ship you will have to work." I said I had to work in every ship I had ever been in. "Ah, but this is different, and you gentlemen out of them big ships; . . . but there! I dare say you will do. Join to-morrow."' (*Youth*, p. 4)

We may recall that in his Author's Note to the volume in which *Youth* was first published, Conrad remarks banteringly of Marlow that the 'origins of that gentleman (nobody as far as I know had ever hinted that he was anything but that) – his origins have been the subject of some literary speculation of, I am glad to say, a friendly nature'. It is as if Conrad is unable to use the word 'gentleman' without irony.

In *The Secret Agent*, the page before Verloc calls Vladimir 'a – a gentleman', Chief Inspector Heat says to Verloc of the Assistant Commissioner, 'I wouldn't trust too much the gentleman who's been talking to you' (p. 211). This could almost be called the 'guilt by association' attack on the term, whereby it is discredited by being used by a discreditable person. 'The End of the Tether' also provides us with a comparable instance when the morally dissolute Mr Sterne remarks of Mr Van Wyk, 'What a thing it was to have a gentleman to deal with!' (p. 310). Mr Van Wyk, of course, *is* a gentleman in the best sense of the word, but Sterne's reason for calling him this depends not upon a recognition of and respect for Mr Van Wyk's finer qualities, but upon the prospect of personal advancement contained in Mr Van Wyk's reliability and honesty.

When Mr Van Wyk first talks with Captain Whalley, there is an interesting use of a cognate term.

> He [Whalley] talked well, without egotism, professionally. The powerful voice, produced without effort, filled the bungalow even into the empty rooms with a deep and limpid resonance, seemed to make a stillness outside; and Mr Van Wyk was surprised by the serene quality of its tone, like the perfection of manly gentleness. (TEOTT, p. 286)

On the one hand, Whalley talks 'without egotism'. But on the other hand his loud, effortless voice may signal something negative; Conradian characters with such voices are recurrently portrayed in a negative manner, as if such voices betoken a false appearance, a misleading guide to their possessors (we can think of Verloc, James Wait and Peter Ivanovitch).

Conrad, in commenting on 'The End of the Tether', was more critical of Whalley than is, I suspect, the average reader;[20] thus in this passage it is hard to say whether his use of 'manly gentleness' is designed as a positive term which escapes the possibly negative connotations of 'gentlemanliness', or whether the term is intended to carry some of these connotations.

Class, race, nation: *The Rescue*

The Rescue remains the work of Conrad's which pays most continued and overt attention to social class. The problematic relationship between Lingard and the 'yacht people' - preëminently Mr and Mrs Travers - has difference of social class as an essential component. Lingard and Mrs Travers think immediately of social class when their thoughts turn to the other's presence.

> Mrs Travers found that Lingard was touching, because he could be understood. How simple was life, she reflected. She was frank with herself. She considered him apart from social organization. She discovered he had no place in it. How delightful! Here was a human being and the naked truth of things was not so very far from her notwithstanding the growth of centuries. Then it occurred to her that this man by his action stripped her at once of her position, of her wealth, of her rank, of her past. (*The Rescue*, p. 167)

The passage is clearly ironic, and shows Mrs Travers at a stage before she has really come to accept the 'mere man' in Lingard, although this is what she thinks she is doing at this moment. For a brief instant she is like the lady patroness of Michaelis in *The Secret Agent* who assumes that the loss of property and class privilege will affect the *nouveaux riches* but not herself, but she quickly realizes that the 'delightful' fact that Lingard has no place in what she takes to be social organization also has implications for herself. In this passage we see Conrad doing in miniature what he does in the large in *The Rescue* as a whole: using a clash between very different individuals to investigate the extent to which personal identity and personality are constructed by membership of a particular social class.

Lingard too treats Mrs Travers as a being outside his range of experience, outside of his own social organization. After Mrs Travers has told him not to look on her as 'a conventional "weak woman" person', and asks if he understands her, he responds:

> 'God knows,' said the attentive Lingard after a time, with an unexpected sigh. 'You people seem to be made of another stuff.'
>
> (*The Rescue*, p. 254)

At a number of key points *The Rescue* raises the possibility that class differences are more significant than national identity. Lingard tells Mrs Travers:

> 'Look here. When I was a boy in a trawler, and looked at you yacht people, in the Channel ports, you were as strange to me as the Malays here are strange to you. I left home sixteen years ago and fought my way all round the earth. I had the time to forget where I began. What are you to me against these two? If I was to die here on the spot would you care? No one would care at home. No one in the whole world – but these two.' (*The Rescue*, p. 158)

'You yacht people'. To Conrad, without doubt, this bitter phrase had a special edge to it. On the opening page of 'Youth' Marlow introduces his companions as follows:

> We all began life in the merchant service. Between the five of us there was the strong bond of the sea, and also the fellowship of the craft, which no amount of enthusiasm for yachting, cruising, and so on can give, since one is only the amusement of life and the other is life itself.
>
> ('Youth', p. 3)

In *The Mirror of the Sea* Conrad remarks sharply that of course

> yacht racing is an organized pastime, a function of social idleness ministering to the vanity of certain wealthy inhabitants of these isles nearly as much as to their inborn love of the sea. (MOS, p. 23)

The 'social idleness' of the Travers party, that idleness which the husband treats as his right and which bores the wife, cuts them off from Lingard in spite of their shared language and culture.

> He swore. 'My people! Are you? How much? Say – how much? You're no more mine than I am yours. Would any of you fine folks at home face black ruin to save a fishing smack's crew from getting drowned?'
>
> (*The Rescue*, pp. 164-5)

Indeed, Lingard has already pointed out that if, as Mrs Travers wishes, he reminds himself of their common culture - 'home' - then what he brings to mind is either the uninterest of people such as Mr and Mrs Travers in his welfare, or a class relationship of master and servant:

> 'I *am* an adventurer,' he burst out, 'and if I hadn't been an adventurer, I would have had to starve or work at home for such people as you.'
>
> (*The Rescue*, p. 134)

One of the reasons why the word 'adventurer' is granted such positive connotations in *The Rescue* seems to be that it is set in opposition to imprisonment within the domestic class structure.[21] This seems to me to have a wealth of significant implications so far as the ideology of imperialism is concerned.

In spite of Lingard's denial of any sense of cultural or racial solidarity, Mrs Travers still attempts to get him to admit to a particular concern for the welfare of his countrymen.

> Mrs Travers sighed.
> 'Yes, it is very hard to think that I who want to touch you cannot make myself understood as well as they [Immada and Hassim]. And yet I speak the language of your childhood, the language of the man for whom there is no hope but in your generosity.
> He shook his head. She gazed at him anxiously for a moment. 'In your memories then,' she said and was surprised by the expression of profound sadness that over-spread his attentive face.
> 'Do you know what I remember?' he said. 'Do you want to know?' She listened with slightly parted lips. 'I will tell you. Poverty, hard work – and death,' he went on very quietly. 'And now I've told you, and you don't know. That's how it is between us. You talk to me – I talk to you – and we don't know.' (*The Rescue*, pp. 218-19)

We can contrast this sad statement with Lingard's earlier confident assertion: 'I am a white man inside and out' (p. 39). In the course of his encounter with the yacht people Lingard finds that his colour, his culture and his nationality do not ensure that he has much in common with those who share these characteristics, indeed he discovers that he is so thoroughly alienated from some white people that he cannot make contact with them, even with a sympathetic individual such as Mrs Travers.

And yet, as seems inevitable in the world of Conrad, any 'natives' who rely upon a sympathetic white man are betrayed, sacrificed because of Lingard's concern for those for whom he feels no cultural responsibility. It is the yacht people who escape unscathed at the end of *The Rescue*, while Immada, Hassim and Jörgenson are destroyed and Lingard's plans are ruined. Does Conrad recognize that individuals may sacrifice their genuine self-interest for the interests of another, or even a rival, social class? Or are we to perceive that in spite of his claims to a sort of proletarian status, Lingard is actually fully involved in the manoeuvres of imperialism (as his reference to himself as an 'adventurer' would suggest)? We certainly have the racialist Shaw bearing witness to the fact that the lower classes (Shaw's speech is rendered unambiguously as non-genteel, and his references to his house and family seem unambiguously to place him as lower-middle-class) can ally themselves with their masters' interests.

It could be suggested that Lingard's clear attraction to Mrs Lingard is the decisive factor, sexuality proving more potent than the bonds of friendship, morality or self-interest, and this cannot be dismissed, although this sexuality is not separate from class. And, moreover, sexual attraction does not save Aïssa or Jewel.

Lingard, like 'Lord' Jim, has an ambiguous placing on the social scale as a result of his overseas successes. In conversation with her husband Mrs Travers reminds him that Lingard, 'is a man of the lower classes' (p. 271), but in addition she draws his attention to the fact that 'he is known also on a certain portion of the earth's surface as King Tom' (p. 274). Lingard, like so many of Conrad's heroes, is a divided man, and his divisions are related to divisions and tensions between nations and cultures. Just as Conrad uses characters of mixed racial descent to expose complexities in human identity and relationships brought about by imperialism, so too he uses Lingard's divided social identity to expose the manner in which social class enters into the formation of individual identity as well as the development of human relationships. Given what we know of Lingard's ambiguous class status it comes as little surprise when he discovers that his own self is divided into antagonistic elements.

> Conflict of some sort was the very essence of his life. But this was something he had never known before. This was a conflict within himself. He had to face unsuspected powers, foes that he could not go out to meet at the gate. They were within, as though he had been betrayed by somebody, by some secret enemy. He was ready to look round for that subtle traitor. A sort of blankness fell on his mind and he suddenly thought: 'Why! It's myself.' (*The Rescue*, p. 329)

The Rescue, in common with so many of Conrad's other works, links its exploration of social class to a concern with the semantics of the word 'gentleman'. For Lingard, whether one is a gentleman or not depends on more than surface characteristics. Talking to Mrs Travers he suggests one reason why he was not trusted.

> I suppose I didn't look enough of a gentleman. Yes! Yes! That's it. Yet I know what a gentleman is. I lived with them for years. I chummed with them – yes – on gold-fields and in other places where a man has got to show the stuff that's in him. Some of them write from home to me here – such as you see me, because I – never mind! And I know what a gentleman would do. Come! Wouldn't he treat a stranger fairly? Wouldn't he remember that no man is a liar till you prove him so? Wouldn't he keep his word wherever given? Well, I am going to do that. Not a hair of your head shall be touched as long as I live!' (*The Rescue*, p. 164)

For Lingard, a gentleman is defined not by his surface attributes but by his principles and his actions; talking to Mrs Travers of d'Alcacer, he comments of the latter's behaviour:

> 'He was trying to make it up between me and your husband, wasn't he? I was too angry to pay much attention, but I liked him well enough. What pleased me most was the way in which he gave it up. That was done like a gentleman.' (*The Rescue*, pp. 258-9)

Lingard's outlook seems to have some authorial support. Of d'Alcacer we read:

> More of a European than of a Spaniard he had that truly aristocratic nature which is inclined to credit every honest man with something of its own nobility and in its judgement is altogether independent of class feeling. He believed Lingard to be an honest man and he never troubled his head to classify him, except in the sense that he found him an interesting character. He had a sort of esteem for the outward personality and the bearing of that seaman. He found in him also the distinction of being nothing of a type. He was a specimen to be judged only by its own worth.
> (*The Rescue*, p. 309)

The paradox, clearly, is that the true aristocrat is possessed of a judgement altogether independent of class feeling. This is not to say that such a person is unaware of class differences; d'Alcacer admits:

> 'Mrs Travers, I will confess to you that I don't feel jocular in the least. But what can he [Lingard] know about people of our sort? And when I reflect how little people of our sort can know of such a man I am quite content to address him as Captain Lingard.' (*The Rescue*, p. 312)

It would be as unsatisfactory to attempt to explain Conrad's abandonment of 'The Rescuer' by reference to his inability to deal with social class as it is, finally, by invoking an inability to deal with love – and this for a number of reasons. Firstly, because class and love are in part linked in *The Rescue*; the attraction which Lingard and Mrs Travers feel for each other is clearly partly sexual (especially on Lingard's part, as passages in 'The Rescuer' which do not appear in *The Rescue* make abundantly clear), but it is a sexuality which has social class as a powerful constituent. Conrad is by no means the first writer to note that a bored upper-class woman and a rough lower-class man may each find that the other's class is in part sexually stimulating. Secondly, because Moser is correct that Conrad *does* have serious problems in dealing with the element of sexual attraction which exists between Lingard and Mrs Travers; the final part of 'The Rescuer' (probably written in 1916) attempts to come to terms with the passionate element in their relationship by displacing it on to external nature, specifically the battle between land and sea. But the attempt is not successful, and little of this part of the manuscript survives in *The Rescue*. And thirdly because there are other elements in 'The Rescuer' which may well also have caused Conrad to abandon the work. The issue of the white man torn between loyalty to 'native' friends and those of his own colour (which is at the centre of *The Rescue*) is of course picked up again in *Heart of Darkness* and *Lord Jim*, and the warnings of the 'gentleman' Mr Wyndham to Lingard in 'The Rescuer' about the danger of white men getting too involved in the humanity of 'natives' both prefigure Kurtz's situation in *Heart of Darkness* and are also very similar to those the 'privileged reader' gives Marlow in *Lord Jim*.

The issue of racial as against human or moral solidarity recurs time and again in Conrad's earlier work, but it is so foregrounded in *The Rescue* that its resolution demanded overt decisions regarding the plot. Conrad abandoned 'The Rescuer' at the point near where such decisions had to be taken. Conrad may well have had difficulty in making such decisions, and this may be connected with the fact that, as Moser points out, proleptic passages critical of Lingard which appear in 'The Rescuer' do not appear in the published version. We must remember that Almayer, Willems and (in a more complex way) Jim are all the subject of authorial criticism; their weaknesses are far more uncompromisingly exposed. It is as if Conrad is unwilling to do this in *The Rescue*; as I have pointed out, the word 'adventurer' is consistently used in a positive, romantic sense in this work (and more frequently and explicitly in 'The Rescuer' than in *The Rescue*). And this unwillingness leads the work into an impasse. To this extent it may be seen to resemble *The Nigger of the 'Narcissus'*, with the important qualification that whereas in *The Rescue* Conrad may have been aware of the problems resulting from the clash between the demands of the Romantic and of the Realistic, in *The Nigger of the 'Narcissus'* he seems not to have been so aware.

For all this, *The Rescue* is not by any means a complete failure. The plot raises important questions concerning the competing claims that race, class, sexuality and friendship make on Lingard, and the answers to these questions proffered by the completed work are not contemptible. The novel makes a very sharp analysis of the claims of national solidarity – claims which Conrad, in his non-fictional writings, seems consistently to have seen as supreme – and finds them (in Lingard's earlier conversations with Mrs Travers) to be undercut by class loyalties. Lingard's betrayal of Hassim and Immada is thus especially tragic, as it goes counter to what he has recognized as his moral responsibility.

There is, however, a tension between the different reasons given for Lingard's effective betrayal of his friends: his solidarity with those of his own race, and his passionate infatuation with Mrs Travers. Jim's betrayal of Jewel is that much more telling precisely because it lacks this confusion of motives: Jim actually loves Jewel, yet betrays her even so.

Conrad's fiction is not, then, as unconcerned with the matter of social class as some of his extra-fictional comments might suggest. This concern takes both overt and indirect forms, and it also ranges from attempts to explore the characteristics of particular social classes to analyses of society which look at the structural place and function of different social classes. At its best Conrad's concern with social class is integrated into other general concerns such as race, imperialism, sexuality, and into a more probing and unstereotyped attempt to explore the mysteries of human social existence. For this reason there are few that will dispute that whatever the perhaps underestimated virtues of *The Rescue*, this work is vastly inferior to *The Secret Agent*.

---

1   'Certain Aspects of the Admirable Inquiry Into the Loss of the *Titanic*' (1912), NLL, p. 247.
2   See Catherine Gallagher, *The Industrial Reformation of English Fiction 1832-1867*, London, Chicago University Press, 1985, and my chapter on *The Nigger of the 'Narcissus'* in the present volume.
3   See my discussion of *Heart of Darkness* in chapter 6.
4   Christine Sizemore, '"The Small Cardboard Box": A Symbol of the City and of Winnie Verloc in Conrad's *The Secret Agent*', *Modern Fiction Studies* 24 (Spring 1978), pp. 23-39.
5   Graham Holderness, 'Anarchism and Fiction'. In H. Gustav Klaus, (ed.), *The Rise of Socialist Fiction 1880-1914*, Brighton, The Harvester Press, 1987, p. 132.
6   Holderness, p. 132.
7   A passage in 'The Rescuer' which does not appear in *The Rescue* is worth quoting here:
      [Mr Travers] was born rich, and in a world of conventional values where it is not a man's intrinsic worth and his mental power but his circumstances and his mental acquisitions alone that count for something, his solemn and well-informed mediocrity served very well his craving for distinction. (p. 234)
    In this 'world' it would seem that 'circumstances' produce something well-nigh indistinguishable from an idle class.
8   Thomas Moser, '"The Rescuer" Manuscript: A Key to Conrad's Development – and Decline', *Harvard Library Bulletin*, Autumn 1956, pp. 325-55.
9   Moser, p. 325.
10 Moser, p. 326.
11 Moser, p. 330.
12 Moser, p. 333.

13 See *The Rescue*, pp. 226, 227; 'The Rescuer', pp. 462, 464.

14 Moser, p. 329.

15 Peter Keating, 'Conrad's *Doll's House*', in Sven Bäckman and Göran Kjellmer (eds.), *Papers on Language and Literature Presented to Alvar Ellegård and Erik Frykman*, Gothenburg Studies in English 60, Gothenburg, 1985.

16 M. H. Abrams, *A Glossary of Literary Terms*, 4th edition, New York, Holt, Rinehart and Winston 1981, p. 100.

17 Martha Vicinus, 'Chartist Fiction and the Development of a Class-Based Literature'. In H. Gustav Klaus (ed.), *The Socialist Novel in Britain*, Brighton, Harvester, 1982, p. 9.

18 Tony Tanner, 'Joseph Conrad and the Last Gentleman', *Critical Quarterly*, 28 (1 & 2), Summer 1986.

19 Tanner, p. 109.

20 See Conrad's comment in a letter to David Meldrum, August or September 1893:

> I am heartened greatly by what you say of the wretched 'Tether'. The old man does not wobble it seems to me. The Elliot [= Eliott] episode has a fundamental significance in so far that it exhibits the first weakening of old Whalley's character before the assault of poverty. As you notice he says nothing of his position but goes off and takes advantage of the information. ....
> A character like Whalley's cannot cease to be frank with impunity. He is not frank with his old friend – such as the old friend is. For, if Elliot had been a genuine sort of man Whalley's secrecy would have been that of an intolerable fool. The pathos for me is in this that the concealment of his extremity is as it were forced upon him. Nevertheless it is weakness – it is deterioration. (CLJC 2, p. 441.)

The passage continues to outline Whalley's decline, while admitting 'that ghost of justification which should secure the sympathy of the reader'.

21 See my chapter on *Nostromo* in the present volume.

3
Race and Class in *The Nigger of the 'Narcissus'*

As I have suggested in the previous chapter, there are two linked problems which make of *The Nigger of the 'Narcissus'* Conrad's problem work: technical confusions in the manipulation of narrative perspective and distance, and ideological uncertainties relating to Conrad's attitudes to the life he is depicting. But what strikes the modern, first-time reader of the novella is perhaps a more pressing and particular problem. When first I read *The Nigger of the 'Narcissus'* as part of an undergraduate course in English literature, what I wanted most of all was a reaction to that word 'nigger' in the title and body of the work – either from within the work itself, or from critical responses to it. Why does Conrad make a black man the centre of this story, and draw attention to him and his blackness in its title? What is the narrative attitude to Wait and his blackness? What is the significance of Conrad's use of the word 'nigger' here? I knew that the word could be used in a relatively neutral manner at the time Conrad was writing – as it is used at the start of 'An Outpost of Progress', for example.

And yet nowhere could I find any answer to these questions. Critics and lecturers concentrated upon *The Nigger of the 'Narcissus'* as a sea story, a reflection of Conrad's years as a mariner and a distillation of the values and qualities this experience had led him to deem essential. Lecturers would address the issue of whether or not Shakespeare's *The Merchant of Venice* included an anti-semitic element, but such matters were not considered when it came to Conrad's novella. And it is only in comparatively recent years that the issue of James Wait's race, and of the significance which this is made to carry in *The Nigger of the 'Narcissus'*, has been discussed by literary critics. What made this silence puzzling to me was that I found it hard to understand that any modern reader could read the novella without being forced to confront the issue of racism. Wait's portrayal seemed so clearly to feed off many stereotypical racist prejudices, and no clear narrative rejection of such elements could be found in the work.

As I read more of Conrad I found this increasingly puzzling, for Conrad's record on racism is generally a very honourable one, especially when seen in the light of his time and circumstances. The Author's Note to *Almayer's Folly* is an admirable assertion of the common humanity of all races, and although, subsequently, I was able to understand the basis of

Achebe's description of the Conrad of *Heart of Darkness* as a racist,[1] I could never accept that a fully contextualized reading of this work could justify such an accusation.

I still find this element of *The Nigger of the 'Narcissus'* problematic, but in a rather different way. The figure of James Wait seems to me to be the visible tip of an iceberg of narrative indecision in this work, a narrative indecision that stems from ideological contradictions and uncertainties in Conrad but which manifests itself most obviously in terms of technical unclarities and blurrings. Of all Conrad's works, *The Nigger of the 'Narcissus'* seems to me to be the most perfect example of the manifest-ation of ideological problems on the narrative plane. And it now seems to me that Conrad's artistic instinct led him to choose the figure of the Negro as the central character in this work with good grounds, for if anything symbolized contradiction and unclarity in the late Victorian popular mind it was the figure of the Negro. After all, although there were many black sailors in Conrad's time (and Conrad had sailed with some), there seems no obvious reason on realist grounds why Conrad should make one the villain of a story designed to say something summarizing about a particular nautical era, especially when the tale also included the figure of Donkin (whatever one thinks of his rôle in the novella).

I refer to *The Nigger of the 'Narcissus'* as Conrad's problem work not to suggest that the work is a failure, or of no artistic value. Indeed, it is precisely because there is so much that is fine – and quintessentially Conradian – about the novella that it represents a problem for us. (No-one, surely, would describe 'The Return' or *The Arrow of Gold* as problem works, unless it is a problem to understand how the writer who produced *Heart of Darkness* and *Under Western Eyes* could also have produced them.) *The Nigger of the 'Narcissus'* is a problem not just because so much that is good in it is mixed in with much that is not, but more because the novella is packed with incoherences, with, literally, failures to cohere, to hang together. I am not referring to the sort of ambiguities and tensions so prized by the New Critics – ambiguities and tensions which can be seen to contribute to a deeper, more complex, artistic unity – but to more funda-mental disunities which present the reader with insoluble and, finally, artistically unrewarding puzzles, rather than with aesthetically productive challenges. Graham Hough has pointed out that the reader is sent back to consider the intentions of a writer far more by an unsuccessful than by a successful work,[2] and perhaps the sort of work that leads us on repeated and frustrating sorties back to the author is that which, like *The Nigger of the 'Narcissus'*, seems to consist of elements which may be unproblematic in themselves, but which fail to hang together, which cannot be combined to produce a satisfying and coherent whole. Writing primarily of *Heart of Darkness* Cedric Watts has suggested that

Critical distinctions between a writer's conscious and unconscious intentions may often be less useful than is the distinction between imaginative intentionality and imaginative unintentionality, for which a basic criterion is this: an apparently anomalous part of a text is imaginatively intentional if predictions based on the assumption of its intentionality are fulfilled within the work.[3]

I have always found *The Nigger of the 'Narcissus'* to contain such 'apparently anomalous parts', and have never succeeded in the sort of successful prediction that would justify the attribution of Cedric Watts's term 'imaginative intentionality' to the novella, either on first or on subsequent readings. And of all of Conrad's major works, this is the one that always seems to send me back to wondering about Conrad's intentions.

It is perhaps wise to dispose of one possible objection to what I have said so far. I have introduced the topic of artistic unity, and it is by now a commonplace that modernist art and the theories it has directly and indirectly generated have repeatedly challenged the traditional assumption that great works of art should (or, by definition, do) manifest a profound unity. As a writer arguably transitional between nineteenth-century realism and twentieth-century modernism Conrad, it might be claimed, produced works of literature which are ill-served by the application of traditionalist concepts such as 'artistic unity'.

My response to this possible objection is that even with a highly modernist novel such as Robbe-Grillet's *The Voyeur*, one can still find a *consistency of artistic purpose* – what Watts refers to as imaginative intentionality. The contradictions in this work confuse the reader on first acquaintance, but before long one realizes that this is what the writer wants – or, at least, the presentation of elements designed to produce such disorientation in the reader gives the work a sort of unity. And, using Watts's yardstick, after a while even the first-time reader of *The Voyeur* can *predict* that the rest of the novel will follow this pattern. It is this consistency of artistic purpose, this sense of comprehensive imaginative intentionality or control, that seems to me to be lacking in *The Nigger of the 'Narcissus'*.

Indeed, attempts to discover such a unity of purpose or of control seem, finally, to create even more problems, ending up by imposing a coherence or consistency on the work which the text cannot justify. Many of the examples of artistic ambivalence which I list below have been discussed before by critics of *The Nigger of the 'Narcissus'*. But it is only comparatively recently that some critics, rather than trying to discover a principle of unity in the work, have instead sought to relate the incoherences to unresolved ideological tensions and contradictions in Conrad the writer. (I am thinking in particular of recent works by Stephen Land

and Michael P. Jones.)[4] My aim in this chapter is to carry this sort of analysis further – particularly with regard to the importance of James Wait's race – and, briefly, to suggest ways in which Conrad appears to have been able to advance his art by apparently learning from the incoherences of this work, to find ways of producing coherent and thematically unified works out of his own divisions and uncertainties.

It is time now to give chapter and verse, to list what I would claim are fundamental incoherences to be found in the novella.

1 Hardly any critic of *The Nigger of the 'Narcissus'* has failed to observe that there are inconsistencies in Conrad's manipulation of point of view in the novella, and this critical recognition is paralleled by a comparable unease on the part of the common reader. It is worth starting with this issue, for although I see it as secondary rather than primary in essence, it may be more apparent to the reader than are what I see as the underlying ideological causes.

Artistic incoherence is not necessarily produced by technical inconsistency in the manipulation of point of view. Many of Conrad's major works exhibit such technical inconsistencies. In *Under Western Eyes*, for example, the teacher of languages tells the reader things which, by his own account of the sources of his information, he could not actually know. And if we accept (which Conrad did not) that Marlow talks for far longer than it is realistic to believe he could possibly have done in *Lord Jim*, then we have another technical inconsistency here, but one which few readers of the novel would deem a significant artistic problem.

It is clearly not inevitably a problem if two characters in a literary work hold different opinions, or if the opinion of one is at variance with that of a personified or non-personified narrator. Nor is it necessarily the case that a work which makes it impossible for the reader to determine between what is supposed objectively to have happened, and what a character merely imagines took place, is artistically flawed – as we see in *The Voyeur*. What generates incoherence is the belief or suspicion that irreconcilable views or perceptions are being presented to the reader in an artistically uncontrolled manner, in a way that either conceals or ignores their irreconcilability, or which even suggests that this irreconcilability is neither artistically planned nor controlled.

From the earliest reviews of the novella mention has been made of the fact that the work appears to have a single narrator who mainly adopts the viewpoint and perspective of an ordinary crew-member of the 'Narcissus', but who sometimes sounds more like an officer and who even becomes omniscient on a number of occasions – at least to the extent of granting us access to the private thoughts of Creighton (p. 21); Singleton (pp. 98-9); Donkin (pp. 143-4; 147; &c.); and James Wait (pp. 147-8). The reader is also made privy to private conversations between the captain and the mate, and between Donkin and James Wait. There are, too, regular shifts between the narrative use of 'we' and 'they' to refer to the crew of the 'Narcissus', often in the same paragraph (c.f. NOTN, p. 66), and in the final four pages of the work the narrator becomes, for the first time, 'I'.

Addressing this problem directly in an article on the novella, John Lester has suggested that, possibly as a result of the influence on Conrad of Charles Dickens's *Bleak House*, of which he was extremely fond, Conrad juxtaposes two separate narrators throughout *The Nigger of the 'Narcissus'*.[5] This just does not seem reconcilable with the evidence of the text, and even if it were to be accepted as true it would be repeatedly impossible to determine which of these two narrators was speaking. As Jakob Lothe puts it, in a subsequent article,

> If we say that there are two narrative voices, one unnamed and one identified, then we make a distinction which broadly corresponds to that between authorial and personal narrative. But then we would also have to say that it is often unclear which voice is speaking.[6]

Lothe argues that 'the identity of the narrative voice in [*The Nigger of the 'Narcissus'*] is obscure'.[7] He suggests that if one attempts to systematize the narrative variations in the novella, the work 'resists such a critical ordering',[8] an important point, and one we can relate to his suggestion that Conrad succeeds in diverting the reader's attention from the question of which voice is speaking in the work, 'and instead makes us focus on the novella's variation of mood - constituted by an elaborate interplay of perspective and distance'.[9] Lothe bases his own analysis on variations in the use of personal pronouns in the novella, and he manages to list no fewer than seven different narrative situations. In a further article, David Manicom covers similar ground, arguing additionally that 'narrators' in fiction are critical constructs based primarily upon point of view, and that in *The Nigger of the 'Narcissus'* we do not have narrating *characters*, as no narrator is seen to perform a single individual action, to speak a single word of dialogue, or to have a single word addressed to him.[10] The point is an important one, but it should be added that the use of 'we' and 'I' in *The Nigger of the 'Narcissus'* does lead the reader to assume the existence of one or more personified and intra-mimetic narrators.

Lothe's suggestions that the work 'resists' an ordering of its narrative variations, and that Conrad 'succeeds in diverting the reader's attention' from the issue of who is speaking in it, are both interesting and revealing, for they confirm a sense shared by many readers that at one level of his creative imagination Conrad senses problems of coherence in *The Nigger of the 'Narcissus'* which he attempts to evade rather than to confront, to mask rather than to explore. We can point more specifically to a number of particular techniques.

As I have argued in my first chapter, Conrad's use of Free Indirect Discourse (FID) does not normally avail itself of the potentialities for ambiguity implicit in the technique. And yet in *The Nigger of the 'Narcissus'* FID is on crucial occasions accompanied by ambiguity, such that it is frequently impossible to be sure whether a particular sentiment should be ascribed to a character or rather to a commenting narrating voice – whether omniscient or personified. Indeed, from what I have said before it should be clear that there is no single narrating 'voice' to which sentiments can unproblematically be ascribed. This creates no difficulties when it is with the description of events or of characters and their thoughts and opinions that we are concerned, but it does when we are interpreting narrative opinions and attitudes. If we are satisfied that James Wait actually said and thought what he is described as having done, then from what source our information comes is of less importance. But when it comes to opinions concerning the crew, or relating to the significance of Wait's race, then the source becomes very important indeed, because it is crucial for the reader to know whether such views are to be ascribed to a crew member or to a narrator with whose values the reader is expected to sympathize.

It is for such reasons that John Lester's comparison with Dickens's *Bleak House* seems to me to be misleading. In Dickens's novel the two narrative voices are clearly defined; we know when we are listening to the anonymous narrator, we know when we are listening to Esther Summerson. Moreover, we quickly get to learn what these two voices know, including what they know of each other; Dickens maintains a relatively strict consistency here. By implication, therefore, we can without too much difficulty work out to what scale of values – positive and negative – the novel commits itself. (Extending this commitment to Dickens himself is no simple matter, but it is possible.) The situation in *The Nigger of the 'Narcissus'* is much more problematic, as we will see.

Reynold Humphries has drawn useful attention to other techniques used in the novella, in particular, the use of passive formulations in such a way as to create a similar ambiguity to that produced by Conrad's use of FID. The use of passive formulations is, of course, a classic means whereby the source of opinions or instructions is concealed. Humphries suggests that the text tries to solve the problem of having a crewman narrator who is both 'a subject of the *énoncé* like any other member of the crew [and] also a subject of the *énonciation* within this *énoncé* inasmuch as he *narrates*'. He suggests that the text tries to solve this dilemma by quite simply pretending that '*there is no narrator at all*', so that 'the events on board ship are often presented as if nobody were relating them, the text disavowing its own activity and encouraging the reader to do the same'.[11] To repeat a point made earlier, I would suggest that *events* cause rather fewer problems than do *opinions* and *interpretations*, for it is in these latter cases that an isolable source is most needed, and it is here that ideological factors are most important.

On a number of occasions passive formulations or FID are used in transitional or linking passages, so that we move between passages which can unambiguously be attributed to a specific source or sources, via 'grey areas', passages of indeterminate authority and origin. A classic example of this is to be found in the description of Wait's face as

> a face pathetic and brutal: the tragic, the mysterious, the repulsive mask of a nigger's soul. (NOTN, p. 18)

Immediately before these words Conrad's use of FID has taken the reader inside James Wait's consciousness, into his private thoughts. We emerge from Wait's mind into - what? Is it a crew member who expresses the racially prejudiced view quoted above? An officer? Or an omniscient narrator to whom we are expected to grant our assent, a narrator expressing views which the novella as a whole underwrites? My own feeling is that my last suggestion comes closest to the way in which most readers read the words in question, for which reason the passage is a very disturbing one. And yet this authorial voice is impossible satisfactorily to pin down; as a result of the ambiguities of point of view in the novella we can rarely make a confident attribution of any views to a narrator who is clearly authorial and reliable.

I will now move on to detail what seem to me to be more specifically ideological incoherences in *The Nigger of the 'Narcissus'*. I would stress, however, that problems of point of view and ideological irresolution are very often hard to separate, are very often two sides of the same coin.

2 The crew of the 'Narcissus' is presented to the reader in strangely contradictory ways. Early on in the novella (p. 25) the bulk of the crew is contrasted unfavourably with those seamen contemporary with the older Singleton. And yet a few pages later (p. 31) we read:

> The men working about the deck were healthy and contented - as most seamen are, when once well out to sea. The true peace of God begins at any spot a thousand miles from the nearest land; and when He sends there the messengers of His might it is not in terrible wrath against crime, presumption, and folly, but paternally, to chasten simple hearts - ignorant hearts that know nothing of life, and beat undisturbed by envy or greed. (NOTN, p. 31)

These are the same men who, we have earlier been told, 'are less naughty, but less innocent; less profane, but perhaps also less believing; and if they had learned how to speak they have also learned how to whine' (p. 25). One cannot help suspecting that the unexpected shifts of tense here ('had' coming where one would have expected 'have') betray a radical uncertainty on Conrad's part concerning point of view: are we with this crew, or looking back on them from a vantage point in the future?

3 We see a comparable contradiction elsewhere. Early on in the novella, on Donkin's first appearance, a passage of sustained and bitter irony at his expense includes the repeated words: 'They all knew him!'. These words are half-echoed later on by James Wait when he tells Donkin to his face, 'Every one knows you' (p. 150). And yet for long periods of the voyage of the 'Narcissus' it seems clear that many crew members do not know him at all, so that if they once did their knowledge has been lost as if in some parodic reversal of the Biblical fall. By page 100 the man they 'all know' is referred to ironically as 'the fascinating Donkin', and in the pages immediately following this it is quite clear that the crew's hearts certainly do not beat 'undisturbed by envy or greed'.

Moreover, as many commentators have remarked, the elegiac view of the crew with which the novella closes is out of key with much that has gone before. By the final paragraph of the work the crew are, 'As good a crowd as ever fisted with wild cries the beating canvas of a heavy foresail; or tossing aloft, invisible in the night, gave back yell for yell to a westerly gale'. Now were it to be the case that we had two (or more) clearly defined and distinct narrators, or even narrative perspectives, then such contradictions would not matter, but would actually contribute to the richness of the work. And, it should be admitted, in a way they *do* so contribute to its richness, both to the range and variety of the life presented and of the views taken of this life. But they also introduce incoherences which, I feel, are far from productive ones.

4 There is a similar oddity in the manner of Singleton's portrayal. We can perhaps refer to his off-ship drunkenness to explain the initially puzzling fact that while at the start of the novella we meet him reading Bulwer-Lytton's *Pelham*, he is unable to sign his name when he receives his pay in the work's final pages. But it seems to me that Conrad gets into more radical tangles by trying to portray him both as totally unthinking and at the same time as an incarnation of nautical wisdom. Thus we encounter Singleton, early on, standing 'still strong, as ever unthinking; a ready man with a vast empty past and with no future, with his childlike impulses and his man's passions already dead within his tattooed breast' (pp. 24-5). Yet a few lines further on Singleton's contemporaries are described as 'Men

hard to manage, but easy to inspire; voiceless men – but men enough to scorn in their hearts the sentimental voices that bewailed the hardness of their fate': something rather hard for unthinking or voiceless men to do one would have thought.

A few more pages on we are told of Singleton that

> Till then he had been standing meditative and unthinking, reposeful and hopeless, with a face grim and blank – a sixty-year-old child of the mysterious sea. The thoughts of all his lifetime could have been expressed in six words, but the stir of those things that were as much part of his existence as his beating heart called up a gleam of alert understanding upon the sternness of his aged face. (NOTN, p. 26)

How *can* a person be 'meditative and unthinking'? Is not this Conrad trying to have his cake and eat it too, trying to see Singleton – like his contemporaries – in two radically different and mutually exclusive ways? The suggestion that certain things call up understanding in Singleton (if the gleam on his face has been correctly interpreted) also seems to have involved a very careful choice of words so that the old sailor is given all the benefits of thought without actually thinking. Compare a much later passage, in which we are told of him that, 'He brooded alone more than ever, in an impenetrable silence and with a saddened face' (p. 98). Is 'brooding' thinking or is it not? The word again seems carefully chosen so as to suggest a process that is not thought but that provides all or many of the benefits of thought.[12] We can note, too, that although Singleton's silence is described as 'impenetrable', this immediately precedes the one passage in which the reader is taken into his thoughts by means of FID.

> For many years he had heard himself called 'Old Singleton,' and had serenely accepted the qualification, taking it as a tribute of respect due to a man who through half a century had measured his strength against the favours and the rages of the sea. He had never given a thought to his mortal self. He lived unscathed, as though he had been indestructible, surrendering to all the temptations, weathering many gales. He had panted in sunshine, shivered in the cold; suffered hunger, thirst, debauch; passed through many trials – known all the furies. Old! It seemed to him he was broken at last. And like a man bound treacherously while he sleeps, he woke up fettered by the long chain of disregarded years. He had to take up at once the burden of all his existence. Old! He moved his arms, shook his head, felt his limbs. Getting old . . . and then?
> (NOTN, pp. 98-9)

First of all, we may note that there is something odd in being told that Singleton had never given a thought to his mortal self, when we have already had it implied that he had no thoughts to give to anything. But it is clear that part of this passage *does* represent Singleton's thoughts: 'Old! It seemed to him he was broken at last'. But the lines preceding this, which follow the description of his brooding alone, could also represent his thoughts, although they are more likely to be read as narrative comment.

It is worthy of note that that which is praised and valued in Singleton's case is condemned in the case of James Wait, who is on one occasion described as 'A thing of instinct – the unthinking stillness of a scared brute' (p. 118). To be unthinking is admirable in Singleton but deplorable in Wait.

There is, moreover, a further irony in the fact that Singleton's voicelessness and muteness are celebrated in such highly articulate prose, a sophisticated form of language which is mocked when used by Wait. Voicelessness is valued not as a general human attribute but as a distinguishing feature of those 'children' who should clearly be seen and not heard. I will come back to Conrad's comparison of the seamen to children, one highlighted in the title given to the American edition of the novella: *The Children of the Sea*. The point is important because it links the ideology perceptible behind the portrayal of the crew of the 'Narcissus' with that underpinning the portrayal of the seemingly childish James Wait.

5 Captain Allistoun is also portrayed in ways that, if not contradictory, are certainly not fully consistent. Early on in the novella we meet him as a man whose captaincy is perhaps tainted with self-seeking pride: 'He loved his ship, and drove her unmercifully; for his secret ambition was to make her accomplish some day a brilliantly quick passage which would be mentioned in nautical papers' (pp. 30-1). Later he comes more and more to function as a symbolic God-figure, a character proleptic of Captain Giles in *The Shadow-Line*: 'He was one of those commanders who speak little, seem to hear nothing, look at no one – and know everything, hear every whisper, see every fleeting shadow of their ship's life' (p. 125). The contrast is not particularly striking, nor does it merit being listed as an incoherence in the work. But it does provide additional evidence that in *The Nigger of the 'Narcissus'* Conrad oscillated between realism and allegory in his portrayal of the 'Narcissus' and its crew.

6 The 'Narcissus' is both compared to and contrasted with the land: 'the ship, a fragment detached from the earth' (p. 29); 'the coast, stretching away straight and black, resembled the high side of an indestructible craft riding motionless upon the immortal and unresting sea. The dark land lay alone in the midst of waters, like a mighty ship' (p. 162). 'The *Narcissus* came gently into her berth; the shadows of soulless walls fell upon her, the dust of all the continents leaped upon her deck, and a swarm of strange men, clambering up her sides, took possession of her in the name of the

sordid earth. She had ceased to live'. (p. 165). I might add that it is not easy to reconcile Donkin's association with the land with the description of the land as 'an indestructible craft'.

One possible explanation is that it is not so much the land as *England*[13] which is compared to a ship, and that Conrad distinguishes between 'land' and 'England' even when these are in one sense identical. In other words there is a particularly ideological thrust behind the descriptions of the land both as like a ship and also as 'sordid earth' to be distinguished from the ship.

I should also make it clear that given such an explanation we are not necessarily dealing with any incoherence here: at the end of the novella, when the end of the voyage might induce a sense of completion in the reader's mind, we are reminded that narrator and men have in a sense moved from one vessel to another. Like *The Shadow-Line*, *The Nigger of the 'Narcissus'* offers us a productive tension between the sense of arrival and completion as end of voyage coincides with end of narrative, and the sense that all endings are also beginnings and there are no final destinations on earth apart from death. The crew of the 'Narcissus' 'sign on' to the ship of England; the captain of *The Shadow-Line* prepares to continue his voyage.

7 It is with regard to James Wait, however, that incoherences are to be found in the greatest abundance. As I have argued, Wait is the visible part of a fault-line that spans the whole of the work, the nodal point at which more far-reaching contradictions are displayed and made apparent. Wait is

(i) a malingerer but also genuinely sick

Critics of *The Nigger of the 'Narcissus'* are still unable finally to make up their minds whether Wait is genuinely sick, and pretending to be a malingerer so as to conceal the fact of his impending death from himself, or whether he actually believes himself to be shamming sickness. The majority opinion at the present time seems to be that Wait is pretending to be shamming so as to avoid recognizing that he is dying. But Seiji Minamida's recent glossary on the novella, commenting upon the captain's statement that Wait has 'been skulking nearly all the passage' (p. 120), argues that

> Captain Allistoun learned from his discharge Jimmy's bad record in his last ship, and had been sure all along that the latter was shamming ill.[14]

Other critics have seen Allistoun's comment as a sympathetic gesture towards Wait, pretending to accept his imposture so as to help him to delay recognition of his impending death. Both explanations are, it seems to me, possible. David Manicom, in an article on *The Nigger of the 'Narcissus'* from which I have already quoted, outlines what are essentially these two alternatives in great detail, and concludes:

> Neither of these two hypotheses concerning Wait's 'illness' can be proven or disproven. The novel's narrative levels allow the two different 'meanings' to play tantalizingly at being the truth behind the lies.[15]

Cedric Watts gives us an equally plausible third alternative which straddles those already mentioned.

> Throughout the voyage, as the text makes clear, [Wait] suffers from tuberculosis (on the first night his 'roaring, rattling cough... shook him like a hurricane'); but when his illness is relatively mild, he exaggerates it in order to malinger, while when the illness becomes mortal, he lies to others and to himself that he is fit.[16]

Conrad seems to go to great lengths to preserve uncertainty; we might think that once it becomes clear that Wait really is dying then the ambiguity would be cleared up, but just about this point comes Wait's confession to Donkin that he has 'done this afore', an admission that might seem to confirm that Wait is, at least in part, malingering. Typically, it is just at this point that Wait coughs violently, thus overlaying the impression of malingering with a reminder of real physical illness. The reader can never be sure whether or not Wait is a malingerer.

(ii) **refined in expression yet also vulgar**
Wait's normal spoken discourse is characterized by its extreme formality and refinement. When he speaks to the mate following the initial mis-understanding concerning his name he even uses a word such as 'mis-apprehended', one we can be confident none of his fellow crewmen would utter. In contrast to the 'mute' (or almost mute) Singleton, Wait speaks like a man reading prose. No other sailor on the ship has access to such 'correct', literary English. And yet when conversing with Donkin shortly before his death he speaks in a colloquial, uneducated manner on a par with the speech of his fellows, using slang terms such as 'chuck' and 'toff', and with a demotic element suggested by non-standard spelling ('wimmen', for example, on page 149 of the novella). Are we to see this as the 'savage' with a veneer of civilized behaviour which is as inadequate in disguising his real nature as are his fine clothes? Or is the fine speech necessitated by Wait's rôle as demonic 'gentleman'? Or is Wait's astonishing range of linguistic registers indicative of the fact that he is all things to all men?

(iii) **brave and courageous yet also cowardly**
'"Get out of this," boomed Wait, courageously' (p. 116). 'He lifted his head and turned bravely at Donkin' (p. 151). Yet while he is being rescued reference is made to 'the agony of his fear' (p. 67), and a later reference alludes to 'the unthinking stillness of a scared brute' (p. 118). It is of course quite possible for any individual to be brave at some times and cowardly at others, and it might conceivably be argued that Wait finds courage in his confrontation with Donkin, perhaps by seeing aspects of himself in the other man. Such an explanation does not have too much textual evidence to back it up, however.

(iv) **urbane yet also primitive**
This particular collision is nowhere better illustrated than in the following passage.

> He stopped short. The folly around him was confounded. He was right as ever, and as ever ready to forgive. The disdainful tones had ceased, and, breathing heavily, he stood still, surrounded by all these white men. He held his head up in the glare of the lamp – a head vigorously modelled into deep shadows and shining lights – a head powerful and misshapen with a tormented and flattened face – a face pathetic and brutal: the tragic, the mysterious, the repulsive mask of a nigger's soul.
>
> (NOTN, p. 18)

The first part of this passage clearly includes represented thought, taking us into Jimmy's consciousness (note the giveaway use of '*these* white men' rather than '*those*'). The resources of FID are utilized to give the reader both the impression that here we have an accurate depiction of Wait's thoughts, and also that the narrator is contemptuous of Wait's pretensions. But even in this first part of the extract the narrative situation is complex, however, as the words 'The disdainful tones had ceased, and, breathing heavily' clearly come from a narrator rather than from Jimmy, who *is* disdainful but does not *think of himself* being so any more than he *thinks* of himself breathing heavily. We then move, however, from Jimmy as sneering aristocrat to Jimmy as distorted brute – a movement which almost inevitably brings along Satanic associations which tie in with other associations of Wait with the devil.[17] It is at this point that the lack of specificity with regard to point of view becomes important. *Who* is it who sees Jimmy's face as brutal and repulsive?

In the course of *The Nigger of the 'Narcissus'* the following words are all applied to or associated with Wait: swagger (p. 17); disdainful (p. 18); condescended (p. 19); contemptuously angry (p. 35); overbearing (p. 35); casual (p. 37); fastidious (used with regard to his appetite: p. 38); languor (p. 105); contempt (pp. 19, 149); superb (assurance) (p. 149).

All of these words are such as are normally associated with upper-class or aristocratic pride and assurance – or with the devil. And yet in contrast we find the following:

> He was afraid to turn his head, he shrank within himself; and there was an aspect astounding and animal-like in the perfection of his expectant immobility. A thing of instinct – the unthinking stillness of a scared brute.
>
> (NOTN, p. 118)

We are led either to the conclusion that Wait is a Satanic figure combining contemptuous self-assurance and pride with animal-like brutality (although Wait's alleged fear does not square with this), or to the conclusion that Wait's refined manner is a thin veneer over his essential brutishness. Or, finally, that Conrad's presentation of Wait is artistically confused, and hovers between irreconcilable allegorical and realistic strategies, strategies which are further complicated by the influence of racially stereotypical elements.

(v) with an imposing, carrying voice, yet weak and powerless
James Wait belongs to a recognizable breed of Conradian characters who are possessed of voices which, without needing to be raised, carry great distances and convey a sense of impressive authority. We can cite Verloc, Kurtz and Peter Ivanovitch as examples. All of these characters are portrayed as being in some way false and hollow. Interestingly, both Kurtz and James Wait die unable to utter more than a whisper. Wait whispers twice in the novella: once in the 'birth' scene when he is rescued, and once when he dies: 'he denied, cursed, threatened – and not a word had the strength the pass beyond the sorrowful pout of those black lips' (p. 151). Wait's powerful voice (along with his assured, articulate speech) has to be understood in the light of Conrad's general attitude towards language and his suspicion of verbal 'eloquence'. Such eloquence is habitually associated with deception by Conrad, and seen in this way Wait's imposing voice can be seen as yet another example of a deceptive veneer, just as his imposing physical appearance conceals the truth of his inner sickness.

Cedric Watts points out that the text repeatedly emphasizes the paradox that Jimmy is physically remarkably light and symbolically remarkably weighty, and this paradoxical view of him complements the contrast between his powerful voice and declining physical strength.[18]

(vi) both loved and hated by his fellows
'We hesitated between pity and mistrust'; '(We all lovingly called him Jimmy, to conceal our hate of his accomplice)': this on the same page as mention of 'this obnoxious nigger' (p. 36)! During the rescue Belfast shouts

to Wait, 'Knock! Jimmy darlint! . . . Knock! You bloody black beast!' (p. 69). During the rescue Wait is described as a 'hateful burden' (p. 72), and as his death nears we read 'Donkin, watching the end of that hateful nigger' (p. 153). Frequently a single sentence will include contradictory elements: 'We knew he was dry and comfortable within his little cabin, and in our absurd way were pleased one moment, exasperated the next, by that certitude' (p. 53). Note how phrases like 'in our absurd way' manage to combine two perspectives here, either those of the crew at the time along with the crew-member's later hindsight, or that of the crew at the time along with an implied authorial narrator. (The crew clearly did not think that their way was absurd at the time.) In this example then the contradictory attitudes towards Wait are recognized by the narrative, are typified as 'absurd', and are attributed to the crew. But this is far from being always the case.

What explanations are there for so many complex and interlocking inconsistencies and incoherences in this work? I do not believe that there is a single, or a simple, available explanation. On one level of argument I would suggest that *The Nigger of the 'Narcissus'*, although by no means Conrad's first work, can still in many ways be seen as an apprentice piece. It is a far more ambitious work than Conrad's first two novels, and this ambition seems to have presented Conrad with problems and difficulties of an order different from those encountered earlier on in his writing career. In particular, during the writing of *The Nigger of the 'Narcissus'* Conrad had to learn how to produce a work that can contain and depict contradictory visions whilst not being mastered by them, uniting them by means of some larger artistic conception. Subsequently Conrad learned, for example, how to displace such tensions and contradictions into a narrator such as Marlow, thereby anchoring them in a way that they are not anchored in *The Nigger of the 'Narcissus'*.

What are these root contradictions which Conrad fails to master in *The Nigger of the 'Narcissus'* and which underlie this work's incoherences? I would wish to isolate two rather different underlying factors: firstly, Conrad's hesitation between what we can term romanticism and realism, and secondly his failure fully to come to terms with Victorian Britain's schizophrenic attitude to the Negro.

Many commentators have found an oscillation between a romanticized and a realistic view of nineteenth-century sailing life in *The Nigger of the 'Narcissus'*. Some have suggested that this oscillation reflects Conrad's own inability to decide what exactly his view of – and relations towards – this life were. It is certainly possible that one reason why Conrad remained so fond of this particular work to the end of his life was that it did hold very different attitudes towards his sea-life in a sort of suspension; not reconciling their contradictions, but effecting some sort of cohabitation between them. It is in *Lord Jim* that Conrad confronts the contradiction as contradiction; at the start of chapter 11 of this novel Marlow remarks:

> Surely in no other craft as in that of the sea do the hearts of those already launched to sink or swim go out so much to the youth on the brink, looking with shining eyes upon that glitter of the vast surface which is only a reflection of his own glances full of fire. There is such magnificent vagueness in the expectations that had driven each of us to sea, such a glorious indefiniteness, such a beautiful greed of adventures that are their own and only reward! What we get – well, we won't talk of that; but can one of us restrain a smile? In no other kind of life is the illusion more wide of the reality – in no other is the beginning *all* illusion – the disenchantment more swift – the subjugation more complete.
>
> (LJ, pp. 128-9)

In *The Nigger of the 'Narcissus'* we find no admission that both illusion and reality, romance and actuality are engendered by the sea – *and that they are opposites and irreconcilable*. The work, by concealing, effectively attempts to deny the existence of such a tension. *Lord Jim*, in contrast, explores and analyses it.

James E. Miller Jr has suggested that

> The iconography of *The Nigger of the 'Narcissus'* was not accomplished without a dangerous compromise between the naturalistic, biographical material and its symbolic transformation.[19]

Conrad's own comments on the work, made at the time of its composition, are evidence of a duality in his intentions. In a letter written while he was writing the work he speaks of producing 'a respectable shrine for the memory of men with whom I have, through many hard years lived and worked'.[20] In another such letter he uses similar words, stating that he 'must enshrine my old chums in a decent edifice'.[21] And by 1903 he can write that

> As a work of fiction *The Nigger* puts a seal on that epoch of the greatest possible perfection which was at the same time the end of the sailing fleet.[22]

'Shrine', 'perfection'; Conrad's terminology in these letters is very revealing. But of course it doesn't really square up all that satisfactorily with what Conrad actually wrote, with the evidence of the text. As we can remember, the epoch of greatest possible perfection is seen in *The Nigger of the 'Narcissus'* as that to which Singleton and his contemporaries belonged. The sailors with whom Conrad sailed might, had they read *The Nigger of the 'Narcissus'*, have found Conrad's 'shrine' a little less than totally complimentary about themselves. What Conrad appears to be doing here is confusing a subjective perfection – the experiences of his youthful years – with an objective one – the end of the sailing fleet. In 'Youth' the distinction is recognized; in *The Nigger of the 'Narcissus'* it is not.

Elsewhere however Conrad refers to the work in rather different terms. Writing again to Edward Garnett, 29 November 1896, he remarks:

> As to lack of incident well – it's life. The incomplete joy, the incomplete sorrow, the incomplete rascality or heroism – the incomplete suffering. Events crowd and push and nothing happens. You know what I mean. The opportunities do not last long enough.
>
> Unless in a boy's book of adventures. Mine were never finished. They fizzled out before I had a chance to do more than another man would. (CLJC 1, p. 321)

Looking at these words it is not hard to see the germ of *Lord Jim* in the contrast between the visions offered by a boy's book of adventures and the opportunities offered by the real world which do not 'last long enough'. In the early part of *Lord Jim* Jim feels 'angry with the brutal tumult of earth and sky for taking him unawares' when the collision takes place (p. 9). By this time Conrad is able to *dramatize* the conflict between the romanticism and realism of the sea, and make it his subject. In *The Nigger of the 'Narcissus'*, in contrast, the conflict is not so much the subject of the work as one of the sources of its incoherence. Commenting upon the final pages of the novella, Michael P. Jones argues that

> Rather than a commentator or a critic, [Conrad] has become an elegist, a kind of pastoral poet singing the praises of a mythical and imaginary past. In the end, Conrad cannot and will not reconcile the detachment of an ironist with the emotional involvement of a participant. And therein lies the final conflict in point of view.[23]

This seems to me to be very well said, but I think that the ideological underpinnings of Conrad's irony and of his realism in *The Nigger of the 'Narcissus'* need to be detailed. In this work narrative irony is never directed towards the officers of the 'Narcissus', but always towards some or all of the crew; it is premised upon highly conservative and hierarchical assumptions. If we contrast the narrative irony of *The Secret Agent* we can note that it is not just the anarchists or those associated with them at whom it is directed; its scope is genuinely comprehensive. (This is one of the reasons why, in spite of the clear visible criticism of the anarchists, the work nonetheless seems in part to underwrite certain aspects of anarchist philosophy.) Conrad's irony in *The Nigger of the 'Narcissus'*, then, seems in tension with his declared aim of enshrining his old chums in a decent edifice. This aim seems actually to have been mastered by a stronger, ideological impulse in the work at times, and these times are characteristically marked by Conrad's use of irony.

Raymond Williams has drawn our attention to the fact that if there is one sure thing about the Golden Age, it is that it has always gone. The further back in time one proceeds, the further back its date is displaced. One aspect of Conrad's contradictory attitude towards the crew in the novella seems to be that it varies very much according to whether Conrad is picturing himself among the crew. Of course, 'Conrad' is not a character in the work; nevertheless, Conrad's real-life attitudes towards the seamen of his sailing days are clearly projected into the work. But the seamen *also* serve a very different function. If at one time they are Conrad's 'old chums', it is apparent that at other times they play a more *representative* rôle in the work, and it is at these times that ideological factors become more intrusive. David Manicom puts the matter as follows.

> *The Nigger of the 'Narcissus'* is a carefully drawn realistic novel that nevertheless continually gazes toward the allegorical. It is possible to accomplish this so convincingly because, as in *Lord Jim* and *Heart of Darkness*, our narrator is both living in *and* interpreting the story.[24]

The difference between *The Nigger of the 'Narcissus'* on the one hand and both *Lord Jim* and *Heart of Darkness* on the other, however, is that Marlow's double attitude towards the events narrated is explained and incorporated into the artistic structure of the works. He admits to it, and tries to tackle its implications. In *The Nigger of the 'Narcissus'*, partly because this work does not have a fully personified intra-mimetic narrator, the contradictions are not explained in terms of the experience and viewpoint of the narrator. Indeed, they are not acknowledged at all. This is why *The Nigger of the 'Narcissus'* presents the reader with problems of a completely different order from those presented to him or her by *Lord Jim* or *Heart of Darkness*. To resolve these problems their ideological roots have to be uncovered by the reader with little help from the work, whereas one of the things that makes both *Lord Jim* and *Heart of Darkness* such powerful works is that they display and analyse their own ideological underpinnings.

At the time of writing *The Nigger of the 'Narcissus'* Conrad seems still to have been hovering between a conservative-paternalist view of the working class (seen at its purest in the admiring description of Singleton, the hard worker who is totally dedicated to his job, is unthinking and accepts authority unquestioningly, and who abandons himself to mindless drunkenness off-duty), and a rather different conservative-reactionary view most apparent in the treatment of Donkin and of his fellow seamen when they are under his influence. This conservative-reactionary ideology is most visible in the younger Conrad, and it tends to disappear and to be replaced by the conservative-paternalist view in his older years. It is expressed in its purest form in Conrad's letter to Spiridion Kliszczewski which I quoted in the previous chapter. The ideology lying behind this outburst is, surely, the same that gives rise to the sarcastic narrative comments in *The Nigger of the 'Narcissus'* about the seamen, who

> inspired by Donkin's hopeful doctrines .... dreamed enthusiastically of the time when every lonely ship would travel over a serene sea, manned by a wealthy and well-fed crew of satisfied skippers. (NOTN, p. 103)

Donkin himself is the parody of the working-class agitator that such an ideology has to create to justify itself. Again, the language used to describe him comes from the same stable as that in Conrad's letter. Donkin is

> The man who can't do most things and won't do the rest. The pet of philanthropists and self-seeking landlubbers. The sympathetic and deserving creature that knows all about his rights, but knows nothing of courage, of endurance, and of the unexpressed faith, of the unspoken loyalty that knits together a ship's company. The independent offspring of the ignoble freedom of the slums full of disdain and hate for the austere servitude of the sea. (NOTN, p. 11)

The passage is rich in ideological polemic. Note how the faith and loyalty that knit together the organic community of the ship have to be *unexpressed* and *unspoken*; there is here a recognition on the part of the ideology that *it must not speak itself*, a recognition that helps to explain why it is that *The Nigger of the 'Narcissus'* cannot confront its own contradictions and incoherences. Indeed, the work itself mirrors this ideology's view of the ship and - clearly, by implication - of society at large. *It will not confront its own divisions and contradictions*, but asserts an organic unity that is revealed as spurious by the hysterical nature of this protestation itself. This is why Singleton has to be 'unthinking', for were he capable of thought he would recognize the incompatibilities in his implicit view of the world. And what is it that is so feared? 'The *independent* offspring of the ignoble *freedom* of the slums full of disdain and hate for the austere *servitude* of the sea'. What is feared is that the exercise of rational thought on the part of the working class will lead to a preference of freedom and independence over servitude. And of course on one level Conrad knows that the seamen do have legitimate grievances: how else can we explain how quickly Donkin persuades his listeners, listeners who we have been told already 'know him' very well? Singleton, incidentally, is just as likely to have come from a slum as is Donkin. It is not really Donkin's origins that Conrad is concerned to attack, but his potential rôle in leading his fellow seamen to stop being 'unthinking' and to begin rationally to consider their situation. Conrad's schizophrenia regarding the seamen of the 'Narcissus' is comparable to that of Dickens concerning his portrayal of the industrial working class in *Hard Times*: it results from a clash between realist and ideological impulses. (And we should also recall Dickens's treatment of 'philanthropy' in *Bleak House* – one of Conrad's favourite novels.)[25]

Such tensions also enter the portrayal of James Wait, although in his case there are additional factors to be considered. Wait is both the symbolic, dark, satanic intruder into the prelapsarian Eden of the ship that represents that 'epoch of the greatest possible perfection', and also the realistically depicted Afro-Caribbean, suffering from a non-symbolic tuberculosis. On the one hand he is the symbolic 'weight' which holds back the ship and makes it 'wait' (his name, in cockney pronunciation, also suggests 'white'). On the other hand, as an unnamed member of the crew observes, 'The man's a man if he is black' (p. 121), or as the Captain adds later on, 'He might have been half a man once' (p. 127) – a comment which partly concedes that before the onset of his disease Wait was as good a human being as any of his white mates.

Such an approach perhaps helps to explain why *The Nigger of the 'Narcissus'* needs *two* agents of corruption: Donkin and Wait. Donkin generally functions as agent of corruption on a realistic level, while Wait performs the same function on a symbolic/mythic plane. It is notable that when he is with Donkin, Wait is realistic Afro-Caribbean, but his relations with the rest of the crew operate on an appreciably less realistic level. (His death at sea allows Conrad to escape the problems that would result from trying to maintain this symbolic/mythic rôle on land.)

An additional problem seems to be, however, that even at sea these two aspects of Wait's rôle leak into one another. And this is partly because of the other factor which makes of Wait such a problematic character in the novella. So many myths concerning the Negro held sway in Victorian England, that portraying a Negro in a purely realistic manner would probably have been impossible. Even the more realistic side of the depiction of Wait contains numerous mythic elements which seem to have their origin in wider social myths about the Negro in Victorian England. And these combine with ideological views of the working class in complex ways. There was, after all, a firm basis for a realistic description of a black sailor in Conrad's time. I have already mentioned that Conrad had sailed with black seamen, and one estimate from 1878 puts the number of coloured sailors engaged in long voyages for the British Merchant Service at 20,000 – of whom 5,000 were Lascars working for the Peninsular and Orient Company.[26]

But this objective basis was overlaid in Victorian public opinion by a mass of myths relating to imperialism and colonialism. Not just this, but even more liberal views – those opposing slavery and colonial brutality, for instance – were often heavily paternalistic in form. And thus paternalism could function as the bridge which joined views of black people and views of the native European working class.

Victorian views of the Negro have been well-documented in recent years, and can be quickly summarized. Firstly, the Negro was seen as racially inferior.

> By unanimous consent, said the *Encyclopaedia Britannica*, the African Negro occupied the lowest position in the evolutionary scale, his abnormal length of arm, prognathism and lightweight brain supposedly affording the best material for 'the comparative study of the highest anthropoids and the human species'. The Victorian fixation with the notion of a 'missing link' becomes apparent here.[27]

Brian Street reports discussion in the Anthropological Society of London about Negro intelligence, suggesting that the Negro child developed until the age of twelve, when the 'sutures' then closed and intelligence stultified.[28]

This opinion is repeated in the *Everyman Encyclopaedia*, 1913 edition:

> The children are described as sharp, vivacious and intelligent, but deterioration commences at puberty, and the full-grown Negro remains childlike, unprogressive, lethargic, without initiation. . . . In the USA and S. Africa, where they are largely Christianized, their acceptance is childish in nature, and their moral status appears unable to rise to the Christian ideal. They have been described as non-moral, rather than immoral, which aptly expresses their undoubted lower stage of development. They are childishly gay, and passionate, with childish rapidity in change of mood; thievish, unreliable, indolent, yet with a childish subordination to authority, and marked faithfulness, yet subject to sudden failure. These points of character united to a marked sensuousness render them a serious social problem in the more progressive and civilized lands, particularly in America.

We can remember that the title chosen by Conrad for his novella in the United States, to meet the objections of a publisher who claimed that American readers would not buy a book with the word 'nigger' in the title, was *The Children of the Sea*. The alleged childishness of the Negro is another bridge reaching over to that native working class represented by the white seamen of the 'Narcissus'. Writing of *The Nigger of the 'Narcissus'* in *Notes on Life and Letters*, Conrad declares of the seamen of his seagoing years that, 'their simple minds had a sort of sweetness' (p. 184). It is clear that a paternalist attitude needs a child or children. In *Under Western Eyes* Peter Ivanovitch's paternalism is expressed in his view of the Russian peasantry as children (he eventually marries one of these children), and in his treatment of Tekla. In *Chance* Marlow's paternalism expresses itself in the view that women are like children (p. 170). In *The Nigger of the 'Narcissus'* Conrad's paternalistic conservatism finds an object in his child-like seamen and in the childish James Wait. There is an interesting contrast to be made with *An Outcast of the Islands*, in which the 'native' Ali expresses the view that white men are like children (p. 297). Conrad seems always to have found it easier to escape from cultural preconceptions with Malays than with Africans.

Christine Bolt confirms that many of these views of the Negro were well established long before the end of the nineteenth century.

> The freedmen were characterized, according to the Victorians – and here is the European racist's most persistent obsession – by their uninhibited sensuality. This was expressed in a passion for eating and drinking, sleeping, dressing up, dancing and sex.[29]

Bolt discusses the debate around Eyre's savage suppression of the Jamaica revolt – a debate in which Charles Dickens was very fully involved in support of Eyre. According to Bolt

> the abolitionist and missionary attempt to demonstrate the essential equality of all men before God seemed disproved by this supposed example of the innate savagery of the Negro – a savagery which permitted, even made essential, savage counter-measures on the part of the superior white race.[30]

Of particular interest is Brian Street's comment that

> Characters who crossed the racial, national and environmental boundaries were important to the Victorians because they helped to define those boundaries . . . Victorians were suspicious, not only of biological hybrids but of those 'cultural hybrids' who had inherited one background but tried to adopt another. These characters, the white man in Africa and the black man in European clothes, present a dilemma which is central to Victorian conceptions of race and culture . . . [31]

It seems clear that such views as I have outlined above have a complex ideological origin. Firstly, they offer a justification for European behaviour in Africa. And secondly, the black man is used as the concealed ideological representative of the native working class, the pastoral scapegoat who can justify the treatment of these native inferiors.

It is no surprise that Conrad is able most effectively to confront and question such views when, in literary terms, he returns to one of these two roots - in 'An Outpost of Progress' and *Heart of Darkness*. The black person subject to most authorial irony in 'An Outpost of Progress' is Makola - who has been westernized. A similar point can be made of Marlow's helmsman in *Heart of Darkness*. Wait's portrayal in *The Nigger of the 'Narcissus'* needs to be seen in the light of complex ideological pressures: not only has he crossed 'racial, national and environmental boundaries', to quote Brian Street, but this in turn allows him to have all sorts of domestic European problems projected on to him in the classic manner of the scapegoat. This seems to be the reason why his portrayal is markedly different from that of Africans and of Malays in other works of Conrad, who are not called upon to bear the sins of Europe in quite the same way. The fact that Victorian society displaced many of its own problems and guilts - especially concerning social class - onto the figure of the Negro, constitutes a key element in the link between Donkin and Wait. Brian Street cites an interesting comment concerning the way in which the Irish had the sins of their English masters projected upon them.

> The almost mechanical way in which Anglo-Saxonists assigned to the Irishman those very traits which were most deplored or despised among the respectable middle and upper classes in Victorian England leaves little room for doubt that the gentlemen who relied upon this stereotype were merely projecting onto an assumedly inferior group all those emotions which lay buried within themselves and which the English social system encouraged - and at times compelled - them to repress. Projection is one of the common consequences of repression.[32]

Douglas A. Lorimer gives us an example of Victorian attitudes to the Negro which could well be partly explained in the same manner:

> Many English commentators described the Southern slaves as lazy, stupid, vicious animals. At other times, and in the eyes of other observers, blacks appeared capable of a saintly, silent endurance of oppression. Mid-Victorian attitudes to the distressed working people of Lancashire displayed a similar ambivalence.[33]

A recent study by Catherine Gallagher has confirmed that from a very early date in nineteenth-century Britain, debates about American Negro slavery became intertwined with arguments concerning the native British working class.[34] Again, the link between Donkin and Wait may be seen to represent complex ideological connections available to the Victorians only in mythic form.

One of the most revealing expressions of Victorian views of black people is surely the 'Nigger Minstrel Show', imported from the United States and assuming a specific identity in Victorian and later England. (The 'Nigger Minstrels' were a regular feature of seaside holidays for me back in the 1950s, and of course British readers of a certain age will recall 'The Black and White Minstrel Show' on television, which survived well into the 1960s.) By the latter half of the nineteenth century

> The comic parts became monopolized by the caricature of the 'negro' dandy with his constantly unrealized pretension to grandiloquence, whereas the tatterdemalion plantation black, particularly as a result of Stephen Foster's songs, became the object, in a much more concentrated fashion, of a sentimental pathos.[35]

It is striking how much this description calls the figure of James Wait to mind: the Negro 'dandy' with a constantly unrealized pretension to grandiloquence, but also the subject of the crew's sentimental pathos. Michael Pickering, from an article by whom the above quotation comes, confirms Douglas A. Lorimer's point that stereotypes of the Negro in Victorian Britain were full of contrasts and contradictions.

> From one side the 'negro' was the faithful, deferential servant; from another the indolent, undisciplined labourer. Turn him again, 'jis so', and one confronts the natural Christian, opposed from an opposite angle by the image of an unregenerate sinner; yet another pair of antithetical popular conceptions show him as a patient, suffering forbearing slave on the one hand, and on the other a brutal, lustful, vengeful savage.[36]

We can summarize much of the foregoing and say that for the Victorians the stereotype of the Negro contained a range of contradictions, many of which were exaggerated displacements of views held of the native working class. Thus the Negro is seen to be

> human yet brute (especially sexually)
> savage yet with pretensions to be refined
> cunning yet stupid
> lazy yet capable of working 'like a Nigger'
> a child and yet an adult
> 'the faithful black' yet untrustworthy
> a pet, yet physically repulsive
> devil but also uncorrupted man

It is no surprise that James Wait's name is represented by a blur in the novella; Conrad's presentation of him reproduces many of the contradictions and incoherences contained in the Victorian stereotype of the Negro.

I have already noted that Conrad seems to have found it far less problematic to escape from the racism of his age when dealing with Malays. We have the splendid Author's Note to *Almayer's Folly* to witness here, and we can also note how, in *The Rescue*, it is the unsympathetic Shaw who refers to Malays as 'niggers', and is the clear recipient of authorial scorn for so doing.[37] There is unambiguous internal evidence in *The Nigger of the 'Narcissus'* that the term 'nigger' was considered to be offensive.

> 'You wouldn't call me nigger if I wasn't half dead, you Irish beggar!' boomed James Wait, vigorously. (NOTN, pp. 79-80)

Lorimer cites Mayhew to confirm that certainly in 1862 black people found this term offensive.[38] Christine Bolt uses the fact that this word gained currency as a term of abuse in India after 1857 to establish the level of Victorian racial prejudice against the Negro. Moreover, in April 1897, a matter of four months before *The Nigger of the 'Narcissus'* started to be serialized, Conrad's friend-to-be Cunninghame Graham published a bitingly sarcastic article entitled 'Bloody Niggers', from which Cedric Watts has quoted the following extract:

> 'Niggers' who have no cannons, and cannot construct a reasonable torpedo, have no rights. 'Niggers' whose lot is placed outside our flag, whose lives are given over to a band of money-grubbing miscreants (chartered or not) have neither rights nor wrongs. Their land is ours, their cattle, fields, their houses, their poor utensils, arms, all that they have; their women, too, are ours to use as concubines, to beat, exchange, to barter for gunpowder and gin . . . Cretans, Armenians, Cubans, Macedonians, we commiserate, subscribe, and feel for . . . But 'niggers', 'bloody niggers', have no friends.[39]

As Watts points out, Conrad read Graham's article in *The Social-Democrat*, and remarked, 'very good, very telling' (LCG, p. 89). How then do we explain Conrad's own quite different attitude to the word 'nigger' in *The Nigger of the 'Narcissus'*? Cedric Watts has suggested that the influence of both Rudyard Kipling and of W. E. Henley may possibly be seen in Conrad's novella. Henley was the editor of the *National Review*, which had agreed to publish *The Nigger of the 'Narcissus'* while Conrad was still writing it, and he was an admirer of Kipling. Henley's opinions were, in Watts's phrase, 'patriotic, royalist, and imperialistic'. A letter from Conrad to the Chairman of a committee formed to establish a memorial to Henley after the latter's death would seem to confirm this. Referring to letters he had written Henley, Conrad adds

> It seemed impossible to tell him on paper that the story he accepted for the Review was written with an eye on him – and yet with no idea that it would ever meet his eye. And that is the strict truth. (CLJC 3, p. 115)

Whatever the reason, in *The Nigger of the 'Narcissus'* not only is the word 'nigger' used by crew members, but also by the narrator – both when speaking as 'we' and also when adopting a more detached and omniscient perspective.[40] And his use betrays no evidence of Conrad's having been affected by Cunninghame Graham's article. (Nor, incidentally, does there seem to be any evidence that Cunninghame Graham reacted against Conrad's use of the word in the novella.)

According to Kenneth Little's book *Negroes in Britain* (first published in 1948), the end of the nineteenth century was a period in which attitudes towards, and notions concerning, the Negro 'seem to have undergone a considerable change'.

> An object for pity becomes very often an object for condescension. The difficulty was that by emancipation the Negro had theoretically ceased to be either. It was no longer possible to regard him merely as the faithful black, a typification of servile devotion and fidelity. It was as if in becoming a 'man and a brother', as one anonymous commentator puts it, 'he forthwith ceased to be a friend'.[41]

It is this 'neither one thing nor the other' sort of attitude which seems to be reflected in *The Nigger of the 'Narcissus'*, and reflected rather than reflected upon; Conrad seems unable to make this indecision the *subject* or focus of the work. Rather, it becomes an element which, because it is not fully recognized and artistically controlled, renders the text of the work unstable and lacking full coherence.

Little's book provides considerable evidence to substantiate the view that there were two especial focal points for prejudice against black people in Conrad's time: sexual relationships between black men and white women, and the physical features of black people. Both of these are referred to in the novella, but their treatment differs markedly and interestingly. With regard to the prejudice concerning inter-racial sexuality, Conrad is able to objectify this and *depict it as a prejudice* by having it expressed by Donkin. It is Donkin rather than the narrator who is so shocked by Wait's claim to have a 'Canton Street girl' waiting for him, one who

'Cooks oysters just as I like . . . She says – she would chuck – any toff – for a coloured gentleman. . . . That's me. I am kind to wimmen,' he added, a shade louder.

Donkin could hardly believe his ears. He was scandalised – 'Would she? Yer wouldn't be any good to 'er,' he said with unrestrained disgust.

(NOTN, p. 149)

The strong implication here is that Donkin's prejudice (which we have witnessed earlier in his view of 'damned furriners') is being mocked and dismissed by the narrator, who seems to share none of Donkin's views concerning the shocking nature of inter-racial sexual contact (we should remember that oysters were reputed to have an aphrodisiac effect by the Victorians). The idea that one so mean and disreputable as Donkin should presume to be 'scandalized' is surely meant to be ludicrously laughable.

The way in which a shocked repulsion from Wait's physical appearance is reported is significantly different in treatment. In this case the commentary comes through direct narrative observation and seems to carry authorial force. *The Nigger of the 'Narcissus'* contains repeated mention of those features stereotypically associated with prejudice against Negroes: thick pouting lips, rolling eyes, flattened nose. It is striking that both in *The Nigger of the 'Narcissus'* and in *Heart of Darkness* Conrad should repeatedly use the word 'mask' in connection with the Negro physiognomy. This may be related to the fact that many British 'nigger minstrels' were actually white men with black masks. But the following comment of Charles Lamb's, quoted by Douglas A. Lorimer, is also of interest here.

In the Negro countenance you will often meet with strong traits of benignity. I have felt yearnings of tenderness towards some of these faces – rather masks – that have looked out kindly upon one in casual encounters in the streets and highways. I love what Fuller beautifully calls – these 'images in ebony'. I should not like to associate with them – to share my meals and my good-nights with them – because they are black.[42]

In its unselfconscious blending of tenderness and repulsion Lamb's statement contains what is recognizably the classic Victorian mixture of contradictory attitudes towards black people. The use of the word mask fits into this pattern in a number of complex ways: on the one hand it contains the implication that physical features are external and non-essential, and that behind 'the mask' a full human being resides; on the other hand there is a refusal to accept that these features are no less human than those of white people, a belief that they must be a mask not a human face.

Thus the description of Wait's face in *The Nigger of the 'Narcissus'* – 'a head powerful and misshapen with a tormented and flattened face – a face pathetic and brutal: the tragic, the mysterious, the repulsive mask of a nigger's soul' – involves many of the contradictions about which I have spoken. The head 'tormented' and 'pathetic' – here we have the voice of paternalist philanthropy. But it is also 'misshapen' and 'flattened', it represents a distortion of the truly human. And, finally, it is 'brutal' and 'repulsive'; it is the face of a being whose humanity is not conceded, a being who is still viewed as a 'nigger', a being lower on the scale of evolution than the white man.

What Conrad seems to have learned about his art from writing *The Nigger of the 'Narcissus'* can be summed up as the realization that he had to be able to dramatize uncertainties and contradictions rather than to attempt to resolve or deny – and thus to be mastered by – them. Conrad's inner conflicts and ambiguities of belief did not disappear upon completion of *The Nigger of the 'Narcissus'*, although he certainly appears to have resolved some of them, as the portrayal of black people in *Heart of Darkness* bears testimony to. But many tensions and contradictions in his mental furniture remained – as they do in all of us. Clearly Marlow was of immense value to Conrad's artistic development. A personified narrator framed by an outer narrator allowed for tensions and uncertainties to be displaced down a narrative chain and thus themselves subjected to scrutiny. And where Conrad does not make use of personified narrators or framed narratives his narrative voices are far more consistent than is the case in *The Nigger of the 'Narcissus'*: think of *Nostromo* and *The Secret Agent*.

Beyond the development of such technical resources, however, it seems as if this work of Conrad's forced him to confront and think through certain inadequately considered attitudes. The conservative-reactionary voice that we find in the letter to Kliszczewski and in the depiction of Donkin appears hardly at all in Conrad's works after *The Nigger of the 'Narcissus'*. And there is a world of difference in the way the Marlow of *Heart of Darkness* comments about those 'with slightly flatter noses than ourselves' and the comments about James Wait's physiognomy in *The Nigger of the 'Narcissus'*. By this time Conrad seems more concerned to perceive the humanity that unites black and white. It is true that his recognition of the humanity of non-Europeans seems always to be more complete in the case of Malays than of Africans, and yet his two African works mark his supersession of a range of myths and prejudices which lie at the heart of the incoherences of *The Nigger of the 'Narcissus'*.

---

1   In a lecture entitled 'An Image of Africa' delivered at the University of

Massachusetts 18 February 1975. An amended version entitled 'An Image of Africa: Racism in Conrad's *Heart of Darkness*' is printed in the third edition of the Norton Critical Edition of *Heart of Darkness* edited by Robert Kimbrough (New York, 1988, p. 251).

2 Graham Hough, *An Essay on Criticism*, London, Duckworth, p. 60.

3 Cedric Watts, *Conrad's 'Heart of Darkness': A Critical and Contextual Discussion*, Milan, Mursia International, 1977, p. 159. (The comment comes in note 20 to chapter 3).

4 Stephen Land, *Conrad and the Paradox of Plot*, London, Macmillan, 1984; Michael P. Jones, *Conrad's Heroism*, Ann Arbor, UMI Research Press, 1985.

5 John Lester, 'Conrad's Narrators in *The Nigger of the "Narcissus"', Conradiana* **XII(3)**, 1980, p. 165.

6 Jakob Lothe, 'Variations of Narrative in *The Nigger of the "Narcissus"'*, *Conradiana* **XXV(3)**, 1984, p. 222.

7 Lothe, p. 217.

8 Lothe, p. 221.

9 Lothe, p. 222.

10 David Manicom, 'True Lies/False Truths: Narrative Perspective and the Control of Ambiguity in *The Nigger of the "Narcissus"'*, *Conradiana* **XVIII(2)**, 1986, p. 105. Bruce Henricksen's article, 'The Construction of the Narrator in *The Nigger of the "Narcissus"'*, (PMLA **103(5)**, October 1988) also has much of interest to say about this topic, looking at the novella in the light of 'Bakhtin's emphasis on the multiple, polyphonic nature of the self'.

11 Reynold Humphries, 'How to Change the Subject: Narrative, Reader and Ideology in *The Nigger of the "Narcissus"'*, *Recherches Anglaises et Américaines*, University of Strasbourg, **XV**, 1982, p. 41.

12 In his essay 'The Unlighted Coast', talking about the young sailor who he met who managed to get in a shot at a Zeppelin, Conrad comments

> I fancy, somehow, that rather than talk of luck so immense that there could be no fit words for it in the world, he would have preferred to brood over it in adequate silence. (TOH, p. 57)

There is some evidence, then, that for Conrad 'brooding' involves a form of non-verbal mental activity. If so, then it is not so much thought, but verbal thought which Singleton lacks. But we are told of Massy in *The End of the Tether* that

> A temper naturally irritable and an amazing sensitiveness to the claims of his own personality had ended by making of life for him a sort of inferno – a place where his lost soul had been given up to the torment of savage brooding. (p. 269)

Here 'brooding' has a far more negative ring about it, roughly equivalent to 'a non-productive nursing of a grievance'. The frequent use of 'brooding' in *Heart of Darkness* is of a different sort, applied recurrently to the non-human, as it is also on one occasion in *Under Western Eyes*.

13 The rhetoric of the closing section of the work suggests that England rather than Britain is the more appropriate term here.

14 Seiji Minamida, '*The Nigger of the "Narcissus"*, Explanatory Notes and Glossary', *Journal of the College of Arts and Sciences*, Chiba University (Japan), b-20, November 30, 1987, p. 143.

15 Manicom, p. 115

16 Cedric Watts, *The Deceptive Text: An Introduction to Covert Plots*, Brighton, Harvester, 1984, pp. 59-60.

17 Wait is associated with the devil on pages 19, 71, 115 and 119 of the novella. We should also bear in mind that this 'intruder' causes a fruit pie to be stolen!

18 *The Deceptive Text*, p. 65.

19 James E. Miller, Jr, 'Trial by Water: Joseph Conrad's *The Nigger of the "Narcissus"*'. Reprinted in John A. Palmer (ed.), *Twentieth-Century Interpretations of 'The Nigger of the "Narcissus"'*, Englewood Cliffs, Prentice-Hall, 1969, p. 37.

20 Letter to T. Fisher Unwin, 19 October 1896. (CLJC 1, pp. 308-9)

21 Letter to Edward Garnett, 25 October 1896. (CLJC 1, p. 310)

22 Letter to Kazimierz Waliszewski, 5 December 1903. Original in Polish, quotation taken from the English translation in Zdzislaw Najder (ed.), *Conrad's Polish Background: Letters to and from Polish Friends*, London, OUP, 1964, p. 240. Also printed in CLJC 3, p. 89.

23 Michael P. Jones, *Conrad's Heroism: A Paradise Lost*, Ann Arbor, UMI Research Press, 1985, p. 62.

24 Manicom, p. 109.

25 Confronting the issue of the racist attitudes in *The Nigger of the 'Narcissus'*, Cedric Watts claims that the work's prejudice is modified by the presentation of Donkin.

> [T]he case for prejudice in *The Nigger of the 'Narcissus'* fails in one obvious respect. The worst character in the book is not Jimmy but the white Londoner, Donkin, who is treacherous, malicious and vicious: a predator, compared with whom Jimmy is sympathetic. Furthermore, Jimmy is subversive not because of his blackness but because of a singular and non-racial characteristic: he is ambiguous, in being a consumptive who lies about the extent of his illness; and thus he belongs to a large family of subversively ambiguous figures in Conrad's fiction, most of whom happen to be white. (*The*

Deceptive Text, p. 74)
What this argument does not recognize is that Conrad's presentation of Donkin involves just as much prejudice as do aspects of his presentation of James Wait; it is just that the prejudice is aimed at a slightly different target.

26 Douglas A. Lorimer, *Colour, Class and the Victorians*, Leicester, Leicester UP, 1978, p. 40.

27 Christine Bolt, *Victorian Attitudes to Race*, London, RKP, 1971, p. 133.

28 Brian Street, *The Savage in Literature: Representations of 'Primitive' Society in English Fiction 1858-1920*, London, Routledge, 1975, p. 73. Street's source is *Anthropological Review*, II, 1964, p. 386.

29 Bolt, p. 41.

30 Bolt, p. 92.

31 Street, p. 111.

32 Cited from L. P. Curtis Jnr, *Anglo-Saxons and Celts*, New York UP, 1968, p. 64.

33 Lorimer, p. 172.

34 Catherine Gallagher, *The Industrial Reformation of English Fiction 1832-1867*, London, Chicago UP, 1985.

35 Michael Pickering, 'White Skin, Black Masks: "Nigger" Minstrelsy in Victorian Britain'. In J. S. Bratton (ed.), *Music Hall: Performance and Style*, Milton Keynes, Open UP, 1986, pp. 70-91.

36 Pickering, p. 85.

37 To do Conrad justice, one should note that in a letter to Kazimierz Waliszewski written 16 December 1903, Conrad reacts to a comment of Waliszewski's about 'l'infériorité des races', and insists that it was rather 'la *différence* des races que j'ai voulu indiquer' (CLJC 3, p. 93). However, in his subsequent references to *Heart of Darkness* and 'An Outpost of Progress' it seems possible that he is thinking of European 'races' rather than of Africans as against Europeans.

38 Lorimer, p. 43.

39 Quoted by Cedric Watts in his introduction to the Penguin edition of *The Nigger of the 'Narcissus'*, Harmondsworth, 1988, p. xxv. Graham's essay is reprinted in Cedric Watts (ed.), *The Selected Writings of Cunninghame Graham*, London, Associated University Presses, 1981.

40 My impression is that up to a comparatively recent date in Britain – probably the late 1950s – this word had a curious double identity. On the one hand it was a term of racial abuse; on the other it had a relatively neutral meaning much like a dead metaphor: way into the 1950s in Britain a particular shade of shoe polish was sold as 'Nigger Brown'. But dead metaphors are rarely completely dead, and the word 'nigger' probably never completely lost its element of racial abuse.

41 Kenneth Little, *Negroes in Britain: A Study of Racial Relations in English*

Society, revised edn with a new Introduction by Leonard Bloom, London, RKP, 1972, p. 229.

42 Lorimer, p. 16.

4
Chance: Conrad's Anti-feminine Feminist Novel

The attack on patriarchy

Given my concluding remarks to the previous chapter it may well seem odd to include *Chance* among those works of Conrad's in which a lack of ideological coherence is related to narrative confusions. After all, this is the fourth of Conrad's works to use Marlow as narrator, and it is also a work in which a particular ideological issue – feminism and women's rights – is recognized as problematic within the text. And yet although *Chance* was Conrad's first significant popular success, it is generally agreed to be the least successful of the Marlow works. And although feminism and women's rights are confronted as a central issue in the novel (more central and important than the theme suggested by the novel's title), there is a lack of clarity in the presentation of this theme which involves Marlow's rôle in the work and which seems to point back to a failure on Conrad's part to make his mind up about the issues the novel raises (or to dramatize these indecisions in an artistically satisfying manner).

There are particular reasons why a renewed concern with *Chance* may be especially appropriate at the present time. Of all Conrad's works, this is the one which devotes most overt and consistent attention to those issues raised by the feminist movement of Conrad's time. Thanks to the resurgence of the Women's Movement in the last decade and a half, readers in the 1980s are probably far better placed to analyse and assess this attention than many previous generations of readers have been. This aspect of *Chance* may well have had much to do with its success upon first publication in 1912; it certainly gives the novel a historical and ideological as well as a literary interest so far as modern readers are concerned.

The consideration of feminist ideas in *Chance* forms part of a larger investigation into Victorian patriarchal ideas. The character of Roderick Anthony's father, the poet Carleon Anthony, is at least partially modelled after the Victorian poet Coventry Patmore, author of that archetypal celebration of the mythic Victorian wife and mother 'The Angel in the House'. The reader of *Chance* is informed by the 'I' narrator that,

> The late Carleon Anthony, the poet, sang in his time, of the domestic and social amenities of our age with a most felicitous versification, his object being, in his own words, 'to glorify the result of six thousand years'

evolution towards the refinement of thought, manners, and feelings.' Why
he fixed the term at six thousand years I don't know. His poems read like
sentimental novels told in verse of a really superior quality.

(*Chance*, p. 38)

The first canto of 'The Angel in the House', 'The Cathedral Close', ends
as follows:

> A tent pitch'd in a world not right
> It seem'd, whose inmates, every one,
> On tranquil faces bore the light
> Of duties beautifully done,
> And humbly, though they had few peers,
> Kept their own laws, which seem'd to be
> The fair sum of six thousand years'
> Traditions of civility.

We are also told of Carleon Anthony that although reading his poetry you
felt as if you were being taken out for a delightful country drive by a
charming lady in a pony carriage,

> in his domestic life that same Carleon Anthony showed traces of the
> primitive cave-dweller's temperament. He was a massive, implacable man
> with a handsome face, arbitrary and exacting with his dependants, but
> marvellously suave in his manner to admiring strangers. These contrasted
> displays must have been particularly exasperating to his long-suffering
> family. (*Chance*, pp. 38-9)

In 1906, a one-volume edition of Patmore's poems had been published
with an introduction by Patmore's biographer Basil Champneys. Conrad
might well have read this introduction at the time that he was attempting
to write *Chance*, or it is possible that he had access to Champneys's 1900
biography of Patmore. (Ideas for the novel can be traced back as early as
1898 in a reference to a projected short-story called 'Dynamite'; Conrad
came back to this story in 1905 and in 1907, in which year he temporarily
abandoned it to work on what became *Under Western Eyes*, picking up the
threads of *Chance* again in 1910.)[1] Champneys's Introduction to the one-
volume *Poems* makes it clear that Coventry Patmore's biography was not
identical to Carleon Anthony's - Patmore was married three times and his
son and daughter from his first marriage both died young - but there are
striking similarities. Patmore's daughter Emily Honoria was a nun, and we
can recall that Marlow says of Mrs Fyne that her father 'had kept her
strictly cloistered' (p. 66). Of Henry, Patmore's son by his first marriage,
Champneys comments that he was, 'a strange and abnormally shy youth,
and therefore reticent in expression of sympathy'.[2] Most interesting,

however, in view of what we are told of Carleon Anthony's domestic bearing, is Champneys's commentary on Patmore's personality.

> In character and appearance Patmore was the exact opposite of the ideal formed of him by the ordinary reader of his earlier poetry, who presumably figured him as a mild sentimentalist. Had they by chance been brought into personal contact with him they would probably have pronounced him haughty, angular, arrogant, austere in mien; dictatorial and unsympathetic in his utterances.[3]

I make these points *not* to argue that Carleon Anthony 'is' Coventry Patmore, but in order to suggest that Conrad chose to incorporate certain classic characteristics of the Victorian Patriarch as exemplified by Patmore in his portrayal of Carleon Anthony. There is a parallel here with Virginia Woolf, who fastened upon comparable characteristics and contradictions in her own father for her portrayal of Mr Ramsay in *To the Lighthouse*.

These echoes and references help to establish that *Chance* cannot just be dismissed as an anti-feminist tract; internal textual evidence can be adduced in support of the thesis that in this novel Conrad was concerned to attack Victorian patriarchal views of women, views which through talk of 'The Angel in the House' seemed to lay claim to a positive disposition towards the female sex, but which in practice were associated with a domestic tyrannizing of wife and children. Thus when Marlow protests that 'A woman is not necessarily either a doll or an angel to me' (p. 53), reference is being made to a form of hypocrisy familiar to Conrad's readers. There can surely be no reader of *Chance* who has failed to detect anti-feminist elements in the novel; it is important that we recognize that the novel also contains an attack on myths concerning 'The Angel in the House'. Such views are more obvious in *Under Western Eyes*: Peter Ivanovitch's 'feminism' and the generally sentimental attitude to women which concludes with his marrying a peasant girl, are set against his cruelty to Tekla and his hypocritical flattery of Madame de S−. And most readers recognize, I think, that in spite of its bitterly ironical treatment of Peter Ivanovitch's feminism, *Under Western Eyes* is not in essence a novel which espouses patriarchal attitudes or which is generally dismissive of women. Why then is it that *Chance* is often taken to be just such an anti-feminist novel? Before attempting to answer this question I would first like to look more closely at another important set of literary references and echoes in *Chance*.

The interrogation of Dickensian stereotypes

In the novel as a whole Dickens is probably a far more important presence than is Patmore. *Chance* is, among other things, Conrad's re-examination of Dickensian myths and ideas concerning women. This, I think, should be of great interest to present-day feminists, who have found many archetypes of modern patriarchal ideas in male novelists of the nineteenth century, and who have found certain patriarchal myths in unusually pure form in Dickens – both in his fiction and in his extra-fictional utterances and writings. Dickens is, of course, a living presence in much of Conrad's fiction, and I suspect that Conrad's debt to his predecessor is too extensive and too profound ever to be more than inadequately charted. In *A Personal Record* (pp. 70-1) Conrad notes that his first introduction to English imaginative literature came through reading *Nicholas Nickleby* in Polish translation in 1870 (when Conrad was 13!). In the earlier *The Mirror of the Sea* Conrad had referred familiarly to Mr Mantalini (p. 167), and at a later stage of *A Personal Record* he makes the following, very revealing comment about *Bleak House*. Referring to his youthful acquaintance Madame Delestang, Conrad remarks that

> In her haughty weariness she used to make me think of Lady Dedlock in Dickens' 'Bleak House,' a work of the master for which I have such an admiration, or rather such an intense and unreasoning affection, dating from the days of my childhood, that its very weaknesses are more precious to me than the strength of other men's work. I have read it innumerable times, both in Polish and in English; I have read it only the other day, and, by a not very surprising inversion, the Lady Dedlock of the book reminded me strongly of the *belle Madame Delestang*.
>
> (APR, p. 124)

Conrad's fiction is packed with possible echoes from *Bleak House*, from his narrators' habit of slipping into the present tense on occasions (apparent as early as *Almayer's Folly*) to the more pervasive debt that *Chance* seems to owe to this work. Two novels in particular suggest a dominating creative engagement with the legacy of Dickens on the part of Conrad: *The Secret Agent* and *Chance*. The nature of this engagement is, though, very different in the two novels. *The Secret Agent* is set in a London whose representative qualities could hardly have been made accessible to Conrad, I feel, without the example of Dickens. The novel's concern with the place of the individual in a town full of privacies and secrets is a concern with symbolic possibilities which Dickens had made available to subsequent novelists, and Conrad's detailed investigation of the symbiotic relation between the domestic and the public, their isolation from and yet dependence upon each other, is an investigation made possible by his great literary predecessor. We see Dickens lurking behind all sorts of odd corners in *The Secret Agent*: in the narrator's early, humorous comment on the crazy street numbering of London, and in the description of the second-hand furniture dealer past which the Professor walks prior to his bumping into Inspector Heat. Most important, however, is Conrad's reversal of the qualities of the animate and the inanimate in *The Secret Agent*, a reversal which is suggestive of a fundamental lack of fit between human needs and aspirations on the one hand, and public systems of value and priority on the other.

The Dickensian presence in *Chance* is of a rather different order. Dickens is actually referred to by name in the course of the work. At the close of chapter 5 Marlow comments:

> 'I remembered what Mrs Fyne had told me before of the view she
> had years ago of de Barral clinging to the child at the side of his wife's
> grave and later on of these two walking hand in hand the observed of all
> eyes by the sea. Figures from Dickens – pregnant with pathos.'
>
> (*Chance*, p. 162)

Dombey and his children, Dorrit and Little Dorrit, perhaps even Little Nell and her grandfather. The young girl faithful to a weak or swindler father or grandfather would suggest *Little Dorrit* or *The Old Curiosity Shop*; the beach scene calls *Dombey and Son* to mind. Bruce Johnson however, has – correctly I feel – stated that it is particularly *Bleak House* of which, of all Dickens's novels, one is reminded by *Chance*.[4] And yet in a sense all of Dickens's works are invoked by Marlow's comment, a comment which appeals to our familiarity with a specific Dickensian *type*: the pure, passive, sad, innocent young girl, devoted and faithful to an older and flawed man. *Chance* is, among other things, Conrad's interrogation of this Dickensian type.

There are other Dickensian echoes and parallels in *Chance*, but they seem in the main to be subservient to this primary act of interrogation. The repeated references to Captain Anthony as 'the son of the poet' utilize a characteristically Dickensian technique, a form of anaphoric reference in which an individual character is first described in a striking way and then referred to by means of increasingly indirect reference to this early description.

For once the element of *tension*, so crucial to Dickens's art, is of considerable importance in a Conradian plot. Whereas in novels such as *Lord Jim*, *Nostromo* and *The Secret Agent* the reader is occupied far more with why and how things happen and much less with what will happen, in *Chance* we are, on our first reading of the novel in particular, gripped by the story, wanting to know what the outcome of the events described will be. And whereas in a novel such as *Nostromo* the reader is told earlier on of the eventual outcome of certain crucial political struggles, in *Chance* Marlow, providing his listeners with details taken from informative discussions he had had with Powell about Flora and Captain Anthony, comments that

> 'I did not ask Mr Powell anxiously what had happened to Mrs Anthony in the end. I let him go on in his own way, feeling that no matter what strange facts he would have to disclose, I was certain to know much more of them than he ever did know or could possibly guess. . . .'
>
> (*Chance*, pp. 310-11)

The concern with maintaining gaps of mystery for the purpose of generating tension and reader curiosity is apparent, and is strikingly un-Conradian.

The swindler de Barral has Mr Merdle as a direct ancestor, and the continued concern of *Chance* for the topic of incarceration is especially reminiscent of *Little Dorrit*. Flora's father feels himself to be imprisoned on board ship, and to the first mate's shock he refers to Captain Anthony as a jailer. And yet the most evocative use of the theme of universal incarceration is that which is related to the position of women. We are told of Mrs Fyne by Marlow that her father had kept her strictly cloistered, and that 'Marriage with Fyne was certainly a change, but only to another kind of claustration' (p. 66). Much later in the novel Marlow remarks, in the context of a discussion of Flora's situation, that

> 'It is the man who can and generally does "see himself" pretty well inside and out. Women's self-possession is an outward thing; inwardly they flutter, perhaps because they are, or they feel themselves to be, encaged.'
>
> (*Chance*, p. 330)

Whereas in a novel such as *Little Dorrit* the prison imagery has a more universal social force – it is Victorian society itself that we are led to see as a sort of prison – in *Chance* imprisonment is related more directly to the situation of women.

> 'I don't mean to say that Flora de Barral was one of the sort that could live by love alone. In fact she had managed to live without. But still, in the distrust of herself and of others she looked for love, any kind of love, as women will. And that confounded jail was the only spot where she could see it – for she had no reason to distrust her father.'
>
> (*Chance*, pp. 353-4)

Perhaps here we need to think not just of *Little Dorrit* but also of *Great Expectations*, for Conrad seems artistically to have perceived how Dickens was able to use the shadow of the prison which hangs over a young woman through her father's incarceration to represent the manner whereby a Victorian father's chosen rôle for his daughter could also be imprisoning in a less literal sense. And the novel in which Dickens uses this symbolic association most consummately is *Great Expectations*.

Of all Dickens's novels, *Bleak House* is the one most overtly concerned with the rôle and position of women. It contains more working women than any other novel by Dickens, and by having Esther Summerson as joint narrator it is able to attempt an exploration of a range of issues related to woman's situation both from inside and from outside. There are some very obvious parallels between *Chance* and *Bleak House*. Mrs Fyne's writing of a work for women with grievances suggests a resemblance with Mrs Jellyby in *Bleak House*, and just as Dickens states that Mrs Jellyby's theoretical concerns take her attention away from those tasks of practical household management which constitute her proper sphere, so too Marlow portrays Mrs Fyne as a woman naturally acute whose perceptiveness is blunted by her authorial concerns.

> '"It was very acute of Mrs Fyne to spot such a deep game," I said .... But then, at that time, when her nightly rest was disturbed by the dread of the fate preparing for de Barral's unprotected child, she was not engaged in writing a compendious and ruthless handbook on the theory and practice of life, for the use of women with a grievance. She could as yet, before the task of evolving the philosophy of rebellious action had affected her intuitive sharpness, perceive things which were, I suspect, moderately plain.' (*Chance*, p. 91)

It is surely not accidental that the Fyne children are badly behaved; like the Jellyby children they are presented as having suffered as a result of a mother who is too occupied with 'grievances' ('causes' in *Bleak House*) to bring them up properly. My own feeling is that such echoes of *Bleak House* are not particularly successful. The parallels are too mechanical, insufficiently integrated into any organically developed theme or piece of characterization in *Chance* – in sharp contrast to *Bleak House*, in which the theme of parental responsibility is pursued by Dickens through a range of interconnected elements. A similar point could be made concerning another echo of *Bleak House* in *Chance*:

> 'It seems that for the last six months .... Flora had insisted on devoting all her spare time to the study of the trial. She had been looking up files of old newspapers, and working herself up into a state of indignation with what she called the injustice and hypocrisy of the prosecution. .... She had reached the conclusion of her father's innocence, and had been brooding over it.' (*Chance*, p. 197)

This seems like a weak echo of *Bleak House*'s Richard Carstone, whose growing obsession with the Chancery suit is finally quite self-destructive.

A weak echo, however, because it leads nowhere in *Chance* – either in terms of plot development or in terms of the characterization of Flora.

It is not in such mechanical or undeveloped echoes of *Bleak House* that the main interest of *Chance*'s Dickensian elements lies, but in the work's less direct and obvious grappling with the complex and contradictory legacy of the Dickensian view of women.

The narrative of *Chance*

One complicating factor with which it is best to deal early rather than late is that *Chance*, unlike *Bleak House*, has no authorial narrator. The novel is narrated by an anonymous but nonetheless personified 'I' who is the recipient of Marlow's narrative, a narrative which itself contains pieces of narrative from Charles Powell and Flora de Barral. Importantly, we are given a clash of opinions and, arguably, of temperaments, between the 'I' narrator and Marlow, something which has no real parallel in the earlier 'Marlow' stories. (Although it should perhaps be noted that whereas in 'Youth' Marlow appeals successfully to the experience and beliefs his audience has in common with him, in *Heart of Darkness* there is a significant gap between Marlow and his listeners, who respond in a more aggrieved manner to some of his rather critical comments about themselves.) The 'I' narrator in *Chance* takes exception to many of Marlow's more hostile generalizations about and characterizations of women, and in the course of the novel Marlow appears to begin to modify his expression of such views out of courtesy to the 'I' narrator.

I call this a complicating factor because it means that it is certainly difficult and probably impossible to move from a reading of *Chance* to the attribution of a coherent set of views concerning feminism to either the novel or to Conrad as actual historical individual. This need not necessarily imply an artistic fault or an aesthetic weakness in *Chance*; such 'complicating factors' might, on the contrary, force the reader to adjudicate between opposed views and to devote attention him- or herself to the problematic issues discussed but not resolved in the work. But in fact this does not seem to have been how most readers have responded to the novel's engagement with feminism. Readers of *Chance* have either tended to have taken the novel to be an anti-feminist tract, or they have found its engagement with the issue of women's rights at best contradictory and at worst blurred and unsatisfactory. I find a parallel with the treatment of race in *The Nigger of the 'Narcissus'* here. Of course, race is not addressed as a theme or problem in the earlier work in quite the same way in which the issue of women's rights clearly is in *Chance*, but nevertheless there is a similarity. In both works narrative hesitations seem traceable back to ideological contradictions or confusions: it is as if Conrad's inability to decide what he believes gets in the way of the novels' narrative clarity.

Thus in spite of what I have said about the clear intention to attack Victorian patriarchal views in *Chance*, Marlow's views have been seen to be so unsympathetic to feminism (named as such) and to women, and to dominate the novel to such an extent, that many readers have found that they cannot merely be taken as opinions dramatized in the novel, but must, rather, be understood as views which the work underwrites. In defence of this argument it can be noted that – as is often the case when Conrad uses a personified narrator – the narrative often seems omniscient and authorial even though it is ostensibly Marlow's. Now this is also true of *Under Western Eyes*, but in this novel the views and opinions of the teacher of languages are far more precisely contextualized – set in the context of his clearly rendered shortcomings of experience and understanding.

One could attempt to make a similar case about the Marlow of *Chance*. There is the clash of views between Marlow and the 'I' narrator to take into account. Moreover, Marlow is himself by no means consistent, and there are internal tensions in his own opinions concerning women. And finally, Marlow is by common critical consent a far less attractive character in *Chance* than he is in those other works of Conrad's in which he has appeared, and the reader's attention is drawn to the more negative aspects of his personality. A critical problem which arises in this connection, however, is that it is not clear to what extent such a negative characterization of Marlow is always fully intended by Conrad – or, to put it another way, it is not clear to what extent negative reactions on the part of readers to. his presentation in *Chance* are artistically controlled or aesthetically productive – as they do seem to be in the case of *Under Western Eyes*.

Marlow's overtly expressed views dominate *Chance* to a far greater extent than they do *Lord Jim* or *Heart of Darkness*, and this fact may have led many readers to treat Marlow's views as authorial and underwritten by the narrative on occasions. The problem is that the conflict of opinions and attitudes between the 'I' narrator and Marlow is not sufficiently contextualized to establish which values the novel as a whole supports. (*Chance* is, perhaps revealingly, Marlow's last appearance in Conrad's fiction. Conrad started *Chance* before *Under Western Eyes*, although the latter novel was published before *Chance*. In *Under Western Eyes* Conrad uses a different personified narrator from Marlow.)

It is not hard to show that *Chance* includes a strongly anti-feminist and even anti-feminine element, of which Marlow's expressed views constitute a considerable but not an exclusive part. We can quickly run through the more negative of such views. As has already been touched upon, Mrs Fyne is presented as a caricature feminist, and although it is Marlow who is responsible for this presentation, the novel does not in any way suggest that his presentation is misleading. Mrs Fyne's masculine dress and succession of different girl-friends (the actual term used) imply relatively unambiguously that she is wholly or partly homosexual in inclination. Her feminism is crude, amoral and intellectually shabby. Not only this, but she does not live by its tenets; Marlow describes her doctrine as follows:

> 'shortly, and as far as my bewilderment allowed me to grasp its naïve atrociousness, it was something like this: that no consideration, no delicacy, no tenderness, no scruples should stand in the way of a woman (who by the mere fact of her sex was the predestined victim of conditions created by men's selfish passions, their vices and their abominable tyranny) from taking the shortest cut towards securing for herself the easiest possible existence.' (*Chance*, p. 59)

And yet when Mrs Fyne believes Flora to have behaved in precise accordance with this doctrine (as a result of having received the letter in which Flora states that she is marrying Captain Anthony although she does not love him), Mrs Fyne tries, inconsistently, to thwart Flora's plans. Her loyalty to a man (her brother) is more powerful than are her 'feminist' principles.

Marlow expresses a wide range of anti-feminist and anti-female opinions. He informs the reader that women are hopelessly impractical, living in a world of their own imagining, a world which could never be put into operation in the real world.

> 'what prevents women – to use the phrase an old boatswain of my acquaintance applied descriptively to his captain – what prevents them from "coming on deck and playing hell with the ship" generally, is that something in them precise and mysterious, acting both as restraint and as inspiration; their femininity, in short, which they think they can get rid of by trying hard, but can't, and never will. Therefore we may conclude that, for all their enterprises, the world is and remains safe enough.'
> (*Chance*, p. 63)

Later on in the novel Marlow suggests that 'what is delightful in women is that they so often resemble intelligent children', although he goes on to restrict this resemblance to the 'crustiest, the sourest, the most battered of them' (p. 171). As we know from racist arguments, to compare a target group to children is a favoured technique for denigration, suggesting charm but immaturity and the lack of self-governing ability. Moreover, to continue the analogy with racist views, what seems offensive in such views of Marlow's is, not least, his recalcitrant refusal to consider that women are individuals, his persistence in offering simple and simplistic (and, as we shall see, contradictory) generalizations.

We have come across such views from Marlow before in *Heart of Darkness*, when his encounters with his aunt and with the Intended led him to express exactly this sort of opinion. In *Heart of Darkness* certain factors clearly act counter to these expressions of opinion. Most importantly, the 'superb' African woman stands in complete contrast to Marlow's aunt and, particularly, to the Intended. Furthermore, it becomes quite apparent that the separation of European women from the realities of the world is a conscious and intended result of the way men treat them, is something that has been imposed upon women by men. (I will expand upon these points in my later chapter on *Heart of Darkness*).

Now although comparable counter-elements can be found in *Chance*, their effect is significantly weaker than in *Heart of Darkness*. Take the following example.

> 'For if we men try to put the spaciousness of all experiences into our reasoning and would fain put the Infinite itself into our love, it isn't, as some writer has remarked, "It isn't women's doing." Oh, no. They don't care for these things. That sort of aspiration is not much in their way; and it shall be a funny world, the world of their arranging, where the Irrelevant would fantastically step in to take the place of the sober humdrum Imaginative. . . .' (*Chance*, p. 93)

This is very reminiscent of a passage in *Heart of Darkness*:

> 'It's queer how out of touch with truth women are. They live in a world of their own, and there had never been anything like it, and never can be. It is too beautiful altogether, and if they were to set it up it would go to pieces before the first sunset. Some confounded fact we men have been living contentedly with ever since the day of creation would start up and knock the whole thing over.' (HOD, p. 59)

In *Heart of Darkness* such views are qualified, as I have suggested, by Marlow's confession that women live in a different world at least in part because men want them to and arrange matters accordingly.

> 'They – the women I mean – are out of it – should be out of it. We must help them to stay in that beautiful world of their own, lest ours gets worse.' (HOD, p. 115)

In *Chance*, replying to the 'I' narrator's objections to his statements about women, Marlow makes a comparable – but, I feel, a weaker – admission.

'to soothe your uneasiness I will point out that an Irrelevant world would be very amusing if women would take care to make it as charming as they alone can, by preserving for us certain well-known, well-established, I'll almost say hackneyed, illusions, without which the average male creature cannot get on. And that condition is very important. For there is nothing more provoking than the Irrelevant when it has ceased to amuse and charm; and then the danger would be of the subjugated masculinity in its exasperation, making some brusque, unguarded movement and accidentally putting its elbow through the fine tissue of the world of which I speak.' (*Chance*, p. 94)

Whereas in *Heart of Darkness* Marlow's argument is essentially a *moral* one – women are the guardians of values which, even if they cannot be put into practice still help to make the world that much better – in *Chance* it seems to be to serve men's pleasing illusions rather than the moral good of the world that women's 'Irrelevant world' has been created and sustained.

A second theme of Marlow's which recurs frequently in *Chance* is that of the passivity of women. Speaking of Mrs Fyne's reaction to Flora's presumed elopement (or worse) with Captain Anthony, Marlow comments to Mr Fyne:

'"[Mrs Fyne] can't forgive Miss de Barral for being a woman and behaving like a woman. And yet this is not only reasonable and natural, but it is her only chance. A woman against the world has no resources but in herself. Her only means of action is to be what *she is*."' (*Chance*, p. 188)

What is involved in a woman's 'being what *she is*' is made clearer by Marlow later on in his narrative.

'And this is the pathos of being a woman. A man can struggle to get a place for himself or perish. But a woman's part is passive, say what you like, and shuffle the facts of the world as you may, hinting at lack of energy, of wisdom, of courage. As a matter of fact, almost all women have all that – of their own kind. But they are not made for attack. Wait they must. I am speaking here of women who are really women. And it's of no use talking of opportunities, either. I know that some of them do talk of it. But not the genuine women.' (*Chance*, p. 281)

What is of interest here is that Marlow specifically discounts a sociological or historical explanation of women's passivity: 'genuine women' do not talk of their lack of 'opportunities' for action. It's worth pointing out that elsewhere in Conrad the argument from 'opportunities' is given a far more sympathetic presentation. In *Nostromo* Decoud, writing to his sister, comments that

'The women of our country are worth looking at during a revolution. The rouge and pearl powder fall off, together with that passive attitude towards the outer world which education, tradition, custom impose upon them from the earliest infancy. I thought of your face, which from your infancy had the stamp of intelligence instead of that patient and resigned cast which appears when some political commotion tears down the veil of cosmetics and usage.' (*Nostromo*, p. 234)

Decoud is, of course, no more an authorial narrator than is Marlow in *Chance* – indeed he is given just as many overt weaknesses as is the latter. And yet his view of women is to a large extent convincing because (extra-textual factors apart) it is substantiated by the behaviour of female characters in *Nostromo*. Mrs Gould's passivity is seen clearly as a function of her social, cultural and emotional entrapment. Antonia, in contrast, *is* positive and able to act.

But even in *Chance* itself the argument that women are as they are because of their restricted opportunities is aired sympathetically – and by Marlow.

'I believe that the girl had been frank with him, with the frankness of women to whom perfect frankness is impossible, because so much of their safety depends on judicious reticences. I am not indulging in cheap sneers. There is necessity in these things.' (*Chance*, pp. 261-2)

As Marlow admits later on in the novel, women are 'the suspected half of the population', and there 'are good reasons for that' (p. 327). He even makes a point to which subsequent feminist theorists have also drawn attention: patriarchy, by encouraging competition between them, makes solidarity between women rarer than it is between men.

'Unfortunately you can't buttonhole familiarly a young girl as you would a young fellow. I don't think that even another woman could really do it. She would not be trusted. There is not between women that fund of at least conditional loyalty which men may depend on in their dealings with each other. I believe that any woman would rather trust a man.'

(*Chance*, p. 209)

Such generalizations, however, need to be more than stated in a novel: they need to be dramatized. We need to be able to witness how Flora's isolation is compounded by her being a woman. And yet she is hard to see that clearly through the fog of Marlow's descriptions of her. Even so, there is some evidence of her ability to be other than passive: in her refusal to tolerate the awfulness of her 'lower-middle-class' relatives, in her leaving the Fynes for Roderick Anthony, in her management of her father, in the glimpses of spirit and annoyance that we are allowed to see in company with Anthony towards the end of the novel.

Such glimpses lead the reader to want to know her better, but after a while Marlow's narrative appears to obscure as much as it reveals of her personality; it is as if Conrad's narrative technique in *Chance* is somehow inappropriate. *Heart of Darkness* does not lead the reader to feel that he or she wants to gain a more intimate acquaintance with characters other than Marlow. Partly this is because the focus of our attention is on Marlow's own mental development, his own response to events in the Congo and his attempts to understand and communicate their significance. In contrast, Marlow is perhaps the character we find least interesting in *Chance*, and our experience of reading the novel often resembles a conversation in which the verbosity of one rather tedious participant prevents our hearing what other, far more interesting participants have to say. There is no getting away from the fact that the Marlow of *Chance* is something of a bore. The reader is left hungering for a fuller view of Flora de Barral and Roderick Anthony, and hoping for less of Marlow. The opposite is true of *Heart of Darkness*; most readers agree with the frame narrator's comment in the following passage.

> 'I don't want to bother you much with what happened to me personally,' he [Marlow] began, showing in this remark the weakness of many tellers of tales who seem so often unaware of what their audience would best like to hear ....' (HOD, p. 51)

We get the occasional glimpse into Flora's thoughts, but we are left with the feeling that we want to know much more. Her expressions of spirit, her annoyance with Anthony, are suggestive of a potentially interesting personality, but we are left with little more than hints to this effect. In *Heart of Darkness*, in contrast, we learn as much about other characters as we wish for: we witness their actions, and their protestations. No more is required. But because the lives of Flora and Anthony are dominated by passivity and restraint during the period covered by *Chance*, only an unfolding of their inner selves will give us the detail that we require. Instead, we have Marlow's undeniably crude generalizations about them – generalizations which, in Flora's case, because they regularly subsume her into the larger category of 'women', are regularly deprived of any particular force. And yet the glimpses of Flora that we get suggest that there is something particular there, something we want to see at first hand and not through the haze of Marlow's generalizations.

Power and sexuality

I have said that *Chance* confronts feminist ideas through an interrogation of Dickensian views of women. It seems to me that alongside this interrogation there is a clear element of self-interrogation. To put it another way: although in *Chance* Conrad seems to flirt with certain female Dickensian stereotypes and to respond to their seductive features, at the same time he forces recognition of their stereotypicality. For example: many commentators have drawn attention to a complex strain of male sexual wish-fulfilment in the Dickensian heroine: pure and innocent, so young as to be almost pre-pubertal, and *dependent*. This element of dependency can take many forms: the natural dependency of youth on the adult world; hopeless, undeclared and unrecognized love for the hero; commitment to an undeserving father; social or economic dependency. What is radically involved in such stereotypes is the production of sexual excitement for the male by power over the woman, a power which to be enjoyed has to be disguised. The man must be able to luxuriate in the feeling that he is being generous and treating the woman as an equal, whilst secretly enjoying his power over her – perhaps without even realizing that he is doing so.

This element is to be found in *Chance*, and it is hard to say to what extent it is recognized for what it is within the text. When Marlow first meets Flora de Barral after what he subsequently learns has been a near suicide attempt, he talks to her 'chaffingly'.

> 'She retorted that, once one was dead, what horrid people thought of one did not matter. It was said with infinite contempt; but something like a suppressed quaver in the voice made me look at her again. I perceived then that her thick eyelashes were wet. This surprising discovery silenced me as you may guess. She looked unhappy. And – I don't know how to say it – well – it suited her. The clouded brow, the pained mouth, the vague fixed glance! A victim. And this characteristic aspect made her attractive; an individual touch – you know.' (*Chance*, pp. 45-6)

It is not surprising that Marlow does not know how to say it; this admission, and the hesitation of his speech at this point, suggest very strongly a resistance to admitting what it is that he finds attractive about Flora which even the most committed anti-Freudian would be hard put to deny. It is an interesting question to what extent the novel (or, if one prefers, Conrad) shares or recognizes this resistance or repression. Leading on from this: is the (presumably male) reader intended to share Marlow's repressed sexual excitement, or to witness and disapprove of it? Before attempting to answer this question, let me give some further relevant examples.

'Flora had tried more than once to free herself, but he tightened his grasp on her arm each time and even shook it a little without ceasing to speak. The nearness of his face intimidated her. He seemed striving to look her through. It was obvious the world had been using her ill. And even as he spoke with indignation the very marks and stamp of this ill-usage of which he was so certain seemed to add to the inexplicable attraction he felt for her person. It was not pity alone, I take it. It was something more spontaneous, perverse and exciting. It gave him the feeling that if only he could get hold of her, no woman would belong to him so completely as this woman.' (*Chance*, p. 224)

Again we have repression: the attraction Roderick Anthony feels for Flora is 'inexplicable'. But inexplicable to him, *not* to Marlow. In this instance it seems clear that Marlow recognizes it for what it is, and makes sure that the reader does too. It is the sexual attraction that power over a woman brings that attracts Anthony, and although his own refusal to admit this makes the attraction inexplicable to him, it is, as I have said, not inexplicable to Marlow or to the reader. The words 'spontaneous, perverse and exciting' surely show indisputably that Marlow recognizes what Anthony does not – 'perverse' is close enough to 'perverted' to make this recognition full and unambiguous.

Anthony, then, has to learn to treat Flora as a human being not as a dependent, as an equal not as a victim. This is why there is a poetic truth in de Barral's view of Anthony as a jailer – not that Anthony is imprisoning the father, but that he is imprisoning the daughter. And Flora's father recognizes this because he himself had looked forward to performing the rôle that he sees Roderick Anthony carrying out. The passage which justifies such a claim makes what – from the perspective of both classical Freudianism and more recent feminist theory – must be seen as a fascinating commentary on de Barral's feelings.

'A residue of egoism remains in every affection – even paternal. And this man in the seclusion of his prison had thought himself into such a sense of ownership of that single human being he had to think about, as may well be inconceivable to us who have not had to serve a long (and wickedly unjust) sentence of penal servitude. She was positively the only thing, the one point where his thought found a resting-place, for years. She was the only outlet for his imagination. He had not much of that faculty to be sure, but there was in it the force of concentration. He felt outraged, and perhaps it was an absurdity on his part, but I venture to suggest rather in degree than in kind. I have a notion that no usual, normal father is pleased at parting with his daughter. No. Not even when he rationally appreciates "Jane being taken off his hands" or perhaps is able to exult at an excellent match. At bottom, quite deep down, down in the dark (in some cases only by digging), there is to be found a certain repugnance. . . . With mothers of course it is different.' (*Chance*, p. 371)

The suggestion that the 'normal father' suffers 'repugnance' at the marriage of his daughter (a marriage which cannot even be confronted directly but has to be referred to as 'parting with his daughter') suggests a level of self-awareness on Marlow's – and, necessarily, on Conrad's – part which justifies my claim that in *Chance* we witness both an inter-rogation as well as an acceptance of certain key sexual stereotypes and male fantasies. Not less interesting is the reference to the need for 'digging', 'down in the dark', a formulation that we can imagine would have gratified Freud himself. On the subject of repression, incidentally, we can cite the testimony of one interview with Conrad published in 1924:

> Questioned about the complexities of meaning in some of his novels, such as the incest theme in *Almayer's Folly*, he was unwilling to explore them and seemed unconscious of the deeper layers which his own unconscious mind had created. . . . he refused to read Freud . . .[5]

The suggested parallel with Almayer's relationship with his daughter in *Almayer's Folly* is unhelpful, and one can sympathize with Conrad's apparent annoyance at the question. Almayer's primary interest in Nina is socio-cultural and economic: through her Almayer will enjoy the social and cultural power of which he has been deprived – his fantasies ('folly') do not seem so much concerned with exercising power *over* her but *through* and with her. Of course, this may be to say no more than that sexual power seems always to be intertwined with and defined in terms of social and cultural power: Anthony feels a thrill of sexual power in Flora's presence because she has been deprived of social and cultural power, because she has no economic resources. And certainly there is a perceptive and tantalizing commixing of social contempt and sexual jealousy in the portrayal of Flora's governess's treatment of her after de Barral's crash.

Marlow as character and narrator

Whatever Marlow's (or Conrad's) ability *consciously* to formulate a theory of father daughter sexuality, of the way in which the pattern of (literal) patriarchal power is reproduced in male sexual fantasies about dependent but pure women, such a theoretical insight is nonetheless displayed to the reader by the text of *Chance*. It is almost as if Conrad has to make Marlow a more authoritarian, patriarchal figure in order to explore the attitudes associated with such figures. Whereas in *Heart of Darkness* and *Lord Jim* Marlow explores and analyses himself for our benefit, in *Chance* we are encouraged to explore and analyse Marlow beyond his own ability to complete such exploration and analysis as he himself initiates. It seems to me that this is both a weakness and a strength of the novel.

Marlow's statements are often symptomatic rather than analytical, responses to a challenge which he will not acknowledge, but to which he responds by means of a counter-attack.

> 'As to honour – you know – it's a very fine mediæval inheritance which women never got hold of. It wasn't theirs. Since it may be laid as a general principle that women always get what they want, we must suppose they didn't want it. In addition they are devoid of decency. I mean masculine decency. Cautiousness too is foreign to them – the heavy reasonable cautiousness which is our glory. And if they had it they would make of it a thing of passion, so that its own mother – I mean the mother of cautiousness – wouldn't recognize it. Prudence with them is a matter of thrill like the rest of sublunary contrivances. 'Sensation at any cost,' is their secret device. All the virtues are not enough for them; they want also all the crimes for their own. And why? Because in such completeness there is power – the kind of thrill they love most. . . .'
>
> (*Chance*, p. 63)[6]

Marlow clearly protests too much – and not just for the 'I' narrator, who interrupts his flow of invective. None of the generalizations Marlow makes concerning women fit Flora, whose story he is telling – but to a large extent they *can* be distributed among the menfolk of *Chance*. Anthony and de Barral want power, Anthony has no caution and if he had he would infuse it with passion, and de Barral has no decency. Marlow displaces his masculine guilt on to the female sex, which he accuses of desiring precisely those things which contemporary feminism was suggesting should be taken away from men. We are not surprised to learn later on in the novel from Marlow that he feels vindictive towards women (p. 150), although he claims that this is attributable to his resentment at the way they treat men as a 'combination of a kid and an imbecile'. But this is not so very far away from the opinion which Marlow has already been revealed to hold of women, some of whom at any rate he has compared with children. Attack is the best defence.

There is plenty of evidence to support the view that the reader of *Chance* is encouraged to view Marlow from a far more critical distance than is the reader of *Heart of Darkness* or *Under Western Eyes*. Marlow's early attribution of malice to Mr Powell the Shipping Master (p. 23) is surely unmerited, and rebounds more upon himself than it does upon Powell. Soon after this cantankerous suggestion, the 'I' narrator describes the man for us.

> Marlow, who was lanky, loose, quietly composed in varied shades of brown, robbed of every vestige of gloss, had a narrow, veiled glance, the

neutral bearing and the secret irritability which go together with a predisposition to congestion of the liver. (*Chance*, p. 32)

But if the 'I' narrator already knows Marlow as a liverish individual, by the middle of the novel even he is forced to admit that, 'I had seldom seen Marlow so vehement, so pessimistic, so earnestly cynical before' (p. 212).

The tone adopted by Marlow in conversation with Mr Fyne also strikes the reader as frequently inappropriate, involving a misplaced humour and an apparent lack of serious concern for Flora and for Anthony. Cedric Watts has suggested that if we build up an transtextual biography of Charles Marlow from those works of Conrad's in which he appears, we uncover a 'sad story',

> for as Marlow ages we hear him gradually become less intelligent and more garrulous: in the later part of *Lord Jim* and for much of *Chance* he is too facile and waffling as philosopher-raconteur, and we regret his ageing. It is a sad story in another respect, too, for this man who had once felt love for Kurtz's fiancée never marries but settles into a long and lonely bachelorhood. In this vast biographical narrative, one crucial piece of covert plotting is indeed the muted, abortive love-relationship in *Heart of Darkness*.[7]

For Watts, 'that long-past meeting with Kurtz's fiancée, who was trapped in the memory of previous love, lends a poignant irony to the ending of *Chance*'.[8] Marlow does not allow Flora to waste the rest of her life in the company only of a dead man's memory, as he allowed Kurtz's Intended so to do. There is an affirmation of life and love in *Chance* which has to be set against the undoubtedly negative aspects of Marlow's view of women – aspects which, if Watts's transtextual argument is accepted, can be explained by recourse to details of Marlow's biography.

As I noted earlier on in commenting upon the debt which Conrad's portrait of Carleon Anthony owes to Coventry Patmore, it is Marlow who protests that a woman is neither doll nor angel to him. Indeed, the passage in which this comment occurs merits being quoted at greater length.

> 'You see, you are such a chivalrous masculine beggar. But there is enough of the woman in my nature to free my judgment of women from glamorous reticency. And then, why should I upset myself? A woman is not necessarily either a doll or an angel to me. She is a human being, very much like myself.' (*Chance*, p. 53)

How can Marlow make such statements at one point, and express the over-generalized condemnations of women which pass his lips at other times? It is as if Conrad has not finally fixed Marlow's character and function in *Chance*, has not finally decided whether he is to be the voice of sanity rejecting idealized views of women held by the 'chivalrous' 'I' narrator,[9] or the crusty bachelor and potential patriarch himself. And this indecision, I suggest, is the result of Conrad's inability to make up his own mind about the claims of the contemporary feminist movement. Earlier I compared Conrad's project in *Chance* with Virginia Woolf's in *To the Lighthouse*. In one sense this seems absurd, given the number of anti-female views contained in the novel. And yet the novel can be defended as an attack on the view of women as angels in the house, and it gives some striking comments about gender characteristics to Marlow. Is not his comment about the woman in his nature reminiscent of Woolf? And the point is repeated later on in the novel, when Marlow notes that Mrs Fyne was making up to him

> 'simply because she had scented in him that small portion of "femininity," that drop of superior essence of which I am myself aware; which, I gratefully acknowledge, has saved me from one or two misadventures in my life either ridiculous or lamentable, I am not very certain which. It matters very little. Anyhow misadventures. Observe that I say "femininity," a privilege – not "feminism," an attitude. I am not a feminist.'
>
> (*Chance*, pp. 145-6)

Marlow's distinction between feminism and femininity may be said to invoke some essentialist idea of gender characteristics, but this is in tension with the suggestion that these characteristics are not neatly distributed between the two sexes. I am also reminded rather strongly of Virginia Woolf – and especially of *To the Lighthouse* – by the following comment of Marlow's:

> 'I call a woman sincere,' Marlow began after giving me a cigar and lighting one himself, 'I call a woman sincere when she volunteers a statement resembling remotely in form what she really would like to say, what she really thinks ought to be said if it were not for the necessity to spare the stupid sensitiveness of men. The women's rougher, simpler, more upright judgment, embraces the whole truth, which their tact, their mistrust of masculine idealism, ever prevents them from speaking in its entirety. And their tact is unerring. We could not stand women speaking the truth. We could not bear it. It would cause infinite misery and bring about the most awful disturbances in this rather mediocre, but still idealistic fool's paradise in which each of us lives his own little life – the unit in the great sum of existence. And they know it. They are merciful.'
>
> (*Chance*, p. 144)

Note that here it is men rather than women who are seen to live in a world of their own, an unreal, idealistic world. And it is women who do not dare to tell the truth to men – whereas we may recall that in *Heart of Darkness* Marlow considered that it would have been 'too dark altogether' had he spoken the truth to the Intended. The picture given at this point of *Chance* seems far more like that which Woolf gives us of her Victorian Patriarch Mr Ramsay, unable to tolerate the truth and demanding that the women around him create a fictional world padded with male flattery and benevolent deception.

Elsewhere in *Chance*, too, Marlow seems to adopt a view of women which is heavily reliant upon the argument from 'opportunities' of which I have already quoted his rejection. When Mrs Fyne talks of her 'crushing impression of the miserable dependence of girls', noting that a young man in Flora's position could have gone to break stones on the road or to enlist (p. 172), Marlow expresses agreement: 'It was very true. Women can't go forth on the high roads and by-ways to pick up a living even when dignity, independence or existence itself are at stake'. Is this not what Virginia Woolf says when writing in *A Room of One's Own* about Shakespeare's sister?

Moreover, Marlow's portrayal of Flora seems very often to contradict some of his own generalizations about women. When de Barral tries to jump out from the cab containing himself and his daughter, she acts decisively.

> 'In this terrible business of being a woman so full of fine shades, of delicate perplexities (and very small rewards) you can never know what rough work you may have to do, at any moment. Without hesitation Flora seized her father round the body and pulled back – being astonished at the ease with which she managed to make him drop into his seat again. She kept him there resolutely with one hand pressed against his breast ....' (*Chance*, p. 366)

This is hardly the passive female, the submissive daughter, the angel in the house. And yet when Marlow, on one of a number of occasions, talks of marriage for himself, we seem to be back with the angel in the house.

> 'Perhaps if I had had a helpful woman at my elbow, a dear, flattering, acute, devoted woman. . . . There are in life moments when one positively regrets not being married. No! I don't exaggerate. I have said – moments, not years or even days.' (*Chance*, p. 136)

The irony makes Marlow's comment difficult to place exactly, and this can be read as a satirical shaft against the 'I' narrator's idealized view of women, but it can also be read in a very different manner.

Has Conrad failed to make up his mind about Marlow in *Chance*, or is he deliberately portraying him as a contradictory or divided individual?

Is Conrad clear that Marlow *is* divided, or do Marlow's contradictory elements reflect contradictions in Conrad himself regarding the rôle and nature of women?

Such questions are difficult to answer, and this difficulty constitutes part of the uneasiness many readers have felt about *Chance*. I believe that Conrad's problems in writing the novel were in part caused by a failure to resolve certain crucial questions in his own mind, not least those asked by the Suffrage Movement during the time that the novel was being composed. The novel has other faults of course; the narrative chain is unnecessarily complicated and seems unproductive; moreover it leads Conrad into a number of impossibilities. But this is also true of other of his novels – *Under Western Eyes*, for instance, a novel which retains its artistic power and cohesion in spite of such technical impossibilities. At base, one suspects that because Conrad had not made up his own mind about 'The Women's Issue', he was unable to create a consistent and artistically rewarding Marlow. *Chance* is a mixture of an anti-feminist novel and an attack on sentimental patriarchal views of 'The Angel in the House', and the mixture is both fascinating and puzzling.

---

1   Jocelyn Baines provides a good chronology of Conrad's interrupted battles with *Chance* in his critical biography.
2   Coventry Patmore, *Poems*, with an Introduction by Basil Champneys, London, G. Bell & Sons, 1906, repr. 1921.
3   Coventry Patmore, *Poems*, pp. xxxvi-vii.
4   Bruce Johnson, *Conrad's Models of Mind*, Minneapolis, U. of Minnesota Press, 1971, p. 12.
5   The quotatation is from an annotation of H-R. Lenormand, 'Note sur un Séjour de Conrad en Corse', *Nouvelle Revue Française* XII (1 Dec. 1924), by Bruce E. Teets & Helmut E. Gerber, *Joseph Conrad: An Annotated Bibliography of Writings About Him*, De Kalb, Illinois, Northern Illinois UP, 1971, p. 526. Ellipses are mine.
6   'Sublunary' means, literally, under the moon – subject to the moon's influence. The term suggests, of course, that women are less rational and more fickle than men, being subject to the influence of the inconstant moon.
7   Cedric Watts, *The Deceptive Text: An Introduction to Covert Plots*, Brighton, Harvester, 1984, pp. 138-9.
8   *The Deceptive Text*, p. 140.
9   We should not overlook hints that the 'I' narrator in *Chance* can be seen as somewhat naïve and foolish. The modern reader may feel encouraged to respond positively to him because he reacts against some of Marlow's anti-feminist and anti-female diatribes, but we should be aware that he does so from a very conventional ('chivalrous') position. And one of his comments to Marlow recalls very strongly Mark Twain's satirical attack

on the novels of James Fenimore Cooper, 'Fenimore Cooper's Literary Offences'. He says to Marlow:

> 'You are the expert in the psychological wilderness. This is like one of those Redskin stories where the noble savages carry off a girl and the honest backwoodsman with his incomparable knowledge follows the track and reads the signs of her fate in a footprint here, a broken twig there, a trinket dropped by the way. I have always liked such stories. Go on.' (p. 311)

If the reference is intended, the 'I' narrator's naïve endorsement of the world of Fenimore Cooper must be indicative of some serious limitations on his part.

II
The Critique of Imperialism

5
'An Outpost of Progress'

'An Outpost of Progress' comes as something of a shock to anyone reading Conrad's fiction in order of its composition, for no matter how familiar we are with Conrad's works this tale stands out as something qualitatively new. The impression of complete artistic assurance never wavers: here is the work in which Conrad first achieves a full maturity of vision and execution which is both technical and intellectual, a work in which the reader feels in the company of a major talent.

That this breakthrough should be associated in his art with Conrad's Congo experiences is not surprising, for Conrad referred to these experiences as a watershed in his life. Edward Garnett reports that

> According to his emphatic declaration to me in his early years at sea he had 'not a thought in his head.' 'I was a perfect animal,' he reiterated, meaning, of course, that he had reasoned and reflected hardly at all over all the varieties of life he had encountered.[1]

Conrad certainly exaggerates here, for the man who was a perfect animal had by his own account already begun the writing of *Almayer's Folly*. Yet Conrad's view of the importance of his time in the Congo is probably not an exaggeration if interpreted more generally, for on the evidence of 'An Outpost of Progress' and *Heart of Darkness* this period of his life seems to have forced him into reflections which were both profound and comprehensive. Conrad's assurance in 'An Outpost of Progress' is that of the writer who knows *how* he wants to say something because he knows *what* it is that he wants to say. Throughout the story it is clear that Conrad sees Kayerts and Carlier and their experiences in terms of their *representative* qualities, and because of this his narrative relationship to them as individuals and as literary characters is unwavering in its manipulation of perspective and orientation and, especially, of distance.[2]

Reading 'An Outpost of Progress', our judgements as readers seem inevitable; it is as if the narrative leaves us only one set of conclusions, even though these are not forced upon us, but merely displayed for our consideration. In this chapter I want to explore the roots of this process. Let me start by looking at a brief passage from near the end of the story.

After meditating for a while, Makola said softly, pointing at the dead man who lay there with his right eye blown out –

'He died of fever.' Kayerts looked at him with a stony stare. 'Yes,' repeated Makola, thoughtfully, stepping over the corpse, 'I think he died of fever. Bury him tomorrow.' (OP, p. 114)

G. Wilson-Knight has suggested that it is at the most tragic moments in Shakespeare's *King Lear* that one is gripped with a desire to laugh – the tragedy having a quality of the grotesque which is both horrifying and comic. The reader of Conrad's 'An Outpost of Progress' is gripped by a similar mixture of ostensibly incompatible emotions at several stages in his or her reading of the work. The passage quoted above is perhaps the most striking example of this: the physical description of Carlier's corpse is horrifying, Kayerts is in a state of shock, and yet Makola's response to the problems posed by Kayerts's shooting of Carlier is almost absurdly comic.

On the surface this might seem a simple matter to explain; Makola's suggestion is dramatically ludicrous, his response seems so inappropriate and at odds with reality that the incongruity is amusing. We laugh, typically, at people unable to come to terms with what seems an obvious reality – half envying them the security of their seemingly inviolable world of illusions. But the humour in the quoted scene is perhaps more complex than this, with roots in some deeper and more serious elements in the work than are apparent upon first consideration.

From the start of 'An Outpost of Progress' it has been apparent that Makola – the ostensible servant – is actually far more in control than are the two white men.[3] And he is in control because he is able to adapt to the dominant needs of imperialism: maximal extraction of wealth disguised by the most convincing lies. His comment to the appalled Kayerts is thus of a piece with the whole imperialist project which he serves. What makes it shockingly comic here is the unexpected reversal: instead of white men creating convincing lies to obscure the truth about the murder of Africans, here we have an African inventing such a lie to obscure the truth behind the death of a white man. There is thus almost a sense of poetic justice at this point in the work, a feeling that Kayerts and Carlier have been consumed by the monster which they served and encouraged. The early description of their living conditions is somehow emblematic of the use of misleading fictions to conceal that which is unpleasant. Their house is 'built neatly of reeds', but the 'plank floor was littered with the belongings of the white men'. A neat outside, an untidy inside: the house is like imperialism itself.

Like *Heart of Darkness*, 'An Outpost of Progress' includes mention of accountancy on its opening page; we are told of Makola that he 'spoke English and French with a warbling accent, wrote a beautiful hand, understood bookkeeping, and cherished in his innermost heart the worship of evil spirits'. Conrad's two 'Congo' works share a common concern with the record-keeping and representation by means of which imperialism accurately monitors and misleadingly accounts for its actions; the accountant in *Heart of Darkness* who is more committed to making correct entries in his books than in dealing with the needs of the dying man whose groans disturb his work, stems from and represents the same reality as do Makola and those he serves.

Surveying the ivory brought to them by Makola's machinations, Kayerts asks him what he gave for it.

> 'No regular trade,' said Makola. 'They brought the ivory and gave it to me. I told them to take what they most wanted in the station. It is a beautiful lot. No station can show such tusks. Those traders wanted carriers badly, and our men were no good here. No trade, no entry in books; all correct.' (OP, p. 103)

Makola is the perfect – even the parody – bureaucrat. So long as the written record is satisfactory and the material end results are satisfactory, then the situation as a whole is satisfactory. Carlier and Kayerts, who know that the situation is far from satisfactory, try nonetheless to salve their consciences through words.

> 'Slavery is an awful thing,' stammered out Kayerts in an unsteady voice.
> 'Frightful – the sufferings,' grunted Carlier with conviction.
> They believed their words. Everybody shows a respectful deference to certain sounds that he and his fellows can make. But about feelings people really know nothing. We talk with indignation or enthusiasm; we talk about oppression, cruelty, crime, devotion, self-sacrifice, virtue, and we know nothing real beyond the words. Nobody knows what suffering or sacrifice mean – except, perhaps the victims of the mysterious purpose of these illusions. (OP, pp. 105-6)

It is this ability of human beings to content themselves with words, to live in a world of words unconcerned with what the words do or do not mean or represent, that 'An Outpost of Progress' recognizes as central to the operations of imperialism. The insight will be developed in both *Heart of Darkness* and *Nostromo*.

After Carlier's death Makola presents Kayerts with a form of words to deal with the situation, behaving as if he assumes that this is what Kayerts wants. (It is hard to tell whether he really does assume this, or whether he is blackmailing Kayerts into an acceptance of what will be most convenient for himself.) But we have already learned, early on in the tale, that the two white men have no critical imagination, are not aware of the potential for insight, control and duplicity which resides in language.

Writing to Edward Garnett soon after the publication of 'An Outpost of Progress', Conrad commented:

> You will understand the reason and meaning of every detail, the meaning of them reading novels and the meaning of *Carlier not* having been armed.
> (CLJC 1, p. 292)

One takes it that it is significant that Carlier is unarmed because he is the soldier: it is the seemingly mild Kayerts who is driven to murder. The passage concerning the reading of novels is worth looking at in detail.

> Their predecessors had left some torn books. They took up these wrecks of novels, and, as they had never read anything of the kind before, they were surprised and amused. Then during long days there were interminable and silly discussions about plots and personages. In the centre of Africa they made acquaintance of Richelieu and of d'Artagnan, of Hawk's Eye and of Father Goriot, and of many other people. All these imaginary personages became subjects for gossip as if they had been living friends. They discounted their virtues, suspected their motives, decried their successes; were scandalized at their duplicity or were doubtful about their courage. The accounts of crimes filled them with indignation, while tender or pathetic passages moved them deeply. Carlier cleared his throat and said in a soldierly voice, 'What nonsense!' Kayerts, his round eyes suffused with tears, his fat cheeks quivering, rubbed his bald head, and declared, 'This is a splendid book. I had no idea there were such clever fellows in the world.' (OP, p. 94)

Carlier and Kayerts lack the ability to read literature critically, and this is directly related to their helplessness. They have never had to explore the relationship between language and reality, have never had to be on guard against the possible duplicities of language. They are able to live in an imaginary world created by fiction while yet remaining unaware of its fictionality, consequently they refer to literary characters as if these were real people. The characters about whom they read help them to see themselves as figures of romance – just as, in *Lord Jim*, Jim's course of 'light holiday reading' helps to create romantic fantasies for him which cut him off from the real world. The passage about the way in which Carlier and Kayerts respond to characters of literary fiction continues, revealingly, with reference to the white men's reading of newspapers.

> They also found some old copies of a home paper. That print discussed what it was pleased to call 'Our Colonial Expansion' in high-flown language. It spoke much of the rights and duties of civilization, of the sacredness of the civilizing work, and extolled the merits of those who went about bringing light, and faith and commerce to the dark places of

the earth. Carlier and Kayerts read, wondered, and began to think better of themselves. (OP, pp. 94-5)

The point seems clearly to be that their inability to cope with literary fiction is related to their inability to cope with a different sort of fiction. They empathize with fictional heroes of romance one minute, and cast themselves as characters in the fictional world created by the propaganda-machine of imperialism the next. However, having so cast themselves, they are unable to accept the fiction as fiction. And when Makola presents Kayerts with a fictional account of the death of Carlier, Kayerts cannot accept it because he knows that it is not true. Makola as typical bureaucrat is not concerned about its truth – merely its efficacy.[4]

If my playing with the different meanings of the word 'fiction' seems far-fetched in this context, a passage to be found in the manuscript of Conrad's *Heart of Darkness* (but not in the published text of the work) suggests that it is not. Talking about the Roman colonization of Britain, Marlow says

> The best of them is they didn't get up pretty fictions about it. Was there, I wonder, an association on a philanthropic basis to develop Britain, with some third rate king for a president and solemn old senators discoursing about it approvingly and philosophers with uncombed beards praising it, and men in market places crying it up. Not much! And that's what I like! No! No! It was just &c.[5]

Makola understands that modern imperialism, unlike that of the Romans, demands 'pretty fictions', and this is what he offers to Kayerts. As we have seen, however, Kayerts has no conception of fiction as a means of concealing an unpleasant reality; for him the fictions that he reads are indistinguishable from reality. As a result, he is unable to accept (or perhaps even to understand) Makola's offer.

It is hardly controversial to point out that Conrad's main target in 'An Outpost of Progress' is that European civilization which is represented by Carlier and Kayerts. From the opening pages of the tale it has been clear that their conception of what civilization consists of is laughably inadequate. Immediately following the lines about the 'home paper' quoted above we can read the following.

> Carlier said one evening, waving his hand about, 'In a hundred years, there will be perhaps a town here. Quays, and warehouses, and barracks, and – and – billiard-rooms. Civilization, my boy, and virtue – and all. And then, chaps will read that two good fellows, Kayerts and Carlier, were the first civilized men to live in this very spot! (OP, p. 95)

The ironic collocation invites the reader to draw a conclusion, a conclusion which is given authorial narrative force at the end of the tale, when Kayerts hears the whistle of the returned steamer.

> Progress was calling to Kayerts from the river. Progress and civilization and all the virtues. Society was calling to its accomplished child to come, to be taken care of, to be instructed, to be judged, to be condemned; it called him to return to that rubbish heap from which he had wandered away, so that justice could be done. (OP, p. 116)[6]

The repetition of words such as 'civilization' and 'virtue' is surely not accidental. Not only does Conrad want to link this passage with Carlier's earlier comments, but it is clear too that he is assuming a familiarity on the part of his contemporary readers with the official propaganda for their imperialist adventures in Africa which the Belgian[7] authorities disseminated - the 'pretty fictions' of Conrad's comment in his manuscript of *Heart of Darkness*. In 1876 King Leopold of Belgium had called a conference in Brussels the purpose of which was to examine the situation in Africa and, in his words, 'to open to civilization the only part of our globe where Christianity has not penetrated and to pierce the darkness which envelops the entire population'.[8]

Suresh Raval has argued that Conrad's *Heart of Darkness* has to be set in the context of an era which was not just one of great industrial development and imperialist success, but also that of idealism in philosophy and politics. He suggests that *Heart of Darkness* brilliantly delineates the moral complicity of idealism with imperialism.[9] In my next chapter on *Heart of Darkness* I will investigate Raval's suggestion in more detail, but at this point I will add that in 'An Outpost of Progress' we learn that imperialism relies as much upon ignorance, concealment and deceit as it does on supportive theories related to (among other things) idealism. Indeed, Marlow's comments to his listeners concerning his early discussion with his aunt, in *Heart of Darkness*, suggest that Conrad saw concealment and deception as a necessary element in the fostering of idealism.

It is certainly noteworthy that Carlier, like Kurtz in *Heart of Darkness*, from accepting the arguments of the 'home paper' that he is engaged in a civilizing mission in Africa, reaches the point where he wishes to exterminate rather than civilize. Kurtz's scribbled comment 'Exterminate the brutes!' is well-known; Carlier responds to the loss of the shot hippopotamus to Gobila's people in a comparable manner.

> It was the occasion for a national holiday, but Carlier had a fit of rage over it and talked about the necessity of exterminating all the niggers before the country could be made habitable. (OP, p. 108)

Both Kurtz and Carlier find that their ideals are unable to survive the first-hand experience of imperialism, even though these same ideals have encouraged and justified imperialism from afar. The complicity of which Raval speaks, then, is hardly a knowing complicity, it is a complicity based upon ignorance, stupidity and moral laziness. What we learn from the description of Carlier and Kayerts reading novels, is that neither of them seem aware that stories can be other than literally true. They are thus completely vulnerable to the lies they read about imperialism, even thinking better of themselves (an important point) when they read these in the discovered 'home paper'. (We can compare the situation of Stevie in *The Secret Agent*, also unaware that lies can be told and similarly vulnerable to the lies that Verloc tells him.)

In a striking passage in the tale, Carlier and Kayerts are compared to released prisoners – physically free but mentally still imprisoned.

> Society, not from any tenderness, but because of its strange needs, had taken care of those two men, forbidding them all independent thought, all initiative, all departure from routine; and forbidding it under pain of death. They could only live on condition of being machines. And now, released from the fostering care of men with pens behind the ears, or of men with gold lace on the sleeves, they were like those lifelong prisoners who, liberated after many years, do not know what use to make of their freedom. They did not know what use to make of their faculties, being both, through want of practice, incapable of independent thought.
>
> (OP, p. 91)

The result of this is that they have no critical judgement; they are unable to distance themselves from their immediate circumstances, or to see these in any larger, explanatory context. In this early work Conrad is already concerned with the 'strange needs' that a society can have, needs which involve the manipulation of human beings possessed of the illusion of self-direction.

> They lived like blind men in a large room, aware only of what came in contact with them (and of that only imperfectly), but unable to see the general aspect of things. (OP, p. 92)

In 'An Outpost of Progress', then, Conrad suggests a connection between the ability to read critically and the ability to distance oneself from one's surroundings, to escape from the imprisoning power of custom, authority and social control. Critical reading, of novels as much as of newspapers, requires the ability to cut oneself off from immediate impressions, to step back from these and to consider alternative explanatory structures into which these can be fitted. Imperialism is able to lie and deceive about what it actually involves, because its servants are either unable or unwilling to question the reports they are given.

Revealingly, 'An Outpost of Progress' itself cannot be read in the manner in which Kayerts and Carlier read the discovered novels. Bakhtin has noted of the novel that one thing distinguishing it from the epic is that the reader can enter the world of the novel, and

> It follows that we might substitute for our own life an obsessive reading of novels, or dreams based on novelistic models . . . [10]

This, in a way, is what Kayerts and Carlier do. Able to enter the world of the novels they read, they are incapable of distinguishing between novelistic world and real world. The reader of 'An Outpost of Progress', in contrast, cannot enter the world of the tale in this way. Whoever the reader, the tale is so written that entry into a separate world within its pages is impossible. No work can *force* a reader to read critically, but 'An Outpost of Progress' does prevent the reader from entering into a separate, novelistic world. This is not the sort of tale into which we can project ourselves, imagining the characters as 'subjects for gossip, as if they had been living friends', and it is worth asking why this is.

A key word here is 'distance'. The sense of intimacy we get in the tale is with the narrator or narrative voice rather than with any of the characters. This is not to suggest that we get a strong sense of a personified narrator in 'An Outpost of Progress', but we do feel that the narrative perspective is a human one and that the observations and judgements we are offered come from a human source. However this human source is so far from being personified that the reader feels unable to enter into its world; it offers us a perspective on rather than an entry into a portrayed world. From this perspective the characters seem far off, observed at such a distance that there is no possibility of emotional empathy. The unqualified narrative contempt, too, makes Carlier and Kayerts less approachable, less joinable in their separate world.

> They were two perfectly insignificant and incapable individuals, whose existence is only rendered possible through the high organization of civilized crowds. Few men realize that their life, the very essence of their character, their capabilities and their audacities, are only the expression of their belief in the safety of their surroundings. (OP, p. 89)

To join such characters, we feel, would be to expose ourselves to the merciless criticism of the narrator. Carlier and Kayerts are *apart* from us, separated from our world by a narrative technique that forces us to observe and analyse them but which makes it impossible for us to enter into their world or their presence.

[The director] made a speech to Kayerts and Carlier, pointing out to them the promising aspect of their station. The nearest trading-post was about three hundred miles away. It was an excellent opportunity for them to distinguish themselves and to earn percentages on the trade. This appointment was a favour done to beginners. Kayerts was moved almost to tears by his director's kindness. He would, he said, by doing his best, try to justify the flattering confidence, &c., &c. Kayerts had been in the Administration of the Telegraphs, and knew how to express himself correctly. Carlier, an ex-non-commissioned officer of cavalry in an army guaranteed from harm by several European Powers, was less impressed. If there were commissions to get, so much the better; and, trailing a sulky glance over the river, the forests, the impenetrable bush that seemed to cut off the station from the rest of the world, he muttered between his teeth, 'We shall see, very soon.' (OP, pp. 87-8)

We can note how Conrad's use of, first, represented speech, and then Reported Speech, both have the effect of cutting us off from the living presence of the characters. It is as if only the substance of what was said merits report; expression, tone, and so on – all these are unworthy of our concern. The final master-stroke is that of the '&c., &c'. Kayerts's speech is so cliché-ridden, so full of conventionalities, that it can be reduced to this formula. The narrator assumes an intimacy with the reader by implying that the reader can fill in the missing words him- or herself, and at the same time implies a weary disdain for Kayerts's mechanical formalities. The disdain hardens into sarcasm in the subsequent sentence, in which we are told that Kayerts knew how to express himself correctly as a result of his having 'been in the Administration of the Telegraphs'. For Kayerts language is a matter of conventions and formalities rather than a means whereby human beings can explore, change and understand their environment and themselves. Carlier, in contrast, thinks only of commissions. Together, Carlier and Kayerts combine some of the diverse characteristics which, in *Heart of Darkness*, we see united in the figure of Kurtz: idealistic and unrealistic rhetoric and eloquence, and amoral pursuit of wealth irrespective of its human cost. The combination – for Kayerts and Carlier as much as for Kurtz – turns out to be lethal and self-destructive.

In an article on 'An Outpost of Progress' J. C. Hilson and D. Timms have pointed out that the final quarrel between the two white men is sparked off by Carlier's calling Kayerts a 'stingy old slave-dealer'. Previous to this, as they say, Kayerts has responded to Carlier's claim that he is sick and so deserves sugar, 'in a peaceful tone'.[11] But when he is called a slave-dealer, we are told that 'There was a surprising flash of violent emotion within him, as if in the presence of something undreamt-of, dangerous, and final' (p. 110). Kayerts cannot bear his actions to be *named*, he cannot tolerate the shattering of his pretty fictions about himself. Conversely,

Carlier can no longer put up with what he sees as Kayerts's hypocrisy. Kayerts responds to Carlier's use of the term 'slave-dealer' by saying 'That joke is in very bad taste. Don't repeat it'. Carlier's reaction is revealing.

> 'Joke!' said Carlier, hitching himself forward on his seat. 'I am hungry – I am sick – I don't joke! I hate hypocrites. You are a hypocrite. You are a slave-dealer. I am a slave-dealer. There's nothing but slave-dealers in this cursed country.' (OP, p. 110)

Carlier's response can be compared, in some ways, to Kurtz's ejaculation 'The horror! The horror!'. It constitutes a refusal to accept pretty fictions any more, an insistence that things be called by their right names – that language make contact with reality rather than remaining in a closed, idealistic sphere of its own. The difference, of course, is that Kurtz is horrified by 'the horror', while Carlier is not. It is Kayerts who is horrified, who wishes to remain safe with his fictions about himself and to pretend that they are real – just as the fictional novels were real to him. The two men who in some ways appear so similar, then, are very different. Kayerts is the bureaucrat, the man who relays messages for others in Africa much as he did in the Administration of the Telegraphs, and who will not face where these messages come from or what reality they describe and bring into being. Carlier is the soldier, the man who has accepted human brutality and the rule of force, and who is not that worried about glossing this over to make it appear other than it is. Both, it is true, are incapable of reading the novels they find in the manner in which they should be read, but – we must suspect – for rather different reasons. Kayerts is unused to testing language against reality; Carlier is not in the habit of allowing language to interfere with his cultivation of his own material interests. It is perhaps the case that Kayerts assumes that the novels are literally true, Carlier that – like all verbal accounts – they are irrelevant, and have no bearing on actual life.

'An Outpost of Progress' is perhaps the first work of Conrad's which we would not have any different from the way it is, a work which has the perfection of great art. And this perfection stems from Conrad's uncompromising analysis of the mechanisms of imperialism. There are no problems relating to point of view such as we find in the almost contemporary *The Nigger of the 'Narcissus'*; the firmly delineated perspective of 'An Outpost of Progress' appears to stem from (and perhaps to contribute to) the steadiness and penetration of Conrad's ideological position. There are no romanticizing or idealizing impulses here; rather, there is the impulse to expose attempts to romanticize or to idealize imperialism. It is for this reason that 'An Outpost of Progress' belongs with works such as *Heart of Darkness* and *Nostromo* rather than with a work such as *The Nigger of the 'Narcissus'*.

1   Edward Garnett (ed.), *Letters from Conrad 1895-1924*, Nonesuch Press, London n.d. [?1928], p. xii.

2   In my comments on narrative distance in 'An Outpost of Progress' I am especially indebted to Jakob Lothe's chapter on this work in his book *Conrad's Narrative Method* (Oxford, Clarendon Press, 1989).

3   This is by no means the first time that such a situation is apparent in Conrad's works. Commenting on *Almayer's Folly*, Cedric Watts argues that

>   One of the major ironies [in this novel] is that though white men are in the foreground, dominating the overt plots, they are often the dupes of the Malays and Arabs in the background who are instigating the covert plots. (Cedric Watts, *The Deceptive Text: An Introduction to Covert Plots*, Brighton, Harvester, 1984, p. 136).

4   In *The Rescue* we learn that Lingard, a character ostensibly very different from Carlier and Kayerts, but nonetheless with something in common with them, has a similar inability to respond to a rather different form of fiction in an appropriate manner. He talks to Mrs Travers of his single experience of an opera.

>   'Fairy stories are for children, I believe,' he said. 'But that story with music I am telling you of, Mrs Travers, was not a tale for children. I assure you that of the few shows I have seen that one was the most real to me. More real than anything in life. (p. 301)

When Mrs Travers says to Lingard, 'I suppose you forget yourself in that story, whatever it was', Lingard agrees – but to his surprise discovers that she has never so forgotten herself in response to art. And yet she has had her romantic illusions, as the reader of *The Rescue* discovers. Conrad suggests, here and in 'An Outpost of Progress', that it is often those seemingly most close to everyday reality who are most vulnerable to the snares of misleading fictions.

5   Quoted in Joseph Conrad, *Heart of Darkness*, Norton Critical Edition, third edn, ed. Robert Kimbrough, New York, W. W. Norton, 1988, p. 10.

6   Note how both 'An Outpost of Progress' and *Heart of Darkness* end with a mention of justice. In the latter work Marlow plays on what is now a little-known proverb, 'Justice – or let the heavens fall' when referring to the fact that the heavens did not fall after his lie to the Intended. The proverb is referred to more explicitly in *Typhoon*, p. 44. and in *Nostromo* on pages 379 and 402. Cedric Watts's note to the *Typhoon* reference in the World's Classics edition of the work cites the original Latin maxim: 'fiat justitia ruat coelum'.

7   The early comment about Carlier's membership of 'an army guaranteed from harm by several European Powers' (p. 88) makes it clear that the imperialist power with which we are concerned in the tale is Belgium. Conrad draws attention to the significance of this phrase in a letter to Kazimierz Waliszewski, 16 December 1903 (see CLJC 3, p. 93).

8 Quoted in Maurice N. Hennessy, *The Congo*, London, Pall Mall Press, 1961. Reprinted in Kimbrough, p. 80.

9 Suresh Raval, *The Art of Failure: Conrad's Fiction*, London, Allen & Unwin, 1986, p. 29.

10 M. M. Bakhtin, *The Dialogic Imagination*, edited by Michael Holquist, translated by Caryl Emerson and Michael Holquist, Austin, U. of Texas Press, 1981, p. 32.

11 J. C. Hilson & D. Timms, 'Conrad's "An Outpost of Progress" Or, The Evil Spirit of Civilization'. In Claude Thomas (ed.), *Studies in Joseph Conrad*, Montpellier, Université Paul-Valéry, 1975, pp. 119-21.

6
Heart of Darkness

What are the key elements in the artistic triumph of 'An Outpost of Progress'? It seems to me that we can sum these up as follows, First, an integrative vision that attempts to *make connections*, to see how a *system* of political and social forces links together the lives and consciousness of the two Europeans, and the Africans upon whose existence they and the powers they serve impinge. Second, a comprehensiveness that excludes the observer in one sense – narrator and readers are not part of the system observed – but includes him or her through the operation of an unflinchingly committed system of values: through a judgemental vision. So that the narrative distance which allows the narrator to present us with a system of productive and causal social and political connections which we can observe dispassionately, is complemented by a passionate (if controlled) human vision which responds with patient pity, with an understanding of the experiential significance of what is depicted. And a key link between the dispassionate observation and the passionate evaluation is provided by irony. In this short story the narrative irony is both distancing and incorporating; it cuts the narrator and the reader off from characters and events, but it links these characters and events to a firmly held set of human values. In this respect there are clear similarities between 'An Outpost of Progress' and *The Secret Agent*.

It is not hard to connect this complex narrative position with the position Conrad must have found himself forced into in the Congo, obliged to observe things for which he felt himself only indirectly responsible, cut off both from his fellow Europeans and from the Africans, but unable not to judge what he saw.

The narrator of 'An Outpost of Progress' is more detached than Conrad must have been from his own Congo experiences. In *Heart of Darkness*, Conrad's use of Marlow allows him to maintain many of the advantages of the narrative of 'An Outpost of Progress' but to complement them with a sense of narrative complicity in the events described. In this novella we again have the same integrative vision that distinguishes 'An Outpost of Progress', but it is complemented by a different sort of human involvement in the events described on the part of the narrative. Instead of the pity of a detached observer we have the guilty complicity of an involved one – and, moreover, an involved narrator who takes care further to involve his listeners/readers. Above all, however, Conrad's artistic achievement is based upon a set of ideological perceptions which, linked together artistically, constitute an understanding of imperialism as a particular *system*, a set of connections, influences and determinations.

The 'murder plot' and the marriage of trade and idealism

In recent years the work of a number of critics has helped us towards a clearer view of Conrad's analysis of imperialism in *Heart of Darkness*. Although I disagree with Ian Watt that a measure of critical consensus in our views of the basic character of Conrad's fiction can be promoted by 'a fairly detailed and literal interpretation of his main works'[1] (surely interpretations of complex literary works necessarily rise above the level of the literal), it is clear that Watt's account of *Heart of Darkness* is genuinely enlightening, both so far as the view of Kurtz as an exemplar of a con-temporary view of Victorian progress is concerned, and also with regard to Conrad's use of impressionist techniques in the novella. In the following pages, however, I would like to draw attention to the work of two other critics, Cedric Watts and Suresh Raval, and to suggest ways in which their treatments of *Heart of Darkness* can be combined and extended. Cedric Watts has published a full-length study of *Heart of Darkness* as well as a further major critical work full of penetrating insights into Conrad's fiction: *The Deceptive Text*.[2] In the latter he has much of value to say about the Faust theme in *Heart of Darkness*, but I also find his comments in the former study concerning the 'murder plot' in the novella most enlightening, for they help to anchor certain of the novella's themes to elements in its plot. One result of clearing up the 'covert plot' of the novella is that certain seemingly opaque statements by Marlow and others which have been granted highly metaphysical interpretations by some critics can be given far simpler explanations. This does not of course rule out subsequent metaphysical interpretations, but it allows them to be built upon a more solid foundation.

In one sense, Raval's study of Conrad picks up a theme that has been treated by Ian Watt and by other critics – Kurtz as an exemplar of a contemporary view of Victorian progress. Raval's account is, however, more specific and (I think) more convincing in its detailing of what precisely it is that Kurtz represents. Let us start by looking at Raval's view more closely.

> It is Kurtz's conviction that every station should be 'a centre for trade of course, but also for humanizing, improving, instructing.' The symbiosis of trade and idealism does not make Kurtz suspicious of the value of idealism which so easily cohabits with commerce and profit. It is logical that Kurtz should be a spokesman for this symbiosis, for the era of great industrial development and imperialist success was also the era

of idealism in philosophy and politics. This idealism was profoundly sanguine, and profoundly blind to the social-economic forces operating in the West and, through the agency of the West, in the rest of the world. And it is Marlow's residual idealism which attracts him to the man who is 'equipped with moral ideas of some sort'.[3]

Raval's use of the word 'blind' is suggestive. We can remember that Carlier and Kayerts were described as being 'like blind men in a large room', and in *Heart of Darkness* the implications of the blindfold around the eyes of the woman in the picture painted by Kurtz are of profound and, I think, very specific significance.

Raval's approach is genuinely helpful to readers attempting to make their way through *Heart of Darkness* (and, perhaps more, through the enormous amount of criticism which it has engendered). At a relatively simple level, a concern with 'the symbiosis of trade and idealism' helps to clarify some obscurities about the actual story[4] of *Heart of Darkness*. We need to understand that this symbiosis is not without tensions and problems, and that on one level *Heart of Darkness* depicts the growth and exacerbation of such problems until the proponents of trade and those of idealism are ranged in hopelessly divided and polarized camps. I feel, however, that the term 'trade' is rather too timid: Raval's discussion makes it clear that what we are really talking about is imperialism, although the word 'trade' might be used as a more acceptably neutral term for apologists of imperialism. This point should be recalled in my own subsequent use of the word 'trade'.

'Symbiosis', however, is exactly the right word. Trade and idealism are portrayed as depending upon each other in *Heart of Darkness*, but at the same time their relationship is not perceived as a genuine collaboration or mixing. Each retains an independence whilst benefiting from and strengthening the other. Thus – as I shall argue – imperialism thrives on an idealism that is ignorant of what that imperialism actually involves. There is therefore no contradiction involved in talking about the marriage of trade and idealism in the same breath as one argues that the idealism we witness in *Heart of Darkness* is kept in artificial isolation, is cut off from the very things which it is used to legitimate. It is again not hard to relate such an analysis to Conrad's own experiences in the Congo.

One reason why this element in the novella is less clear to the reader of *Heart of Darkness* than it might be, is that it is unclear to Marlow in his early days in Africa, and perhaps remains partly unclear to him even at the close of his narrative. Marlow gets to Africa not quite as an innocent abroad – his earlier remarks to his aunt make that clear – but unprepared for the level of brutality and hypocrisy he is to encounter there, and also unaware of the precise lines of battle within the camps of the white men. And as the reader learns of these details along with

Marlow, at certain stages of an initial reading of the work some things can be as puzzling to us as they were (and, to a degree, remain) to Marlow. And this is where Cedric Watts's analysis of the covert plot of the novella is extremely helpful.

Newly arrived at the Central Station, Marlow is informed that his steamer is at the bottom of the river

> 'I did not see the real significance of that wreck at once. I fancy I see it now, but I am not sure – not at all. Certainly the affair was too stupid – when I think of it – to be altogether natural. Still . . . But at the moment it presented itself simply as a confounded nuisance.'
>
> (HOD, p. 72)

The remark is tantalizing, and not just to the reader making his or her first acquaintance with the novella. My own view is that the most successful attempt to decode these comments of Marlow's can be found in Watts's account of the novella's covert plot: the struggle for dominance between opposed groupings among the white men, and what Watts has further suggested is actually an account of the murder of Kurtz by that party whose interests he is seen to threaten. Marlow discovers bit by bit that even before his arrival he has been assigned to a particular interest or grouping, one which includes Kurtz and the 'very high personage in the Administration' who, at the behest of Marlow's aunt,[5] obtains Marlow his job and even writes to Kurtz about him. As the brickmaker of the Central Station tells Marlow,

> '"You are of the new gang – the gang of virtue. The same people who sent him specially also recommended you. Oh, don't say no. I've my own eyes to trust." Light dawned upon me. My dear aunt's influential acquaintances were producing an unexpected effect upon that young man.'
>
> (HOD, pp. 79-80)

What, then, the 'real significance of that wreck' is, we are never told directly, but we can infer that Marlow comes to suspect that deliberate sabotage has been arranged in order to do down a representative of 'the gang of virtue', and to isolate Kurtz from help for as long as possible so as to secure his death. Watts explains the matter as follows.

> At Marlow's first interview with the manager, he is asked how long it will take to repair the wreck. 'How can I tell?' says Marlow, and receives the reply: 'Well, let us say three months before we can make a start [upstream]. Yes. That ought to do the affair.' Marlow therefore considers him 'a chattering idiot', but adds: 'Afterwards .... it was borne in upon me startlingly with what extreme nicety he had estimated the time requisite for the "affair".'

The repair is delayed because there are no rivets at the Central Station. There are, however, rivets in abundance at the Outer Station, and a message could summon them; but evidently Marlow's request is never sent.[6]

Watts's account has the virtue of, among other things, explaining the manager's awkwardness and embarrassment on first meeting Marlow and having to talk to him about his sunken ship.

'He paid no attention to my explanations, and, playing with a stick of sealing-wax, repeated several times that the situation was "very grave, very grave." There were rumours that a very important station was in jeopardy, and its chief, Mr Kurtz, was ill. Hoped it was not true. Mr Kurtz was . . . I felt weary and irritable. Hang Kurtz, I thought. I interrupted him by saying I had heard of Mr Kurtz on the coast. "Ah! So they talk of him down there," he murmured to himself. Then he began again, assuring me Mr Kurtz was the best agent he had, an exceptional man, of the greatest importance to the Company; therefore I could understand his anxiety. He was, he said, "very, very uneasy." Certainly he fidgeted on his chair a good deal, exclaimed, "Ah, Mr Kurtz!" broke the stick of sealing wax and seemed dumfounded by the accident. Next thing he wanted to know "how long it would take to" . . . I interrupted him again. Being hungry, you know, and kept on my feet, too, I was getting savage. "How could I tell?" I said. " I hadn't even seen the wreck yet – some months, no doubt." All this talk seemed to me so futile. "Some months," he said. "Well, let us say three months before we can make a start. Yes. That ought to do the affair."' (HOD, p. 75)

Read in the manner Watts suggests, what we witness here is a man guiltily afraid that his subterfuge will be discovered, worried about the extent of Kurtz's reputation, but praising Kurtz to a man he assumes to be of the same party as Kurtz. And, finally, 'That ought to do the affair' then becomes sinisterly ambiguous: both 'That ought to be enough time to get the boat operational again' (which is surely how most readers read it on first acquaintance with the novella), and 'That ought to be long enough to destroy Kurtz'. This last reading seems that much more likely when compared with a much later comment of Marlow's:

'The manager was very placid, he had no vital anxieties now, he took us both in with a comprehensive and satisfied glance: the "affair" had come off as well as could be wished. I saw the time approaching when I would be left alone of the party of "unsound method."' (HOD, p. 147)

It is of course true that the manager denies involvement in any such plan against Kurtz, in the discussion he has with his uncle which Marlow overhears as he is lying flat on the steamboat. The uncle stresses the influence Kurtz must have had with the Administration, commenting, 'Is it not frightful?' (p. 89), and adds soon after that 'The climate may do away with this difficulty for you'. Marlow then hears snatches of conversation, culminating in the two agreeing that the 'pestilential fellow' (the Russian) should be 'hanged for an example'. The conversation continues:

> '"Certainly," grunted the other; "get him hanged! Why not? Anything – anything can be done in this country. That's what I say; nobody here, you understand, *here*, can endanger your position. And why? You stand the climate – you outlast them all. The danger is in Europe; but there before I left I took care too – " They moved off and whispered, then their voices rose again. "The extraordinary series of delays is not my fault. I did my best." The fat man sighed. "Very sad." "And the pestiferous absurdity of his talk," continued the other; "he bothered me enough when he was here. 'Each station should be be like a beacon on the road towards better things, a centre for trade of course, but also for humanizing, improving, instructing.' Conceive you – that ass! And he wants to be manager! No it's – "' (HOD, p. 91)

The reader is left in the same position as Marlow, knowing that there is a conspiracy against Kurtz but unsure whether this actually involves a plot to delay relief so as to hasten his death. The reader also learns from this passage that Kurtz's idealistic views on the ways in which trading can be carried out in Africa contribute to the rivalry which he inspires.

How can we characterize the 'parties' whose struggle for dominance forms a hidden but determining thread in the story unfolded in the novella? It is here that Raval's argument that Kurtz represents an attempt to combine trade with idealism is enlightening. Asked who Kurtz is, the brickmaker first of all describes him as the chief of the Inner Station, then, in response to Marlow's sarcasm, indulges in irony.

> '"He is a prodigy," he said at last. "He is an emissary of pity, and science, and progress, and devil knows what else. We want," he began to declaim suddenly, "for the guidance of the cause entrusted to us by Europe, so to speak, higher intelligence, wide sympathies, a singleness of purpose." "Who says that?" I asked. "Lots of them," he replied. "Some even write that; and so *he* comes here, a special being, as you ought to know."'
> (HOD, p. 79)

Those opposed to this party may not constitute a tightly-knit group. It is clear that the manager wishes to hold on to power and his position; his vulnerability lies in Kurtz's connections in Europe and the amount of ivory Kurtz sends back.

'"Anything since then?" asked the other, hoarsely. "Ivory," jerked the nephew; "lots of it - prime sort - lots - most annoying, from him." "And with that?" questioned the heavy rumble. "Invoice," was the reply fired out, so to speak.' (HOD, pp. 89-90)

It is 'most annoying', of course, because this provision of ivory strengthens Kurtz's position; it seems that Kurtz has indeed managed successfully to unite trade and idealism - a combination which the manager clearly sees as a potent threat to his own security.

Ⅹ It is important to note that Marlow's interest in Kurtz (an interest which culminates in a feeling of commitment to him), grows only slowly. Marlow's narrative makes it clear that his initial reaction to the feuding and plotting is one of 'a plague on both your houses'.

'There was an air of plotting about that station, but nothing came of it, of course. It was as unreal as everything else - as the philanthropic pretence of the whole concern, as their talk, as their government, as their show of work.' (HOD, p. 78)

'I had plenty of time for meditation, and now and then I would give some thought to Kurtz. I wasn't very interested in him. No. Still, I was curious to see whether this man, who had come out equipped with moral ideas of some sort, would climb to the top after all and how he would set about his work when there.' (HOD, p. 88)

I fretted and fumed and took to arguing with myself whether or no I would talk openly with Kurtz; but before I could come to any conclusion it occurred to me that my speech or my silence, indeed any action of mine, would be a mere futility. What did it matter what any one knew or ignored? What did it matter who was manager? One gets sometimes such a flash of insight. The essentials of this affair lay deep under the surface, beyond my reach, and beyond my power of meddling.' (HOD, p. 100)

In the second of the above quotations we see that Marlow's interest in Kurtz starts to develop because, as Raval suggests, Kurtz has come out 'equipped with moral ideas of some sort'; Marlow wants to see whether Kurtz *can* unite idealism and successful trade - or imperialism. *Is* it possible to be both principled and successful in an imperialist context? This is the question that seems to take hold of Marlow's imagination. At this point Kurtz fascinates Marlow much as Gatsby fascinates Nick Carraway in *The Great Gatsby*.[7] The third quotation suggests that Marlow has moved beyond a concern for Kurtz as individual while on the trip up the river; the *personal* issue no longer interests him and he no longer feels the need to warn Kurtz about the machinations and plotting of the manager of the Central Station. He no longer believes that he has the power to intervene in such issues, and feels that 'the essentials of this affair' are beyond his control. He realizes that what one man can or cannot do is relatively irrelevant; what interests him now is the operation of the larger system.

After the attack on the boat in which the helmsman is killed, Marlow finds himself thinking of Kurtz and regretting the fact that Kurtz is now dead - which he assumes to be the case. The terms of Marlow's regret are very interesting, and the passage in which they can be studied needs to be cited in full in spite of its length.

> 'There was a sense of extreme disappointment, as though I had found out I had been striving after something altogether without a substance. I couldn't have been more disgusted if I had travelled all this way for the sole purpose of talking with Mr Kurtz. Talking with. . . . I flung one shoe overboard, and became aware that that was exactly what I had been looking forward to - a talk with Kurtz. I made the strange discovery that I had never imagined him as doing, you know, but as discoursing. I didn't say to myself, "Now I will never see him," or "Now I will never shake him by the hand," but, "now I will never hear him." The man presented himself as a voice. Not of course that I did not connect him with some sort of action. Hadn't I been told in all the tones of jealousy and admiration that he had collected, bartered, swindled, or stolen more ivory than all the other agents together? That was not the point. The point was in his being a gifted creature, and that of all his gifts the one that stood out preëminently, that carried with it a sense of real presence, was his ability to talk, his words - the gift of expression, the bewildering, the illuminating, the most exalted and the most contemptible, the pulsating stream of light, or the deceitful flow from the heart of an impenetrable darkness.' (HOD, pp. 113-14)

At this point Marlow realizes that Kurtz's idealism cannot be put into practice; its practical effect is limited to that of acting as camouflage, as 'deceitful flow'. Marlow's interest is in Kurtz as intellect, as idealist, as *a man with ideas*, but he is forced to concede that these ideas are as impractical as are those of his aunt. Marlow's curiosity may be partly explained by the recollection that he himself had also been described in words identical to those used of Kurtz.

> 'In the course of these confidences it became quite plain to me I had been represented to the wife of the high dignitary, and goodness knows to how many more people besides, as an exceptional and gifted creature - a piece of good fortune for the Company - a man you don't get hold of every day.' (HOD, p. 59)

It is not surprising that with such a recommendation Marlow is taken to be of the gang of virtue upon his arrival at the Central Station, nor that he starts to identify himself with Kurtz to a certain extent.

Right at the start of his narrative Marlow makes it clear that, for him, imperialism can only be justified by having an idea behind it:

> 'The conquest of the earth, which mostly means the taking it away from those who have a different complexion or slightly flatter noses than ourselves, is not a pretty thing when you look into it too much. What redeems it is the idea only. An idea at the back of it; not a sentimental pretence but an idea; and an unselfish belief in the idea – something you can set up, and bow down before, and offer a sacrifice to. . . .'
>
> (HOD, pp. 50-1)

The passage quoted comes at the end of a paragraph which has started with Marlow's suggestion that 'What saves us' (in contrast to the Roman conquerors of Britain) 'is efficiency – the devotion to efficiency'. Efficiency and the idea, trade and idealism. Indeed, the idea which Marlow has in mind may consist in part of a concern with efficiency, a belief that the imperialist venture is justified by its bringing of greater efficiency to those lands which are brought under its sway.

Marlow's growing curiosity about Kurtz, then, is a growing interest in him as a possible exemplar of the successful fusion of trade and idealism, a living proof that imperialism can be justified by being built on an idea, by transforming the inefficient to the efficient. Kurtz is distinguished from the other white men Marlow meets in Africa (the Russian excepted) by the fact that he really has believed in his idea, it has not been a 'sentimental pretence' as is the philanthropy of the pilgrims, it is not just a belief in appearances – as in the case of the manager.

> '"It is very serious," said the manager's voice right behind me; "I would be desolated if anything should happen to Mr Kurtz before we came up." I looked at him, and had not the slightest doubt he was sincere. He was just the kind of man who would wish to preserve appearances. That was his restraint.' (HOD, p. 106)

Cedric Watts remarks on this passage:

> The manager is sincere in the sense that although he hopes Kurtz will die, he truly wishes to 'preserve appearances': he wants Kurtz to die after, rather than before, the relieving party arrives. His restraint, then, lies in hypocritically concealing his treachery under the cloak of propriety. Compared with this, the restraint of the cannibals, who evidently consider the whites unappetizing but openly display their hunger for human flesh, is admirably free from perversity.[8]

The more Marlow learns of the manager and the other white men in the Central Station the more contemptible he finds them: they are concerned only to extract the maximum amount of wealth under the possible cover of philanthropic sentiments. But the more he learns of Kurtz the more interested he becomes in him, as a man who may have had 'an idea', who may genuinely have tried to unite idealism and trade, to develop an imperialism justified by sincerely philanthropic motives.

Such a reading produces at least one problem, however. How do we explain Marlow's contempt for the keeping up of appearances of the manager, and his apparent respect for that of the Company's chief accountant?

> 'I respected the fellow. Yes; I respected his collars, his vast cuffs, his brushed hair. His appearance was certainly that of a hairdresser's dummy; but in the great demoralization of the land he kept up his appearance. That's backbone. His starched collars and got-up shirt-fronts were achievements of character. He had been out for nearly three years; and, later, I could not help asking him how he managed to sport such linen. He had just the faintest blush, and said modestly, "I've been teaching one of the native women about the station. It was difficult. She had a distaste for the work." Thus this man had verily accomplished something. And he was devoted to his books, which were in apple-pie order.
>
> 'Everything else in the station was in a muddle, – heads, things, buildings. Strings of dusty niggers with splay feet arrived and departed; a stream of manufactured goods, rubbishy cottons, beads, and brass-wire set into the depths of darkness, and in return came a precious trickle of ivory.' (HOD, p. 68)

Marlow's respect for the accountant is doubly puzzling as it seems that the accountant's attitude is typical of a heartless, inhuman order dedicated only to the maximal extraction of wealth. That he represents the arrogant, self-interested exercise of power is clear from his remarks about having taught one of the native women to produce his immaculate laundry – along with his 'slight blush' and his admission that she 'had a distaste for the work'. A page later we are told of his chilling remark, 'When one has got to make correct entries, one comes to hate those savages – hate them to the death', a remark that makes him a fitting symbol for the whole imperialist project observed by Marlow. And the process of exchange of rubbish for ivory detailed in the second of the two paragraphs quoted above also has a representative appropriateness: all the accountant is concerned with is what goes out and what comes in – what he can write up in his accounts. What neither he nor his account-books have any concern for is what happens in 'the depths of darkness' when exchange takes place: just as the Europeans in the domestic power are quite uninterested in what happens *in* Africa, they are merely concerned with what goes in there and what comes out. (This is one of the reasons why the depiction of the French warship firing into the depths of the land has such a powerful symbolic force: it captures certain crucial aspects of the imperialist venture and its underlying attitudes). As I have suggested, in his concern for 'correct entries' the accountant may remind us of Makola in 'An Outpost of Progress', who combines the same concern for accurate book-keeping along with unconcern for human suffering and exploitation. What, then, are we to make of Marlow's respect for the accountant?

It is possible that we should see Marlow's respect in the context of his relative inexperience at this point of the narrative – that we are meant to understand that his respect is the respect of the narrated rather than the narrating Marlow, still unaware of the duplicities of imperialism. It is also possible that Marlow is himself a narrator who is less morally reliable than many commentators on Conrad's novella have assumed, and that such passages as the above are designed to trigger off the reader's suspicions with regard to the acceptability of Marlow's opinions. But a third option is open to us. The accountant's concern for his immaculate dress and appearance is neither hypocritical nor self-interested. It does not conceal anything, it does him no good. It can thus be taken to represent a determination to maintain some set of standards independent of their immediate benefits. In this he stands out: 'Everything else in the station was in a muddle'. (Again, we may remember that in 'An Outpost of Progress' the white men are provided with a house 'built neatly of reeds' which they proceed to make extremely untidy.) The accountant can thus be seen to have some inner resources, something inside himself which, when all restraint is removed, keeps him living in a manner not determined purely by the desire to indulge his own lusts and desires.[9] The manager, in contrast, wants to keep up appearances in a rather different way – he wants to keep them up in order to *conceal* what is going on underneath.

The more Marlow learns about Kurtz, of course, the more he discovers that a successful combining of trade and idealism has not taken place, that Kurtz's ideals – his 'idea' – consist but of words.

> 'I was cut to the quick at the idea of having lost the inestimable privilege of listening to the gifted Kurtz. Of course I was wrong. The privilege was waiting for me. Oh, yes, I heard more than enough. And I was right, too. A voice. He was very little more than a voice.' (HOD, pp. 114-15)

Given what Kurtz has been seen by Marlow to represent earlier on in the novella, the judgement is a damning one. The 'idea' supporting and justifying imperialism, that idealism that can be happily married to profitable trade, is so much hot air. It is language without any substantial referent, words as 'the deceitful flow from the heart of an inpenetrable darkness' rather than as 'the pulsating stream of light'.

In the course of his African experiences Marlow confirms not just that imperialism is 'not a pretty thing', but that it is not actually subservient to *any* idea. The ideas are there, but the idealism which they constitute is valuable as camouflage and as a means to deceive, rather than as a genuinely controlling impulse. Imperialism is helped by being covered with a smokescreen of idealism, and idealistic beliefs help to convince people of the worth of imperialism. A comment of Decoud's to Mrs Gould in Conrad's later work *Nostromo* is of great relevance here:

> '[Charles Gould] cannot act or exist without idealizing every simple feeling, desire, or achievement. He could not believe his own motives if he did not make them first a part of some fairy tale.'
>
> (*Nostromo*, pp. 214-15)

Cedric Watts makes a similar point.

> There are also evident connections between *Heart of Darkness* and Conrad's most ambitious novel, *Nostromo* (1904). A central figure is Gould, the determined mine-owner who, like Kurtz, has ventured boldly in the idealistic belief that by developing the material resources of the land he would be bringing the torch of humane progress to it: he would simultaneously be conquering the recalcitrant material environment and the recalcitrant force of human lawlessness. Like Kurtz, however, he becomes the victim of the environment.[10]

I do not think that it is adequate to see either Kurtz or Charles Gould as victims of 'the environment', however. Gould in particular seems to cope with the task of subduing the physical environment rather well. It is something less tangible that subdues both characters: something nearer to what in *Nostromo* we get to know as 'material interests'.

In other words, the link between idealism and imperialism is not fortuitous, it is functional. Just as we see how the two white men Carlier and Kayerts, in 'An Outpost of Progress', think that much better of themselves after having read about 'Our Colonial Expansion' and 'the rights and duties of civilization' in the 'home paper' they discover, so too Marlow's aunt thinks well of the imperialism Marlow is sent to serve and further because of the 'rot let loose in print' (p. 59) that she reads. We are, in other words, dealing here with the ideological support granted by idealism to imperialism.

It is clear at many points in the text of *Heart of Darkness* that women are given a particular responsibility and function so far as the preserving of idealism is concerned, and at this stage I would like to look more closely at this aspect of the novella's treatment of the relationship between idealism and imperialism.

The women of *Heart of Darkness*

The chain of worship and betrayal that we witness in *Heart of Darkness* is completed by Marlow's own worship of that more perfect world inhabited by women, a worship which leads him to lie to the Intended and thus to perpetuate the cycle of lies that fuels imperialism. Given Conrad's reputation as a very masculine writer, more concerned with the world of male than of female experience, it is salutory to recall that three female characters each play an indispensable rôle in *Heart of Darkness* – Marlow's aunt, the 'wild and gorgeous apparition of a woman' the reader presumes is Kurtz's African mistress, and Kurtz's Intended. There is additionally Kurtz's portrait of the blindfolded female, and there are the two women knitting black wool met by Marlow in the Company's office in Europe, women whose resemblance to the Fates of classical mythology is clearly intended. Their appearance in the novella suggests that women may have a significant rôle to play in determining various fates in *Heart of Darkness*. The blindfolded woman suggests that this determining influence may not be a knowing or intended one. The parallel with what I have already argued about the rôle of idealism in the imperialist venture should, I hope, be apparent.

What becomes apparent if we consider the three main female characters in the novella, is that in *Heart of Darkness* issues of gender are inextricably intertwined with matters of race and culture. To start with, we should note that the following comments made by Marlow about 'women' are clearly aimed at *European women*: they do not apply to the African woman. Nor do they apply to working-class European women; Marlow's statement is both culture- and class-limited.

> 'Girl! What? Did I mention a girl? Oh, she is out of it – completely. They – the women I mean – are out of it – should be out of it. We must help them to stay in that beautiful world of their own, lest ours gets worse. Oh, she had to be out of it.' (HOD, p. 115)

The women are 'out of' the man's world just as effectively as Kurtz's ideas and values are out of the horrific world he constructs in Africa. And just as Kurtz's ideas and values become weakened and impoverished by this isolation, so too do the women who are out of it, imprisoned in their 'beautiful world of their own', end up as debilitated and sterile as the Intended. The remarks quoted above are all of a piece with Marlow's earlier comments about women, comments inspired by his aunt's adoption of the 'rot let loose in print and talk' which leads her to picture him as 'an emissary of light, something like a lower sort of apostle' (p. 59).

'It's queer how out of touch with truth women are. They live in a world of their own, and there had never been anything like it, and never can be. It is too beautiful altogether, and if they were to set it up it would go to pieces before the first sunset. Some confounded fact we men have been living contentedly with ever since the day of creation would start up and knock the whole thing over.' (HOD, p. 59)

What Marlow describes as the 'world of their own' of women in the above passage has much in common with the world of Kurtz's ideals, which he does actually try to set up and which does go to pieces before too many sunsets because some 'confounded fact' starts up and knocks the whole thing over. And indeed, just as Marlow's aunt 'got carried off her feet' (p. 59), so too Kurtz 'had kicked himself loose of the earth' (p. 144).

In a work which, I have argued, explores the fate of an idealism betrayed into a corrupting alliance with imperialism, European women perform an important symbolic function. At the same time as they provide us with a relatively straightforward and realistic depiction of European middle-class women of the time, they also serve a larger representative function, portraying that idealism which the domestic imperialist powers use as apology for their exploitation. This idealism is, paradoxically, nurtured apart from that for which it offers an apology: the activities of the European powers in the subject countries dominated by imperialism. If this argument is accepted, then it must also be accepted that the idealism in question is a weak, emaciated, and unhealthy creature. Neither Marlow's aunt nor Kurtz's Intended could be said to be possessed of any striking features suggestive of energy or practicality. With his aunt Marlow has a last decent cup of tea for many days 'in a room that most soothingly looked just as you would expect a lady's drawing-room to look' (p. 59). It is one of the the functions of women and that idealism which they represent to 'soothe' those off to do imperialism's dirty work. Marlow's patronizing tone when talking of his aunt is however mild in contrast to the powerful connotations of death and disease to be found in the description of the Intended's home.

'The bent gilt legs and back of the furniture shone in indistinct curves. The tall white marble fireplace had a cold and monumental whiteness. A grand piano stood massively in a corner; with dark gleams on the flat surfaces like a sombre and polished sarcophagus.' (HOD, p. 156)

The Intended herself is a thing of black and white, of sickliness and death. She has no energy, no living presence.

'She came forward, all in black, with a pale head, floating towards me in the dusk. ....

This fair hair, this pale visage, this pure brow, seemed surrounded by an ashy halo from which the dark eyes looked out at me.'

(HOD, pp. 156-7)

Note how words connotative of idealism such as 'pure' and 'halo' are made to seem unhealthy and corrupted in this description. This seems to me to support the argument that the way in which European women are portrayed in *Heart of Darkness* serves to strengthen the novella's depiction of idealism as weak, unhealthy and corrupted.

The black–white imagery of *Heart of Darkness*, the effect of which comes to a climax in the meeting between Marlow and the Intended, is complex. An analysis of its function in the passage quoted above would not be easy, and in the novella as a whole it cannot unproblematically be reduced to any schematic system of symbolic meaning. Conrad seems concerned to undercut simple symbolic associations in his use of this imagery, to disabuse the reader of the belief that good and bad can be straightforwardly defined and neatly compartmentalized. Very often in the novella we can observe a process of change from white to black: the centre of Africa is white on the map, but turns out to be a place of darkness; the Intended is pale and fair, but her dark eyes and the darkness falling in her room suggest that her very purity is productive, however unknowingly, of evil. The complexity of this pattern of imagery also seems to me to have something to say about the marriage of trade and idealism in the work: just as we no longer accept the conventional association of white with purity and virtue by the end of the novella, so too we see that idealism can be corrupted by association with evil forces. The challenge to our conventional views at the level of the novella's imagery duplicates and reinforces the challenge made by the work to other conventional views.

It is apparent from the quoted passage that the Intended's capacity is for devotion, not for living. Existence in a world of their own, then, does not seem to produce any sort of enviable life for European women, but more a sort of living death. And inside the white tomb, black decay and corruption can be found. A disembodied idealism, far from preserving the good, may actually foster the bad. If we accept such an interpretation of aspects of the black–white imagery of the novella, we will have to consider critically Marlow's view that if women are kept confined to that 'world of their own' this may help to make our own (that is, the world of men) better.

The contrast to the Intended offered by Kurtz's African mistress could not be sharper.

'She walked with measured steps, draped in striped and fringed cloths, treading the earth proudly, with a slight jingle and flash of barbarous ornaments. She carried her head high; her hair was done in the shape of a helmet; she had brass leggings to the knee, brass wire gauntlets to the elbow, a crimson spot on her tawny cheek, innumerable necklaces of glass beads on her neck; bizarre things, charms, gifts of witch-men, that hung about her, glittered and trembled at every step. She must have had the value of several elephant tusks upon her. She was savage and superb, wild-eyed and magnificent; there was something ominous and stately in her deliberate progress.' (HOD, pp. 135-6)

Where the Intended is static and passive, she is active and forceful; where the Intended has the odour of death about her, she is the personification of life; where the Intended is a thing of black and white, she is ablaze with colour; where the Intended is refined to the point of etiolation, she is 'savage and superb'; and where the Intended is clad in mourning, she is clad for war. Moreover, while the Intended has an air of oppressive sterility about her, Marlow says of the African woman that 'the immense wilderness, the colossal body of the fecund and mysterious life seemed to look at her, pensive, as though it had been looking at the image of its own tenebrous and passionate soul' (p. 136).[11] This aspect of the contrast is particularly important: the Intended and the idealism she represents are sterile; nothing will come of them but death. But the powerful life of the African woman is, like the wilderness reflected in her, passionate and fecund.[12]

The contrast is in tune with others in the novella: between, for instance, the boat 'paddled by black fellows' seen by Marlow on his way to Africa, and the lifeless French man-of-war shelling 'enemies' inland. Marlow sees in that African actuality which is untouched by imperialism an energy, a concentrated life that contrasts with the sterility seen in a European idealism cut off from reality. The life of the African woman is all of a piece: there is no division of ideals and aspirations from actuality, no separation between her and her life activity. This being so, the over-whelmingly positive description which the reader is given of her serves as a critique of the life of the Europeans, divided between sterile ideals and brutal 'horror'. I should add, however, that if we look at the two women together we recognize, I think, a familiar pattern: woman as devoted and chaste spirit, and woman as sensual and sexual flesh. But this reproduction of a well-known stereotypical pattern is not itself restricted to the patriarchal ideology that fosters and benefits from it, for in juxtaposing the two women the narrative of *Heart of Darkness* draws attention to the process whereby women are dehumanized by being divided into spirit and body and are denied the full humanity that requires possession of both.[13]

There are critics who find Marlow's (and Conrad's) account of the African woman melodramatic and unconvincing, just as there are many who find the closing scene between Marlow and the Intended to strain after an effect which it fails to achieve, and it is true that if these scenes are considered in isolation then a convincing case against them can be made along these lines.

> All of these objections [to the final scene with the Intended] seem to have their base on aesthetic grounds, but it could be contended that the problem here too is essentially ideological, since Marlow's response to the Intended is the result of a particular kind of anti-feminism that pervades the novella and may well reflect Conrad's own inadequate response to the feminine. The attitudes of Victorian patriarchy structure the response to women and to savages in the same way, by imposing a sentimental and reductive definition upon the object that removes the necessity of actually looking at it.[14]

This is an interesting suggestion, but one which I find mistaken. And the mistake is similar to that which accuses the Conrad of *Heart of Darkness* of racism. For the ideological force of the presentation of the Intended can be tapped only when this presentation is set alongside that of Kurtz's African mistress. It is when the two are seen as two aspects of a patriarchal view of women that the ideological thrust of the work comes into focus, just as Conrad's presentation of Africans in *Heart of Darkness* has to be set against his description of Europeans and of the system they impose upon Africa.

The gender divisions referred to by Marlow are not, of course, just a literary matter, not just a question of the work's symbolic patterns of meaning, nor can they be considered separately from the imperialist brutalities which are recounted in *Heart of Darkness*. The Intended's sterile isolation depicts realistically the separation of those in the domestic culture from full knowledge of what is being done in their name in Africa, while at the same time it is also an accurate portrayal of some of the results of the differential treatment of men and women in the European culture. It is European men who are sent to Africa to further the aims of imperialism; but we see European women – ignorant of what their menfolk are really doing for imperialism – offering powerful ideological support to them. What *Heart of Darkness* suggests to the engaged reader is that the division of ideal and action, of theory and practice, is effected in part by means of the division of genders.

The African woman in *Heart of Darkness* is one of a number of 'native' women in Conrad's fiction who are betrayed through their love for, or involvement with, a white man. Aïssa is betrayed by Willems, Jewel by Jim. And both Hassim and his sister Immada are effectively betrayed by Lingard in *The Rescue*. In Conrad's first published novel *Almayer's Folly*, implicit authorial approval is accorded Nina's decision to reject the possibility of a white husband, to turn her back on the race of her father, and instead to follow Dain. In *Lord Jim* Jewel says to Marlow: 'He has left me .... you always leave us – for your own ends', and on the penultimate page of the novel Marlow says of Jim that he 'goes away from a living woman to celebrate his pitiless wedding with a shadowy ideal of conduct' (pp. 348, 416). These two comments are extremely suggestive, and bring to mind a range of significant implications. On the strictly literal level, one is reminded that an aspect of imperialism has always been that of the sexual exploitation of 'native' women by male representatives of the exploiting power, an exploitation which does not typically involve any permanent commitment to the women involved, who are always left for the personal 'ends' of the men concerned. But it is striking how Marlow's comment on Jim at the end of *Lord Jim* can also be applied to Kurtz, who also leaves a 'living woman' to celebrate a 'pitiless wedding with a shadowy ideal of conduct'. (Both the African woman and the Intended are abandoned by Kurtz, albeit in different ways.) Kurtz's 'pitiless wedding' is not a happy one, and he apparently finds in the African woman qualities which are lacking in the Intended and which he cannot resist. Kurtz is morally responsible for turning the Intended into a living corpse, and then unable to resist the attraction of a woman possessed of precisely that life which European culture has denied the Intended. (Many of Conrad's contemporary readers would doubtless have seen Kurtz's relationship with the African woman as further evidence of his degeneration, and there is some textual evidence that this is how Marlow sees it. But I do not think that the work as a whole can unproblematically sustain such a reading.)

Kurtz manages to destroy both women. As I have said, in different ways, he abandons both. So positive and forceful is the impression given off by the African woman that it is not hard to forget that she too has the word 'tragic' applied to her more than once in the work.

> 'Her face had a tragic and fierce aspect of wild sorrow and of dumb pain mingled with the fear of some struggling, half-shaped resolve. She stood looking at us without a stir, and like the wilderness itself, with an air of brooding over an inscrutable purpose.' (HOD, p. 136)

Perhaps Conrad believes that like Taminah in *Almayer's Folly*, she lacks the language and the self-knowledge to isolate and explore the source of her pain, which Marlow describes as 'dumb'. But of course the reader is never allowed to witness her speech or her thoughts, and this narrative restriction may represent both a limitation of Conrad's experience and of his ideological outlook. (It contrasts strikingly with his ability to make us privy to the speech and thoughts of his Malays.)

When the steamer leaves, taking Kurtz away from her, we are told that

'Only the barbarous and superb woman did not so much as flinch, and stretched tragically her bare arms after us over the sombre and glittering river.' (HOD, p. 146)

The gesture is recalled by Marlow later on, during his meeting with Kurtz's Intended.

'She put out her arms as if after a retreating figure, stretching them black and with clasped pale hands across the fading and narrow sheen of the window. Never see him! I saw him clearly enough then. I shall see this eloquent phantom as long as I live, and I shall see her, too, a tragic and familiar Shade, resembling in this gesture another one, tragic also, and bedecked with powerless charms, stretching bare brown arms over the glitter of the infernal stream, the stream of darkness.'

(HOD, pp. 160-1)

The linking together of the two women at this juncture in the narrative makes an important point. Both women are tragic, both have been betrayed by Kurtz. Putting women on a pedestal, cutting them off from reality, and restricting them to a world of sterile ideals and lifeless illusions is as destructive as treating a woman purely as the recipient of passion.

The duplicities of imperialism work their way through into human relationships through – among other things – their connection with gender divisions in the domestic culture. (Another way of looking at the matter is to say that imperialism involved the projection of divisions and duplicities already existing in Europe on to the exploited lands. 'Native' women were thus slotted into a rôle previously occupied by poor women in the domestic cultures. No doubt many like Kurtz who never left Europe had their Intendeds and their mistresses just like Kurtz – even if the mistresses were white. As I argued in my chapter on *The Nigger of the 'Narcissus'*, common attitudes could encompass 'niggers' and members of the domestic working class.)

Talking of Jewel in *Lord Jim* Marlow says that her indifference, 'more awful than tears, cries, and reproaches, seemed to defy time and consolation' (p. 348). Of the Intended in *Heart of Darkness* Marlow observes that 'I perceived she was one of those creatures that are not the playthings of Time. For her he had died only yesterday' (p. 157). In both cases a 'native' woman has been removed from time by association with a European man: has been effectively removed from the process of living. And in *Heart of Darkness* this separation in some ways results from a set of disembodied and unreal ideals which are imposed upon women by men. The Intended's isolation from the reality of Kurtz is a part of imperialism's nurturing of spurious ideals, ideals which function more as camouflage than as active principles or guides to action.

'"He was a remarkable man," I said, unsteadily. Then before the appealing fixity of her gaze, that seemed to watch for more words on my lips, I went on, "It was impossible not to – "

'"Love him," she finished eagerly, silencing me into an appalled dumbness. "How true! How true! But when you think that no one knew him so well as I! I had all his noble confidence. I knew him best."

'"You knew him best," I repeated. And perhaps she did. But with every word spoken the room was growing darker, and only her forehead, smooth and white, remained illumined by the unextinguishable light of belief and love.' (HOD, p. 158)

The Intended's forehead seems here to symbolize her unshakeable idealism; unaware of the horror of the world, believing herself to have known Kurtz better than anyone, she is actually more and more isolated, and more and more reduced by her isolation. The whiteness of her forehead parallels Kurtz's own 'ivory' head: unhealthy, unnatural; and illumined by a light which – like the light held by the painted woman in Kurtz's picture – fails to help its blind owner to see. The picture is proleptic of Marlow's final scene with the Intended in a number of ways.

'Then I noticed a small sketch in oils, on a panel, representing a woman, draped and blindfolded, carrying a lighted torch. The background was sombre – almost black. The movement of the woman was stately, and the effect of the torch-light on the face was sinister.' (HOD, p. 79)

The painted woman is as cut off from her surroundings as is the Intended; her torch, like the Intended's idealism, is apparently aimed at illuminating the darkness, dispelling ignorance, but 'the effect of the torch-light on the face was sinister'. Ideals held in blind ignorance of reality do not bring good, but its opposite. The picture helps to support the argument that the novella associates the isolation of European women with the isolation of idealism from that which it is being used to underwrite.

Why does Marlow remark that perhaps the Intended did know Kurtz best? Is it that she understood his dreams, his ideals, and that these were the true centre of Kurtz, that which could explain both sides of the corrupted idealist? Or is this an indication of Marlow's limitations, of his own desire to maintain a separate world of imagined ideals, a world in which Kurtz's reality would be measured not by his actions but by his expressed values, his disappointed dreams – 'a shadow insatiable of splendid appearances, of frightful realities; a shadow darker than the shadow of the night, and draped nobly in the folds of a gorgeous eloquence' (p. 155)?

A brief comparison of the final pages of *Heart of Darkness* with those of *Under Western Eyes* prompts some relevant observations. In the later novel, Nathalie Haldin is led to recognize the fact that her ideals have been cut off from the world, have failed to make contact with those realities they have claimed to be concerned to alter. As a result, she travels back to Russia, seeking to renew her contact with these lost realities at first hand. In contrast, *Heart of Darkness* ends with Marlow's decision to maintain the ignorance of the Intended, to keep her in the dark – however much he claims that it 'would have been too dark – too dark altogether' to tell her the truth about Kurtz.

Does this difference represent a change in Conrad's own views about the need to keep women in that 'world of their own' the existence of which makes 'ours' (i.e. men's[15]) a little better? A case could be made for such a judgement, but it seems to me to ignore the fact that it is Marlow rather than Conrad who argues that women should be kept in that 'world of their own' in *Heart of Darkness*. What the novella gives us is not what Conrad the man thought about women, but Conrad's artistic insight into the way in which gender divisions enter into the duplicities of imperialism. I have suggested that the African woman and Kurtz's Intended can be seen as classic examples of female stereotypes: passive virgin and knowing, active woman. The novella suggests that imperialism was able to inherit these stereotypical female rôles and to put them to work for itself, a work that in turn further intensified the domestic oppression of the female sex. (If we wanted an illustration of the distance that separates Conrad from Dickens, his debt to the earlier novelist notwithstanding, we could point to the way in which these familiar female stereotypes are held up to more rigorous criticism in *Heart of Darkness* than ever they are in any of Dickens's works.) And one of the reasons why Conrad's engagement with male-female relationships is so much more satisfactory in *Heart of Darkness* than it is in *Chance* is that in the former work such relationships are seen in a very precisely drawn determining context.

In Conrad's manuscript of *Heart of Darkness*, in the passage in which Marlow says that women must be helped to stay in that beautiful world of theirs, lest ours gets worse, the following words follow the words 'ours gets worse':

> 'That's a monster-truth with many maws to whom we've got to throw every year – or every day – no matter – no sacrifice is too great – a ransom of pretty, shining lies – not very new perhaps – but spotless, aureoled, tender.'[16]

These words make Marlow's position seem far more vulnerable and morally unsound, and they suggest that Marlow's propensity to set up gods or idols to whom ransoms of pretty, shining lies (pretty fictions?) can be paid, and for whom 'no sacrifice is too great', is one which unites him morally with Kurtz. Marlow's choice of the nightmare of Kurtz would thus be seen as a choice of idealism rather than trade or imperialism, but an idealism which is guilty of complicity in imperialism's wrongdoings, an idealism which Marlow should recognize not just as powerless but also as corrupt, which Kurtz himself does in his final outburst.

The women of *Heart of Darkness* are not the only symbolic representatives of an idealism apologetic to imperialism. In a different way the Russian can also be seen in this way, and at this stage I would like to turn briefly to consider him.

The Russian

Marlow's meeting and conversation with the young Russian focus and crystallize a number of the themes already discussed. The Russian worships Kurtz for his ideas, for his cultural attainments, for his idealism. He repeats several times that Kurtz has enlarged his mind, and claims that Kurtz has been shamefully abandoned (back to the murder plot!) – 'A man like this, with such ideas' (p. 132). Kurtz's personality has overwhelmed him: 'You don't talk with that man – you listen to him' (p. 123), and Marlow perceives that the Russian's worship of Kurtz is unthinking and without reservations.

> 'I did not envy him his devotion to Kurtz, though. He had not meditated over it. It came to him, and he accepted it with a sort of eager fatalism. I must say that to me it appeared about the most dangerous thing in every way he had come upon so far.' (HOD, p. 127)

It seems that the Russian's rôle in *Heart of Darkness* is to exemplify the fatal attraction that pure idealism can present to a particular kind of *man*; one naïve, disinterested and romantic. The portrayal of the Russian thus complements that of the European women of *Heart of Darkness*. On the first page of the third section of the novella the word 'glamour' is used of the Russian three times by Marlow. 'Glamour' is a favoured word of Conrad's, appearing in many of his works and typically suggestive of the romantic associations youth imposes upon otherwise unremarkable events, actions or places (the word is used to some effect, not surprisingly, in 'Youth'). Of the Russian we are told that

> 'The glamour of youth enveloped his particoloured rags, his destitution, his loneliness, the essential desolation of his futile wanderings. For months – for years – his life hadn't been worth a day's purchase; and there he was gallantly, thoughtlessly alive, to all appearance indestructible solely by the virtue of his few years and of his unreflecting audacity.
> ....

If the absolutely pure, uncalculating, unpractical spirit of adventure had ever ruled a human being, it ruled this be-patched youth.' (HOD, p. 126)

The Russian, we may propose, represents that romantic spirit of adventure from which imperialism recruits so much of its muscle-power in the domestic land. His 'unreflecting' mind is completely taken over by Kurtz's rhetoric (he thinks that it has merely been 'enlarged'). His admiration for this rhetoric, we should note, leads him unreservedly to defend Kurtz's brutal actions – the heads on the poles, the attack on the steamer, even the offer of violence and death to himself in order to obtain some ivory. The Russian thus stands for a sort of romantic male delusion peculiar to imperialism, testimony to the fact that physical danger and adventure along with elevated ideas and culture combine to make a very potent, and morally destructive, mixture.

The fact that the Russian is young is of great significance. Youth is the time of idealism. It is hard not to associate the Russian's youthful wonder at Kurtz's ideas with Conrad's report of his own idealism and subsequent disillusion concerning the white centre of Africa. In his essay 'Geography and Some Explorers' Conrad talks of having dreamt of going to the Congo, struck as he was with the story of David Livingstone. Eighteen years afterwards, on board a steamboat moored to the bank of an African river, his sentiments are rather different.

> A great melancholy descended upon me. Yes, this was the very spot. But there was no shadowy friend to stand by my side in the night of the enormous wilderness, no great haunting memory, but only the unholy recollection of a prosaic newspaper 'stunt' and the distasteful knowledge of the vilest scramble for loot that ever disfigured the history of human conscience and geographical exploration. What an end to the idealized realities of a boy's daydreams! (LE, p. 17)

The shadowy friend found by the young Russian fills his head with 'ideas in general' so that, unlike Conrad, his 'idealized realities' do not come to an end in Africa. The Russian turns a blind eye to Kurtz's vile scramble for loot as a result of being overpowered by Kurtz's rhetoric; he is swept off his feet by Kurtz's conversation, a conversation which touches not on specific matters, but on generalities.

> '"We talked of everything," he said, quite transported at the recollection. "I forgot there was such a thing as sleep. The night did not seem to last an hour. Everything! Everything! . . . Of love, too." "Ah, he talked to you of love!" I said, much amused. "It isn't what you think," he cried, almost passionately. "It was in general. He made me see things – things."'
> (HOD, p. 127)

The Russian is as inarticulate as, we infer, Kurtz is articulate. Kurtz's eloquence has bewitched and mastered him, but he is incapable of repeating the substance of what Kurtz said, although we can assume that Kurtz's talk of love was general enough to avoid mention of either the Intended or the African mistress. It is a commonplace of Conradian criticism that the Russian's multi-coloured garb calls to mind the multi-coloured map of the world described earlier in the novella by Marlow. And as these colours betoken the ownership of territories by European powers, we may surmise that in some sense just as all Europe has contributed to the making of Kurtz, so all imperialist possession is somehow represented by the Russian. We may draw particular attention to the description of his pockets:

> 'One of his pockets (bright red) was bulging with cartridges, from the other (dark blue) peeped "Towson's Inquiry," etc., etc.' (HOD, p. 140)

The marriage of seamanship with firepower is most appropriately associated with the colours red and blue, colours particularly associated with the British flag and with British imperialism. And this association is strengthened by the Russian's very positive attitude towards the British, and towards English sailors.

In *Under Western Eyes* the teacher of languages tells Miss Haldin – who in her way is as vulnerable to idealistic protestations and illusions as is the young Russian in *Heart of Darkness* – that 'The most idealistic conceptions of love and forbearance must be clothed in flesh as it were before they can be made understandable' (UWE, p. 106). This is precisely what Kurtz does not do: he speaks only of love in general. The clothing in flesh takes place elsewhere, and it does not bring the words 'love and forbearance' to mind. Marlow remarks ironically to the Russian, when Kurtz appears, borne in a stretcher, 'Let us hope that the man who can talk so well of love in general will find some particular reason to spare us this time' (p. 133). The irony hits at the heart of Marlow's – and Conrad's – objections to a particular sort of idealism. It is cut off from everyday reality. It neither helps us to see the world realistically, nor to act effectively or morally in it. Instead, it serves as a smokescreen for the most appalling brutalities and hypocrisies.

Marlow and Kurtz

We are left, however, with a further problem. The Russian's admiration for Kurtz is seen clearly to be a delusion. Why though does Marlow maintain some solidarity with Kurtz?

> 'The pilgrims looked upon me with disfavour. I was, so to speak, numbered with the dead. It is strange how I accepted this unforeseen

partnership, this choice of nightmares forced upon me in the tenebrous land invaded by these mean and greedy phantoms.' (HOD, p. 147)

'However, as you see, I did not go to join Kurtz there and then. I did not. I remained to dream the nightmare out to the end, and to show my loyalty to Kurtz once more.' (HOD, p. 150)

After Kurtz's famous ejaculation, 'The horror! The horror!', Marlow comments

'I like to think my summing-up would not have been a word of careless contempt. Better his cry – much better. It was an affirmation, a moral victory paid for by innumerable defeats, by abominable terrors, by abominable satisfactions! But it was a victory! That is why I have remained loyal to Kurtz to the last, and even beyond, when a long time after I heard once more, not his own voice, but the echo of his magnificent eloquence thrown to me from a soul as translucently pure as a cliff of crystal.' (HOD, pp. 151-2)

How do we explain this reaction of Marlow's – a reaction which, the above passage makes clear, may also help us to understand why Marlow lies to Kurtz's Intended? Put another way: why does Kurtz's 'cry' impress Marlow so positively towards him? Kurtz's own insight comes only at the very last. Shortly before his death he seems still to believe in the possibility of an imperialism guided by ideas, in the fusion of trade and idealism.

'Sometimes he was contemptibly childish. He desired to have kings meet him at railway-stations on his return from some ghastly Nowhere, where he intended to accomplish great things. "You show them you have in you something that is really profitable, and then there will be no limits to the recognition of your ability," he would say. "Of course you must always take care of the motives – right motives – always."' (HOD, p. 148)

And soon after this he dies, having cried out, 'The horror! The horror!' At this stage the reader surely expects Marlow to be completely disillusioned with Kurtz. And yet this does not seem to be the case.

This is the site of what is perhaps the best-known critical crux in *Heart of Darkness*, and it raises a number of complex questions which can only be answered in the light of an interpretation of the whole text. A very brief, summary answer to why Marlow admires Kurtz for his despairing cry might be that Marlow remains convinced of the need for ideals even in the face of their manifest powerlessness or of the self-deception which they involve. However much Kurtz's ideals fail him, they provide our only hope of making the world better, of moderating the behaviour of those freed from external restraints. This at any rate is the burden of Marlow's own explanation of why he lied to the Intended.

> 'I laid the ghost of his gifts at last with a lie,' he began, suddenly. 'Girl! What? Did I mention a girl? Oh, she is out of it – completely. They – the women – I mean – are out of it – should be out of it. We must help them to stay in that beautiful world of their own, lest ours gets worse.' (HOD, p. 115)

Idealism may not be all-powerful, Marlow's argument seems to run, but it offers a modifying influence which may have some positive effect on human behaviour. But if this *is* what Marlow is seen to believe, it is not what the reader can conclude from the novella as a whole, and such a view of Marlow's assumptions necessarily leads the reader towards a critical attitude towards Marlow.

But Kurtz's cry can also be seen as 'a moral victory' (as Marlow terms it), in as much as it involves a perception and recognition of the betrayal of his previous ideals: he does not attempt to conceal or deny the depth of his degeneration, the extent of his moral collapse. And in a context characterized primarily by duplicity and dishonesty, this openness stands out as a moral victory. (Recall my comments on the accountant's lack of duplicity and on Marlow's admiration for him.) Moreover, as I pointed out in my first book on Conrad, with his cry Kurtz brings his words back into contact with reality, rather than using them in a closed sphere apart from the actualities to which they ostensibly refer.

The problem of the extent to which the reader of *Heart of Darkness* is encouraged to view Marlow, his beliefs and actions, more critically than he himself does, is a difficult one. Take Marlow's comment – quoted earlier – that the only thing that redeems 'the conquest of the earth' is 'the idea'.

> 'An idea at the back of it; not a sentimental pretence but an idea; and an unselfish belief in the idea – something you can set up, and bow down before, and offer a sacrifice to. . . .' (HOD, p. 51)

The terminology of worship and sacrifice is one which should arouse our suspicions. Kurtz has had himself set up, bowed down to, and offered sacrifices, and the result has been his utter moral collapse. We may presume that worshipping an idea may be as destructive to the idea as worshipping the man is seen to be to the man. Kurtz's worship of the idea prevents him from recognizing what it is sanctioning, just as the Intended's worship of Kurtz cuts her off from his reality.

By the end of *Heart of Darkness*, then, Marlow should be able to see that the idealism represented by Kurtz and by his Intended is the opposite of beneficial: instead of guiding imperialism towards principled actions, it offers a disguise for its unprincipled actions; instead of being an influence for moral good it is an agent of corruption. (A similar point could be made of *Nostromo*, in which Charles Gould's unshakeable conviction that he is in the right makes him so much more complete a servant of American imperialism as represented by the financier Holroyd; and just as a 'wall of silver bricks' comes to divide Gould from his wife, so Kurtz seems almost to turn into ivory. Kurtz and Gould hope to invest the winning of wealth with human values, but instead human values are enslaved by the needs of the winning of wealth. The attempt to use 'material interests' or profit to serve altruism or idealism ends in the domination of altruistic sentiments or ideals by those same material interests or profits.) The idealist in *Heart of Darkness* falls further than the mere looters, commits worse crimes than those unproblematically concerned to line their own pockets. (The Faustian element in *Heart of Darkness* uncovered by Cedric Watts is especially relevant here). The culminating point of 'every altruistic sentiment' is 'Exterminate all of the brutes!'

Intellect and solidarity

The Russian says of Kurtz, 'He hated all this, and somehow he couldn't get away';

> '"When I had a chance I begged him to try and leave while there was time; I offered to go back with him. And he would say yes, and then he would remain; go off on another ivory hunt; disappear for weeks; *forget himself among these people – forget himself – you know*."'
>
> (HOD, p. 129; my italics)

We should remember that Marlow specifically says that Kurtz's intellect was undamaged.

> 'And I wasn't arguing with a lunatic either. Believe me or not, his intelligence was perfectly clear – concentrated, it is true, upon himself with horrible intensity, yet clear ....
> But his soul was mad. Being alone in the wilderness, it had looked within itself, and, by heavens! I tell you, it had gone mad.' (HOD, p. 144)

Kurtz's intellect is cut off from human sanity just as his ideals are; 'a sane intellect and a mad soul' is not a bad way of describing the imperialism portrayed in *Heart of Darkness* (we can recall Marlow's earlier remarks about 'what saves us is efficiency – the devotion to efficiency').

Kurtz, as we are told several times in the course of *Heart of Darkness*, is nothing but a voice – a 'disembodied voice'. Conrad returns throughout his works to the fact of the detachability of voice from belief; it offers him a perfect symbol of unsubstantiated belief, mere surface appearance unrepresentative of inner strength. As I have pointed out elsewhere, in Conrad's fiction those with eloquence, those able to speak well or with voices that carry without effort on their part, are consistently subjected to moral condemnation. Not only is the detachability of language from belief and accurate reference a *symbol* for moral insubstantiality and duplicity, it is also a *means* whereby this duplicity is effected.

> 'Kurtz discoursed. A voice! a voice! It rang deep to the very last. It survived his strength to hide in the magnificent folds of eloquence the barren darkness of his heart. Oh, he struggled! he struggled! The wastes of his weary brain were haunted by shadowy images now – images of wealth and fame revolving obsequiously round his unextinguishable gift of noble and lofty expression. My Intended, my station, my career, my ideas – these were the subjects for the occasional utterances of elevated sentiments.' (HOD, p. 147; a comparable passage appears on p. 115.)

Kurtz's heart is dark not just because it is corrupt but also because it is secret, concealed, uncharted even by him – until his final ejaculation. The 'eloquence' which surrounds it serves to conceal not to reveal its reality, serves to cut it off from the outside world rather than to join it to that world. What is striking, too, about the above passage is the jumbling together of intellectual, material and human 'possessions' in his mind: 'My Intended, my station, my career, my ideas'.

The desire for *possession* corrupts human relationships, work and intellect: Kurtz is rightly described by Marlow as having a 'weirdly voracious aspect, as though he had wanted to swallow all the air, all the earth, all the men before him' (p. 134). Marlow learns from the Russian at one point in the narrative that 'Evidently the appetite for more ivory had got the better of the – what shall I say? – less material aspirations' (p. 130). We might sum up a constant theme in Conrad's work and, especially, in *Heart of Darkness*, as the conviction that the attempt to marry material and immaterial aspirations ends always in the taking over of the latter by the former. The attempt to combine trade and idealism, to reconcile the gaining of immense profit with philanthropic and altruistic ideals, has completely corrupted those ideals – just as it is seen to do in Conrad's later work *Nostromo*, in which not only the ideals of Charles Gould, but those of Holroyd and of the politically impotent author of *Fifty Years of Misrule* are seen to miscarry.

Kurtz's ideas, his 'principles', are imposed upon his natural self like clothes on a body, and they do not enter into his real self because Kurtz lacks knowledge of that self. His one attempt to look within himself leads not to knowledge but to madness. The wilderness had awakened *'forgotten* and brutal instincts' (p. 144). Only at the last does the knowledge of his 'deficiency' come to him.

> 'But his soul was mad. Being alone in the wilderness, it had looked within itself, and, by heavens! I tell you, it had gone mad. I had – for my sins, I suppose – to go through the ordeal of looking into it myself. No eloquence could have been so withering to one's belief in mankind as his final burst of sincerity. He struggled with himself, too. I saw it, – I heard it. I saw the inconceivable mystery of a soul that knew no restraint, no faith, and no fear, yet struggling blindly with itself.' (HOD, p. 145)

Note the final 'blindly'; if one wishes to struggle with oneself, as one has to in order to behave correctly, one must fight to gain as full a knowledge of one's own heart of darkness as is possible. This Marlow is able to do, but Kurtz is not. Observable here is an idea stressed in Conrad's 'An Outpost of Progress', that civilized society denies its members knowledge of themselves because of its creation of a sophisticated system of external restraints.

Kurtz is not identical to Carlier and Kayerts in 'An Outpost of Progress', but he nonetheless shares their ignorance of their inner selves and their lack of a 'deliberate belief'. Like them he has ideals – although theirs are contemptible and his are grandiose. But however grandiose, they offer him as little support in the wilderness as they are given by their own tawdry beliefs.

What is wrong with idealism, then, is its impracticality, its failure to engage with the reality of humanity, its belief in a mankind without the negative impulses and potentialities which a lack of external restraint will release. A more sombre view of humankind – including of oneself, Marlow suggests – will stand more chance of bringing good to the world than abstract principles or ideals which believe they can sup with the devil without using a very long spoon.

Conrad – and Marlow – returns to the deceptive lure of ideas in the later *Lord Jim*. Jim and Kurtz do not, on the face of it, appear to have that much in common, and yet both can be seen as individuals who have been unable to resist a crucial temptation because in some sense their will has been sapped by their intellect, by ideas, and by a failure to recognize and to accept their inner strengths and weaknesses. Indeed, it is perhaps their ideas and ideals which have prevented an honest appreciation of the strengths and weaknesses of their inner selves. The parallel may become clearer if one notes how the following comments of Marlow's about Jim could appropriately be applied to Kurtz.

> 'I don't mean military courage, or civil courage, or any special kind of courage. I mean just that inborn ability to look temptations in the face

– a readiness unintellectual enough, goodness knows, but without pose –
a power of resistance, don't you see, ungracious if you like, but priceless
– an unthinking and blessed stiffness before the outward and inward
terrors, before the might of nature, and the seductive corruption of men
– backed by a faith invulnerable to the strength of facts, to the contagion
of example, to the solicitation of ideas. Hang ideas! They are tramps,
vagabonds, knocking at the back-door of your mind, each taking a little
of your substance, each carrying away some crumb of that belief in a few
simple notions you must cling to if you want to live decently and would
like to die easily!' (LJ, p. 43)

The passage continues in much the same vein, going so far even as to
praise that 'good, stupid kind we like to feel marching right and left of us
in life, of the kind that is not disturbed by the vagaries of intelligence and
the perversions of – of nerves', of which Marlow finds Jim to be outwardly
typical. (Compare Marlow's comment on Kurtz's *Report* in *Heart of Darkness*: 'But this must have been before his – let us say – nerves, went
wrong' [HOD, p. 117].) Marlow's speech in *Lord Jim* may seem at times
to be almost a hymn to stupidity; certainly it shares Marlow's repeated
conviction in *Heart of Darkness* that it is not thanks to the *intellect* that one
is granted the strength to resist temptation. And indeed there is a
suspicion of the intellect in Conrad which recurrently tempts him to value
unimaginative stupidity over intelligence, perhaps most notably in *The
Nigger of the 'Narcissus'*. What is clear is that Conrad (and Marlow)
believed abstract ideas, 'ideas in general', an idealism cut off from the
world it pronounced upon, to be more dangerous than dulness or obtuse-
ness; it was left to E. M. Forster to explore the evils that unimaginative
and stupid obedience to duty could lead to in a colonial context. One sure
way to avoid the dangers of idealism, the pitfalls of intellectualism, of
course, is to be so stupid that one has hardly ideas or ideals at all, and
occasionally Conrad seems attracted to this solution. But it is not a
satisfactory or a satisfying solution, and Conrad always seems finally to
reject it, and to go on to consider ways in which the intellect can contribute to correct behaviour without leading us into temptation.

It is possible to see much of Conrad's oevre as an attempt to explore
ways of protecting the individual against the perils of self-consciousness,
against the inadequacies of the intellect. *Heart of Darkness* is, among other
things, a very important staging-post in this continuing concern of
Conrad's. The novella warns that any attempt to marry the intellect to the
needs of imperialism will result in an unequal match, one in which the
intellect will end up the subdued partner. Many of Conrad's works of
fiction stress that it is solidarity with other human beings that allows the
individual to escape from at least some of the limitations of his or her
isolated intellect. And because imperialism involves no such solidarity –

even between those Europeans who stand to benefit materially from it – it cannot present a context in which the intellect and its ideals can flourish.

1 Ian Watt, *Conrad in the Nineteenth Century*, London, Chatto, 1980, p. x.
2 Cedric Watts, *Conrad's 'Heart of Darkness': A Critical and Contextual Discussion*, Milan, Mursia International, 1977; Cedric Watts, *The Deceptive Text: An Introduction to Covert Plots*, Brighton, Harvester, 1984.
3 Suresh Raval, *The Art of Failure: Conrad's Fiction*, London, Allen & Unwin, 1986, pp. 29-30.
4 I adopt what has become the conventional distinction between 'plot' and 'story' here. 'Story' is the actual events narrated prior to and independent of this narration; 'plot' is these events as narrated. Watts's use of the term 'murder plot', of course, involves a quite different use of the word 'plot'.
5 Marlow's aunt actually knows 'the wife of a very high personage in the Administration, and also a man who has lots of influence with' (someone unstated); (p. 53). This chain of influence through wives is reminiscent of some of the complex chains of mediation in Conrad's *The Secret Agent*.
6 Watts, *Conrad's 'Heart of Darkness'*, p. 84.
7 There are interesting parallels between the two writers. See Peter L. Hays and Pamela Demory, '*Nostromo* and *The Great Gatsby*', *Études Anglaises* 4, 1988, pp. 405-17.
8 Watts, *Conrad's 'Heart of Darkness'*, p. 106.
9 Although his 'slight blush' suggests that his mistreatment of the native woman may extend to making use of her sexually.
10 Watts, *Conrad's 'Heart of Darkness'*, p. 152. See also my chapter on *Nostromo* in the present volume.
11 Cedric Watts examines the treatment of Kurtz's relationship to the African woman in terms of the Faust legend, which he sees as 'the most important "supernatural" covert plot' in *Heart of Darkness*. Kurtz's relationship with the African woman is thereby compared to Faustus' embracing of the image of Helen of Troy.
> Kurtz, like Faust, has been tempted to make a diabolic pact, sacrificing his soul for worldly gratification. If Faustus's fate was sealed when he embraced a devil who appeared in the guise of the seductive Helen, Kurtz has embraced the spirit of the wilderness in the form of his black mistress: the wilderness has 'loved him, embraced him, got into his veins, and sealed his soul to his own', and the black mistress is presented (in similarly inferior 'Conradese') as an incarnation of that wilderness .... (Cedric Watts, *The Deceptive Text: An Introduction to Covert Plots*, Brighton, Harvester, 1984, p. 79).

The reading is an interesting and convincing one in general terms, but is perhaps most strained with this particular comparison.

12 Marlow's comment that the African woman 'must have had the value of several elephant tusks upon her' can be taken a number of ways. Either it suggests that this woman, too, is corrupted by the love of wealth or (I think more likely) that in using the ivory to provide decoration and display, she represents a more vital and straightforward life than the Europeans.

13 An article which explores the links between the two women in some detail is Mahmoud K. Kharbutli, 'The Treatment of Women in *Heart of Darkness*', *Dutch Quarterly Review* 17(4), 1987, p. 242-3.

14 Peter Hyland, 'The Little Woman in the Heart of Darkness', *Conradiana* 20(1), 1988, p. 4.

15 And not all men, of course, but those men who needed an idealistic gloss on what they were doing out in the world: not black men, nor white working-class men.

16 Quoted from Conrad's manuscript in Joseph Conrad, *Heart of Darkness*, Norton Critical Edition, edited by Robert Kimbrough, third edition, New York, 1988, p. 49.

7
Nostromo: Adventurers and Fairy Tales

Something that no one willed

Nostromo is the third and final major work of Conrad's in which an analysis of imperialism is to be found, and the key advance in Conrad's understanding of imperialism is apparent in this novel's concern with the factors which *determine* the events depicted. Neither 'An Outpost of Progress' nor *Heart of Darkness* provided the reader with any theory as to what the dominant and determining motor force of history is. But *Nostromo* insists at length that it is not the consciousness of human beings which is primary in this movement, but other, non-human forces: 'material interests'. Thus a significant concern in *Nostromo* is with self-deception; the novel is full of characters who think that they are the masters of history but who are in fact its slaves and puppets.

Writing of *Nostromo* in his *An Introduction to the English Novel*, Arnold Kettle argues that the novel 'succeeds most wonderfully in capturing the truth of social movement', and he quotes a passage from a writer who he admits it is extremely improbable that Conrad ever read: Frederick Engels.

> History makes itself in such a way that the final result always arises from conflicts between many individual wills, of which each again has been made what it is by a host of particular conditions of life. Thus there are innumerable intersecting forces, an infinite series of parallelograms of forces which give rise to one resultant – the historical event. This again may itself be viewed as the product of a power which, taken as a whole, works *unconsciously* and without volition. For what each individual wills is obstructed by everyone else, and what emerges is something that no one willed.[1]

We get a comparable insight into the the forces behind the historical event early on in *Nostromo*, when Sir John talks to his chief engineer.

> This was not the first undertaking in which their gifts, as elementally different as fire and water, had worked in conjunction. From the contact of these two personalities, who had not the same vision of the world, there was generated a power for the world's service – a subtle force that

> could set in motion mighty machines, men's muscles, and awaken also in human breasts an unbounded devotion to the task. (*Nostromo*, p. 41)

It is the interaction between people of different vision that produces 'a power for the world's service', or for its subjection. But Sir John and his chief engineer get, we are led to assume, the results they want. In contrast, those characters in *Nostromo* who actually live in Costaguano get very little of what they want.

Applied to the political and historical events of *Nostromo* Engels's comment is strikingly appropriate, but if one takes it further it can be seen to apply, too, to what happens to each of the important characters in the work. In different ways, all of the major characters of the novel (with the arguable exception of Dr Monygham) end up not just in a different situation from what they had planned or expected, but as different persons from what they thought they were or had hoped to become. Decoud, the *boulevardier* and dilettante who enjoys mocking his native country's politics to Parisian acquaintances, ends up planning and helping to execute a key political coup. Nostromo, the man who wants only to be respected, to live a life of public adulation, ends up despising himself and his secret enslavement to the silver. In the case of the Goulds the end result is most markedly at variance with their earlier dreams and intentions.

And these are the characters who play a crucial rôle in the politics of Costaguana. It is the characters who are ineffective, cut off from political realities and influence – Captain Mitchell, Viola – who remain unchanged, retaining a secure and relatively unchallenged sense of themselves. Even when Captain Mitchell feels 'in the thick of things', we are told that it was, 'with a strange ignorance of the real forces at work around him' (p. 136). One should perhaps add that Viola has a past of active political involvement, which prefigures what we are to witness in *Nostromo*: the events which he helped to bring about in this past were not what he and his fellows wanted and fought for, and he too ended up a different person from what he presumably was at the start of his career as a Garibaldino. Viola's political career is as proleptic of the course of events in the novel as is the story of the lost gringos with which the novel opens.

Looked at from the perspective of the 1980s, the political events depicted in *Nostromo* seem utterly familiar and predictable. We regularly read bits of the novel in the morning newspaper: American and British investment in Latin America accompanied by political pressure and military threat (or action); civil war, and secession; poverty, oppression and cruelty; class-struggle and nationalist revolt. Nothing that happens in *Nostromo* nor the reasons for its happening, which Conrad's narrative techniques lay absolutely bare – surprises a modern reader. Yet everything that happens seems to surprise those who have made it happen, and that includes what happens to themselves.

Foremost among those who become that which they have not expected to become are, of course, Mr and Mrs Gould. Conrad almost seems to go out of his way to inform the reader early on in the novel how the Goulds see themselves and each other, and all of their assessments are rendered incorrect by the passage of time.

Conrad's adventurers

We read early on in the work, for instance, of Mrs Gould's great confidence in her husband.

> He had struck her imagination from the first by his unsentimentalism, by that very quietude of mind which she had erected in her thought for a sign of perfect competency in the business of living. (*Nostromo*, p. 50)

We have Gould's own word for it that this is more or less how he sees himself. He compares himself to Holroyd, the American capitalist.

> In comparison to the correctness of his [Gould's] aim, definite in space and absolutely attainable within a limited time, the other man appeared for an instant as a dreamy idealist of no importance. (*Nostromo*, p. 78)[2]

And he tells his wife:

> 'Any one can declaim about these things, but I pin my faith to material interests. Only let the material interests once get a firm footing, and they are bound to impose the conditions on which alone they can continue to exist. That's how your money-making is justified here in the face of lawlessness and disorder. It is justified because the security which it demands must be shared with an oppressed people. A better justice will come afterwards. That's your ray of hope.' (*Nostromo*, p. 84)

Gould is very clear, moreover, that he is no mere profiteer. He tells his wife that

> 'Uncle Harry was no adventurer. In Costaguana we Goulds are no adventurers.' (*Nostromo*, p. 64)

Charles Gould is then, according to himself and his wife at the start of the novel, unsentimental, one who pins his hopes on material interests rather than abstract ideals, not a sentimentalist, and not an adventurer. All of these assessments are explicitly and authoritatively controverted later on in the novel – sometimes by the Goulds themselves. Decoud repeats at great length to Mrs Gould his conviction that her husband is an idealist and a sentimentalist.

> A puzzled look came upon Mrs Gould's face, and Decoud, approaching, explained confidentially –
> 'Don't you see, he's such an idealist.' (*Nostromo*, p. 214)[3]

Mrs Gould flushes pink and responds 'wonderingly' to this comment, but when Decoud goes on to argue to her that Charles Gould has idealized 'the existence, the worth, the meaning of the San Tomé mine', there is an ironic response on the part of the authorial narrator which makes it clear that Decoud has hit the nail on the head:

> He must have known what he was talking about. Mrs Gould, ready to take fire, gave it up suddenly with a low little sound that resembled a moan. (*Nostromo*, p. 214)

Two pages later, Decoud tells Mrs Gould that he believes that her husband can be drawn into his plan, 'like all idealists, when he once sees a sentimental basis for his action'. In his letter to his sister, Decoud repeats these charges, repeatedly referring to Gould's idealism and sentimentality.

It is via the consciousness of Gould himself that his much earlier claim that neither he nor his family were adventurers is controverted.

> After all, with his English parentage and English upbringing, he perceived that he was an adventurer in Costaguana, the descendant of adventurers enlisted in a foreign legion, of men who had sought fortune in a revolutionary war, who had planned revolutions, who had believed in revolutions. For all the uprightness of his character, he had something of an adventurer's easy morality which takes count of personal risk in the ethical appraising of his action. (*Nostromo*, p. 365)

The word 'adventurer' is an important one for Conrad, and his use of it demonstrates quite clearly his awareness of the fact that Europeans who claimed that they were seeking adventure might actually be better described as adventurers – individuals seeking plunder. In his essay 'Geography and Some Explorers' Conrad notes of Tasman the explorer that 'there was a taint of an unscrupulous adventurer' in him (LE, p. 8). He adds,

> The voyages of the early explorers were prompted by an acquisitive spirit, the idea of lucre in some form, the desire of trade or the desire of loot, disguised in more or less fine words. But Cook's three voyages are free from any taint of that sort. (LE, p. 10)

The comment encapsulates a key political and moral insight of Conrad's, one which keeps him relatively free of the jingoism or imperial apologetics that so many writers contemporary to him suffered from. It is in *Heart of Darkness* that Conrad most directly confronts the habit of disguising the acquisitive spirit in 'more or less fine words', but this impulse also constitutes a significant element in *Nostromo*. Charles Gould's fine words seem very down-to-earth, without pretence: he puts his trust in material interests not in declamations. And yet he too is forced to recognize that he and his uncle Harry are, good intentions notwithstanding, correctly described as adventurers. In like manner Lingard in *The Rescue*, another white man convinced of the sound morality of his intervention in the affairs of 'native' people, is forced to accede to the accusation that he is an adventurer.

> 'I *am* an adventurer,' he burst out, 'and if I hadn't been an adventurer, I would have had to starve or work at home for such people as you.'
> *(The Rescue, p. 134)*

As I have already argued, however, Conrad's use of the word 'adventurer' in *The Rescue* is significantly different from that which we find in subsequent works. Conrad's more mature use of the word 'adventurer' displays a clear awareness of the fact that European men engaged in what seemed like boys' adventures could in fact be adventurers engaged in dubious activities in the service of imperialism. Admittedly, Conrad would not have used precisely these words to express this belief, but *Heart of Darkness*, *Lord Jim* and *Nostromo* all confirm his artistic perception of this truth. In Conrad's major fiction the semantics of the word 'adventurer' is complex. The word is used on numerous occasions in *The Rescue*, and yet more frequently in the earlier 'The Rescuer' manuscript. In both it is applied to many different characters. Almost without exception, the word 'adventurer' is used positively in *The Rescue*/'The Rescuer', and this is a measure of Conrad's failure to subject the romantic-escapist element in his artistic vision to any sustained discipline or scrutiny in this work. The following passage gives the flavour that the term consistently enjoys in 'The Rescuer', and also in the published *The Rescue*:

> She [Mrs Travers] found she understood him [Lingard]; she understood him as though she also had been an adventurer of the sea knowing no power on earth but that of his own impulses, free to pursue the wild shapes of dreams in sunshine or starlight.[4]

It is true that both in its manuscript and its much later, published form, *The Rescue* implies a critique of adventurers by the way it shows Lingard responding to the rival claims of race, friendship and sexuality. But this critique has not worked its way through into an analysis of the semantics of the word 'adventurer'. Whenever the romantic in Conrad dominates the realist in him, the negative elements in the semantics of 'adventurer' tend to be suppressed. In 'Karain', for example, Karain himself is described as 'an adventurer of the sea, an outcast, a ruler – and my very good friend' (TOU, p. 8).

In *Lord Jim* the word is seen to have two sides, the glamorous and romantic one familiar from *The Rescue*, and another, darker side involving robbery and oppression which is there only by indirect implication in *The Rescue*. Both Jim and Stein are associated with the word. We are told of Jim that

> He, on his side, had that faculty of beholding at a hint the face of his desire and the shape of his dream, without which the earth would know no lover and no adventurer. He captured much honour and an Arcadian happiness (I won't say anything about innocence) in the bush, and it was as good to him as the honour and the Arcadian happiness of the streets to another man. (*Lord Jim*, p. 175)

At this stage in the recounting of Jim's history, the word still has mainly positive connotations, as its association with the word 'lover' here indicates. And yet in retrospect we can see that Jim's 'desire' and his 'dream' are still in thrall to 'the sea-life of light literature' that has infected him as a boy. It is for this reason that he appeals to Stein (referred to by Marlow as an adventurer on page 203 of the novel). Stein too mixes a dangerous search for plunder with romantic idealism. Conrad is more uncompromising in *The Mirror of the Sea*, when he describes the East Wind as a 'subtle and cruel adventurer without a notion of honour or fair play' (p. 94). And in *The Mirror of the Sea* the idealized Dominic Cervoni

> takes his place in my memory by the side of the legendary wanderer on the sea of marvels and terrors, by the side of the fatal and impious adventurer, to whom the evoked shade of the soothsayer predicted a journey inland with an oar on his shoulder, till he met men who had never set eyes on ships and oars. (MOS, p. 183)

At the level of his mature creative insight Conrad saw clearly that there were two sides to the term 'adventurer'. There was the glamorous side – the romantic life pictured in adventure stories for boys. And there was the dark underside of cruelty and plunder. Within this complex semantics we are again made witness to the marriage of idealism with imperialism, the marriage in which in the long run idealism is revealed to be the deceived partner. In his essay 'Well Done' Conrad attempts to explain what he believes to be the distinction between a mere adventurer and a worker in adventurous conditions:

> The mere love of adventure is no saving grace. It is no grace at all. It lays a man under no obligation of faithfulness to an idea and even to his own self. Roughly speaking, an adventurer may be expected to have courage, or at any rate may be said to need it. But courage in itself is not an ideal. (NLL, p. 189)

> There is nothing more futile under the sun than a mere adventurer.
>
> ....
>
> The successive generations that went out to sea from these Isles went out to toil desperately in adventurous conditions. A man is a worker. If he is not that he is nothing. Just nothing – like a mere adventurer. (NLL, p. 190)

These comments do attempt to deconstruct the complex significance that the term 'adventurer' had in Conrad's time, and that there is a darker side is clearly recognized. But problems remain. Charles Gould is, after all, a worker, a man who toils desperately in adventurous conditions. But he is, nevertheless, an adventurer – by his own admission. Moreover, he has convinced himself that his development of the San Tomé mine has been for the best of moral reasons. Even so, he is later forced to admit that he is nonetheless an adventurer, one who has, like Lingard, decided that it is better to intervene in the lives of 'natives' than to live a life of poverty at home.[5]

So far as *Nostromo* is concerned, Charles Gould's realization that he himself is an adventurer has to be set in the context of the earlier appearance of this term in the novel. On its second page we are told of the tradition that many adventurers of olden time had perished in the search for gold, and the 'gringos' who disappear in this search are referred to as the 'impious adventurers' (p. 5). Decoud, talking to Antonia, remarks:

> 'No, but just imagine our forefathers in morions and corselets drawn up outside this gate, and a band of adventurers just landed from their ships in the harbour there. Thieves, of course. Speculators, too. Their expeditions, each one, were the speculations of grave and reverend persons in England. That is history, as that absurd sailor Mitchell is always saying.' (*Nostromo*, p. 174)[6]

'That absurd sailor Mitchell', ironically but appropriately enough, becomes himself one of those grave and reverend persons in England in due course; retiring there with his fortune invested in the San Tomé mine.

A further irony is that Decoud too becomes an adventurer. Of him and Nostromo, alone in the lighter after the collision, we are told:

> There was no bond of conviction, of common idea; they were merely two adventurers pursuing each his own adventure, involved in the same imminence of deadly peril. (*Nostromo*, p. 295)

What is lacking in the outlook of the adventurer is any commitment to a wider moral purpose, any fellow-feeling with another human being. The acquisitive individualism of the adventurer may have fuelled many romantic dreams, but this point in his career Conrad can clearly see its anti-human implications. By this point in *Nostromo*, then, Conrad's critique of the word 'adventurer' serves as additional support to the larger argument that there is a fundamental incompatibility between material interests pursued by self-seeking individuals, and common human needs.

Referring earlier to Suresh Raval's comments about 'the symbiosis of trade and idealism', I concluded that *Heart of Darkness* demonstrated the impossibility of such a symbiosis. If we compare Conrad's comments on adventure and adventurers in the essay 'Well Done' with his exploration of this issue in *Heart of Darkness* and *Nostromo* we find, I think, that the symbiosis of trade and idealism which is viewed as a possibility in the essay is revealed as an illusion in the two novels. Indeed, in the essay this possibility is linked to what can justifiably be termed the encouragement of wilful blindness.

> For the great mass of mankind the only saving grace that is needed is steady fidelity to what is nearest to hand and heart in the short moment of each human effort. In other and in greater words, what is needed is a sense of immediate duty, and a feeling of impalpable constraint.
> (NLL, pp. 190-1)[7]

The injunction is presented in positive terms: steady fidelity to what is nearest to hand and a sense of immediate duty. But it clearly carries a related negative implication: *no* fidelity to what is a long way away; *no* sense of any complex or highly mediated duty. It seems entirely appropriate that such sentiments should lead Conrad into a reference to *The Nigger of the 'Narcissus'* a few pages later on in his essay. It is in this earlier work that 'the great mass of mankind', represented by the ordinary seamen, is seen as fit for nothing higher than 'steady fidelity to what is nearest to hand and heart in the short moment of each human effort'. It is a mark of the superiority of later works such as *Heart of Darkness* and *Nostromo* to *The Nigger of the 'Narcissus'* that the above sentiments seem inadequate to them. Indeed, in *Nostromo* it is Nostromo's restriction to a steady fidelity to what is nearest to hand and heart in the short moment of each human effort that prevents him from seeing that he is betraying himself.

Mrs Gould is just as good an example as her husband of a person who changes into the opposite of her youthful self. Her initial idealism and sentimentality are pointed out early on in the novel. We are told with reference to her first visitors from abroad in Sulaco that

> Perhaps had they known how much she was inspired by an idealistic view of success they would have been amazed at the state of her mind as the Spanish-American ladies had been amazed at the tireless activity of her body. She would – in her own words – have been for them 'something of a monster.' (*Nostromo*, p. 67)

A little later we are informed that

> even the most legitimate touch of materialism was wanting in Mrs Gould's character. The dead man of whom she thought with tenderness (because he was Charley's father) and with some impatience (because he had been weak), must be put completely in the wrong. Nothing else would do to keep their prosperity without a stain on its only real, on its immaterial side! (*Nostromo*, p. 75)

Prosperity is stained by being desired for itself, just as Conrad wrote of Tasman that there was the taint of the unscrupulous adventurer about him. But Mrs Gould's rejection of the materialist ambitions of her husband's father is self-deceiving, for she fails to realize the extent to which the whole Gould project is still enslaved to material interests. It should be stressed that Mrs Gould's idealism is an important, perhaps even a *necessary*, contributory factor so far as her husband's adventurism is concerned. Her support is indispensable to Charles Gould in his struggle for the mine, however egocentrically he interprets and rewards this support. The situation is not new in Conrad's work; I suggested that a similar case could be made with regard to the contribution the idealism of the Intended makes to the service Kurtz renders imperialism. In both examples a woman's idealism allows a man to become a ruthless servant of imperialism – an adventurer – while pretending to himself and others that he is inspired by selfless and disinterested ideals.

Mrs Gould changes in a direction contrary to the change she experiences in her husband. Decoud, writing to his sister, says of her that 'She may have been sentimental once' (p. 239). By implication, she is not any longer. By this time she has begun to recognize the contribution her sentimentality has made to her husband's enslavement by the mine. The woman to whom Gould proposes is a sentimentalist and an idealist. Much later, we are told

> With a prophetic vision she saw herself surviving alone the degradation
> of her young ideal of life, of love, of work – all alone in the Treasure
> House of the World. The profound, blind, suffering expression of a pain-
> ful dream settled on her face with its closed eyes. In the indistinct voice
> of an unlucky sleeper, lying passive in the grip of a merciless nightmare,
> she stammered out aimlessly the words –
> 'Material interests.' (*Nostromo*, p. 522)

Mrs Gould perceives, as if in a dream, the truth. But she is still 'lying
passive'; her idealism has unfitted her for active struggle against material
interests, just as much as it has facilitated her husband's enslavement to
them.

Fairies and fairy tales

In my previous book on Conrad I suggested that it was a substantial insight of Conrad's to perceive how important to imperialism was the
masking of the acquisitive spirit by fine words. Charles Gould feels pity for
the parliamentarians who put their trust in words, 'while murder and
rapine stalked over the land' (p. 368). But he too conceals unpleasant
facts from himself by means of pretty fictions. Decoud tells Mrs Gould that
her husband

> cannot act or exist without idealizing every simple feeling, desire, or
> achievement. He could not believe his own motives if he did not make
> them first a part of some fairy tale. The earth is not quite good enough
> for him, I fear. (*Nostromo*, pp. 214-15)

He repeats the point a short time afterwards; 'Life for me is not a moral
romance derived from the tradition of a pretty fairy tale. No, Mrs Gould;
I am practical. I am not afraid of my motives' (p. 218).

David Leon Higdon and David Rude have recently discovered that
Conrad either wrote or translated a fairy tale himself some time near the
beginning of his writing career. 'The Princess and the Page' is an
unexceptional work described on its title page as 'A True Fairy Tale for
Grown-up Princesses' and telling a sad little story about a page who
sacrifices himself so that a spoiled and ungrateful Princess may live.
Higdon and Rude point out that 'during the late 1880s and 1890s the
British reading public witnessed an unexpected interest in and publication
of numerous *Kunstmärchen* or art fairy tales'[8], and they remark further:

> Assuming that none of the characteristics of the tale were invented by
> Conrad, he may well have been attracted by the irony of the narrative
> voice, so distant from and yet so disapproving of the Princess, or he might
> have been intrigued by the situational ironic contrasts between the

plentiful fields and orchards and the starvation of the Princess, the idealized selfless love of the Page and the egotistical mind of the Princess, or the final contrast between the Page's selfless sacrifice and the Princess's contempt for the food with which his death provided her.[9]

They add that it is 'easy to forget at times that Conrad's women are every bit as destructive as Thomas Hardy's and D. H. Lawrence's'.[10] But the situation in this fairy story is in some ways like a reversal of that which we find in *Nostromo*. Instead of a man's selfless sacrifice we have that of Mrs Gould; instead of a woman's egotistical mind we have the enormous if unrecognized egotism of Charles Gould.

Conrad makes some relatively dismissive comments concerning the fairy tale in his essay on John Galsworthy.

> For the fairy tale, be it not ungratefully said, has walked the earth in many unchallenged disguises, and lingers amongst us to this day wearing, sometimes, amazingly heavy clothes.
>
> ....
>
> But the secret of the long life of the fairy tale consists mainly in this, I suspect; that it is amusing to the writer thereof.
>
> ....
>
> The pride of fanciful invention; the pride of that invention that soars (on goose's wings) into the empty blue is like the intoxication of an elixir sent by the gods above. And whether it is that the gods are unduly generous, or simply because the sight of human folly amuses their idle malice, that sort of felicity is easier attained pen in hand than the sober pride, always mingled with misgivings, of a single-minded observer and conscientious interpreter of reality. This is why the fairy tale, in its various disguises of optimism, pessimism, romanticism, naturalism and what not, will always be with us. And, indeed, that is very comprehensible; the seduction of irresponsible freedom is very great; and to be tied to the earth (even as the hewers of wood and drawers of water are tied to the earth) in the exercise of one's imagination, by every scruple of conscience and honour, may be considered a lot hard enough not to be lightly embraced. (LE, p. 126)[11]

It is as if Conrad is attracted by certain symbolic patterns and archetypal situations to be found in the fairy tale, at the same time as he rejects the escapist element inherent in the genre and, indeed, uses mention of the fairy tale as an indication of a selfish flight from reality. What is clear from this essay is that Conrad believed that the writer was faced with the same clear alternatives as was any human being considering his or her relationship to the world: either to surrender to 'the pride of fanciful invention', or to become 'a single-minded observer and conscientious interpreter of reality'. In different ways, both Mr and Mrs Gould have succumbed to the attractions of the former alternative, although Mrs Gould grows to realize and to regret this fact. She realizes, indeed, that she has been a character in her husband's fairy stories.

> Small and dainty, as if radiating a light of her own in the deep shade of the interlaced boughs, she resembled a good fairy, weary with a long career of well-doing, touched by the withering suspicion of the uselessness of her labours, the powerlessness of her magic. (*Nostromo*, p. 520)

Much earlier in the novel, Mrs Gould had been referred to as resembling 'a fairy, posed lightly before dainty philtres dispensed out of vessels of silver and porcelain' (p. 52). Her illusions, as much as those of her husband for which she has provided support, have their origin in silver.

Gould thinks himself a realist, as far away from believing in fairy tales as can be imagined. And yet this is not the way Decoud sees him. In the quotation I have already given in which Decoud tells Mrs Gould that 'Life is not for me a moral romance derived from the tradition of a pretty fairy tale' (p. 218), Decoud is referring obliquely to Charles Gould. The chief engineer, too, sees the fairy-tale aspect of life in Costaguana. Talking to Dr Monygham of the plan to hide the silver, he says:

> It sounds like a comic fairy tale – and behold, it may come off; because it is true to the very spirit of the country. (*Nostromo*, p. 315)

Even the 'privileged passenger' introduced towards the end of the novel, listening to Mitchell's pompous record of the birth of the new republic, listens 'like a tired child to a fairy tale' (p. 487). The cumulative effect of all these references is to convince us that the Europeans in Sulaco are living an unreal life in a world whose real contours they cannot see. Just as Lord Jim fails to make proper contact with the real world because of his youthful infatuation with light holiday literature, so Charles Gould is cut off from an insight into what he is actually doing by the magic of the fairy tales to which he is mentally in thrall. As I have pointed out before,[12] Decoud perceives that fairy tales somehow help Gould to act effectively in this world, but 'effectively' only in a limited sense. They enable him to become a very efficient servant of imperialism, but they do not help him to understand or serve his or his wife's human needs. There is a parallel here with the way in which the unreal ideals of such as the Intended are actually seen to contribute to the plunder in Africa in *Heart of Darkness*.

Like any good fairy story, *Nostromo* involves wealth and power; the Goulds end up in the treasure house of the world. But they do not live happily ever after. The roots of their unhappiness can be traced back to the start of the novel, to before their marriage.

Charles Gould (the Gould family, established in Costaguana for three generations, always went to England for their education and for their wives) imagined that he had fallen in love with a girl's sound common sense like any other man, but these were not exactly the reasons why, for instance, the whole surveying camp, from the youngest of the young men to their mature chief, should have found occasion to allude to Mrs Gould's house so frequently amongst the high peaks of the Sierra.

(*Nostromo*, p. 46)

From the beginning Charles Gould is cut off from the reality of his wife by his imagination. Just as his father's mind is overpowered in a particular way as a result of his being well-read in light literature (the echo of *Lord Jim* is striking), so his is corrupted by fairy tales. The passage quoted above is ambiguous as to whether Gould really had fallen in love, and imagined that it was with his wife-to-be's sound common sense, or whether he merely imagined that he had fallen in love. But what is clear is that Charles Gould is as misinformed about his wife-to-be's 'common sense' as she is about his unsentimentalism. What is more, the ironic parenthetic comment about the Goulds always going to England for their education and their wives suggests that Gould is far more in the grip of the conventions of his expatriate culture than he is aware, that his choice of wife is far less a choice of a specific individual than he believes.

From this point on, we are regularly reminded that Charles Gould is so wrapped up in his own visions, so egocentrically concerned with his fairy tales, that he never succeeds in making any real contact with his wife at all.

Charles Gould did not open his heart to her in any set speeches. He simply went on acting and thinking in her sight. This is the true method of sincerity. (*Nostromo*, p. 60; the final sentence is, surely, deeply ironic.)

But now he was actually not looking at her at all; and his expression was tense and irrational, as is natural in a man who elects to stare at nothing past a young girl's head. (*Nostromo*, p. 63)

Mrs Gould heroically concealed her dismay at the appearance of men and events so remote from her racial conventions, dismay too deep to be uttered in words even to her husband. She understood his voiceless reserve better now. Their confidential intercourse fell, not in moments of privacy, but precisely in public, when the quick meeting of their glances would comment upon some fresh turn of events. She had gone to his school of uncompromising silence, the only one possible, since so much that seemed shocking, weird, and grotesque in the working out of their purposes had to be accepted as normal in this country. (*Nostromo*, p. 165)

'One could close one's eyes to the glare,' said Mrs Gould. 'But, my dear Charley, it is impossible for me to close my eyes to our position; to this awful . . .'

She raised her eyes and looked at her husband's face, from which all sign of sympathy or any other feeling had disappeared. 'Why don't you tell me something?' she almost wailed.

'I thought you had understood me perfectly from the first,' Charles Gould said, slowly. 'I thought we had said all there was to say a long time ago. There is nothing to say now. There were things to be done. We have done them; we have gone on doing them. There is no going back now. I don't suppose that, even from the first, there was really any possible way back. And, what's more, we can't even afford to stand still.'

'Ah, if one only knew how far you mean to go,' said his wife, inwardly trembling, but in an almost playful tone.

'Any distance, any length, of course,' was the answer, in a matter-of-fact tone, which caused Mrs Gould to make another attempt to repress a shudder. (*Nostromo*, pp. 207-8)

The seemingly Jamesian indirection of this last exchange is perhaps misleading. James's characters talk in this way because there are things they wish to know which cannot be mentioned openly. But so far as Charles Gould is concerned there really *is* nothing to say now; because he has attached himself to the development and protection of 'material interests' there is no longer any need for human intercourse; as Dr Monygham tells Mrs Gould at the end of the novel,

'No!' interrupted the doctor. 'There is no peace and no rest in the development of material interests. They have their law, and their justice. But it is founded on expediency, and is inhuman; it is without rectitude, without the continuity and the force that can be found only in a moral principle. Mrs Gould, the time approaches when all that the Gould Concession stands for shall weigh as heavily upon the people as the barbarism, cruelty, and misrule of a few years back.' (*Nostromo*, p. 511)

It is because the development of material interests is *inhuman* that Charles Gould no longer has anything to say to his wife, for the assessment of the human implications of what he does is irrelevant to this development. His humanity is given expression only in fairy tales preserved by that good fairy his wife – just as the Intended preserves Kurtz's ideals for him in *Heart of Darkness*, preserves them safely far away from anywhere where they might actually threaten to have some effect on events.

It is clear from many passages in *Nostromo* that Charles Gould's passion for his wife has been transferred to the mine. Mrs Gould is one of a number of women in Conrad's fiction whose idealism contributes indirectly to the destruction of their relationship with the man they love.

The Intended, Jewel and Mrs Gould contribute an essential support to the commitment that Kurtz, Jim, and Charles Gould maintain in their service of imperialism. This support is inspired by an idealistic vision of what that service can entail, but this idealistic vision is crushed by the unrecognized logic of the service. *Nostromo* is thus the last and most self-conscious of those works of Conrad which investigate the tragic marriage of idealism and imperialism. It is the most self-conscious because the service that idealism renders to imperialism, and the destruction that it receives in return, are unambiguously and overtly exposed in this work.

At the start of this chapter I argued that *Nostromo* provides us with a theory of the motor force of history, that in its concern with the power of material interests it attempts a *causal* explanation of imperialism which goes beyond anything we can see in 'An Outpost of Progress' or *Heart of Darkness*. But Dr Monygham's above-quoted comments remind us that although there are elements of a deterministic theory of history in *Nostromo*, the novel also offers the reader a non-determinist alternative: that of a moral principle. The final conclusion of this novel is surely that however powerful material interests may be, the tragedy is for human beings to believe that such interests alone will bring about human betterment, for human betterment will come only from active struggle in pursuit of a moral principle.

---

1   Arnold Kettle, *An Introduction to the English Novel*, vol. 2, London, Hutchinson, repr. 1962, p. 77. Engels's comment comes in a letter to J. Bloch, 21 September, 1890.

2   Writing to his sister, later on, Decoud refers to Holroyd as an 'utter sentimentalist' (p. 240).

3   In his letter to his sister, Decoud refers to Gould's passion for the mine, which has crept into 'his cold and idealistic life', and also to Gould's 'sentimental unfaithfulness', which surrenders his wife's happiness and life to the seduction of an idea. There seems little doubt but that these sentiments have authorial support.

4   'The Rescuer', manuscript of *The Rescue*, The British Library, Ashley manuscript 4787, p. 539. Earlier on in 'The Rescuer' Shaw tells Lingard that the worst name he had ever heard people call the captain was 'adventurer' (p. 40). It is clear that Shaw does not consider this a very bad name, and this chimes in with the dominant attitude towards the term in the rest of the manuscript. It is a measure of Conrad's maturing as an artist that the picture is quite different in *Nostromo*.

5   Given Conrad's attitude towards adventurers, it is somewhat inappropriate for Robert LaBrasca to refer to him in this manner: 'He was an adventurer who had spent 20 years at sea before immersing himself in the

literary profession'. (Robert LaBrasca, 'Two Visions of "The Horror"', reprinted in the third edition of the Norton Critical Edition of *Heart of Darkness*, ed. Robert Kimbrough, London 1988, p. 289). Perhaps, though, Conrad might have allowed that his early days gun-running for Spanish Carlist rebels justified use of the description.

6   I comment upon the double meaning of the word 'speculation' here in my previous book on Conrad.

7   Compare my comments in the previous chapter concerning the passage in *Lord Jim* in which Marlow seems to be recommending stupidity as a refuge from the snares of the intellect.

8   '"The Princess and the Page": An Unpublished Conrad Manuscript', *Nineteenth-Century Literature* 43(2), September 1988, p. 240.

9   Higdon and Rude, p. 242.

10 Higdon and Rude, p. 242.

11 There is a relevant running discussion of fairy tales in 'Prince Roman' which should perhaps be noted. Starting from the comment that the notion 'we children' had of princes 'was mainly literary, and had a glamour reflected from the light of fairy tales', the tale's narrator proceeds to contrast the actual life of Prince Roman with the expectations aroused by such fairy-tale associations. One comment deserves quotation. Having mentioned that in fairy tales princes always appear young, charming, heroic and fortunate, the narrator continues: 'Yet, as well as any other children, we could draw a firm line between the real and the ideal' (TOH, p. 33). It is his lack of this childish ability that makes fairy tales so destructive to Charles Gould.

12 See *Joseph Conrad: Language and Fictional Self-Consciousness*, pp. 60-5.

III
The Uses of the Imagination

8
Typhoon

In the three chapters following I shall look in turn at three of Conrad's fictional works which, although very different, are all concerned with the moral implications of interpretation. In *Typhoon, Under Western Eyes*, and 'The Tale' central characters are faced with the problem of making sense of the world from limited information, of constructing a picture of some sort of totality from isolated clues. Thus in different ways all of these works explore the functioning and the limits of human imagination. And because all of the characters concerned are isolated in different ways and have no direct access to the reality they need to understand if they are to act correctly, each of these works is concerned with the question raised by Ian Watt: alienation, of course, but how do we get out of it?

In *Typhoon* the problem of interpretation occurs at different levels: MacWhirr has to make sense of the omens of bad weather that are presented to him, those many characters who receive written letters have to interpret these, and the reader is encouraged to set his or her own interpretative experiences in reading the work against the imaginative procedures depicted in the work. Once again, then, the functioning of narrative has a moral thrust: it enacts processes which model larger interpretative activities necessary for human survival in the extra-literary world.

The people who live in Razumov's world in *Under Western Eyes* exist for him a jumble of disconnected parts. Like MacWhirr, he too has to 'read' these parts and construct some sort of an imaginative whole from the clues that he has. And, as in *Typhoon*, this process of interpretation is mirrored at different narrative levels. *Under Western Eyes* is full of 'readings', of people, events, writings. And these acts of interpretation interact with and mirror both Razumov's attempts to interpret isolated clues and also the reader's attempts to make sense of the novel as a whole.

In one sense all novels are detective stories. On the basis of clues, of bits of information, readers have to imagine whole worlds. Descriptions of characters and events in a novel are like those mansions constructed for Hollywood films which consist of imposing façades with nothing behind them. Like the cinema audience we have, in the act of reading, to construct an imaginative whole from partial evidence. The problems of *reading*, then, parallel the problems met with by MacWhirr, Razumov and the Captain of 'The Tale', such that in all three of the works I have mentioned reading has a moral dimension.

Stephen K. Land has argued, persuasively, that *Typhoon* can be illuminated by seeing it in relation to *Lord Jim*, claiming that the shorter work stands to the longer in the relation of 'an exercise in thematic inversion'.[1] He points out that whereas *Lord Jim* (the completion of which work preceded Conrad's writing of *Typhoon* by a matter of just over a month) deals with an imaginative and romantic hero who is destroyed by an ultimately unbridgeable gap between the realm of his aspirations and that of implacable facts, *Typhoon* 'is a study of a hero who thinks and operates on a purely factual level'.[2] Land's case is a strong one, and *Typhoon* in its early pages certainly gives the impression of being a work written to explore a particular formula.

> Having just enough imagination to carry him through each successive day, and no more, he was tranquilly sure of himself; and from the very same cause he was not in the least conceited. It is your imaginative superior who is touchy, overbearing, and difficult to please; but every ship Captain MacWhirr commanded was the floating abode of harmony and peace. It was, in truth, as impossible for him to take a flight of fancy as it would be for a watchmaker to put together a chronometer with nothing except a two-pound hammer and a whip-saw in the way of tools. Yet the uninteresting lives of men so entirely given to the actuality of the bare existence have their mysterious side. (*Typhoon*, p. 4)

If the opening sentences of this passage seem to suggest that Conrad is more interested in exploring a thesis than creating a complex character, the final quoted sentence indicates that perhaps something more than this can be expected. We should note that it is MacWhirr's *life* rather than his consciousness which we are told may be more complex and obscure than might be expected: one of the lessons suggested by *Typhoon* is that the process of active living, of grappling with problems along with one's fellows, may be creative of mental profundity in even the most unimaginative. Land's suggestion that *Typhoon* can be seen as a sort of mirror-reflection of *Lord Jim* can, therefore, be taken further. Whereas *Lord Jim* presents us with a hero whose imagination cuts him off from effective action in the world of everyday reality, *Typhoon* gives us one whose lack of imagination does not render him immune to the educative powers of experience, especially when this experience is of an extreme kind.

Land also suggests that Mr Jukes, the chief mate, 'is a paler version of Jim, a young, relatively inexperienced, but highly promising officer endowed with a hyperactive imagination'.[3] We are reminded that Jim was also a chief mate.

The opening pages of *Typhoon*, then, present us with a pair of rather schematically drawn characters, characters seemingly created to explore a thesis rather than to present human life in its full complexity and contradictoriness. And yet from this rather simplistic opening the work moves to a far more complex and rich exploration of a range of recognizable Conradian issues: the functioning of the imagination; the educative power of experience; human solidarity and human isolation; work as an escape from isolation and as a route to the discovery of the truth about oneself, others and the world; and an attempt to isolate those factors which enable (or prevent) effective human communication.

Part of the artificiality involved in the creation of a character totally lacking in imagination is avoided, or disguised, by portraying Captain Mac-Whirr as an eccentric who is perceived as such by his fellow officers. This is one of Conrad's works in which humour plays an important part both in establishing a particular tone, and also in making the main characters appear more human and more complex.[4] Jukes's performance with Mac-Whirr's umbrella (observed by the amused Rout), and his conversation with the captain concerning the ship's flag, help to build up a more believable and seemingly realistic social environment in the work.

One of the issues explored in *Typhoon* can be termed the imagination–communication–knowledge dialectic. To what extent is imagination a necessary prelude to and constituent of our knowledge of the world and of successful communication in it? So far as written communication is concerned, the answer to this question given in the work would appear to be, 'To a very large extent'. There are many letters written in *Typhoon*, so many that one cannot help wondering whether Conrad was consciously or unconsciously influenced by the epistolary novel in his writing of the work. *Typhoon* bears some particularly strong resemblances to Tobias Smollett's novel *Humphry Clinker*; the parallels between MacWhirr and Matt Bramble, and Jukes and Jerry Melford, are particularly noticeable. The characters who we meet in *Typhoon* are fervent letter-writers, and their activities allow Conrad's work to benefit from some of the traditional advantages of the epistolary novel: a range of varied perspectives on the same set of experiences, and the revealing of personality and inner truths through characters' own words. (It is true that we are told that the second mate never writes any letters, and does not seem to hope for news from anywhere [p. 28], but even here the non-writing of letters is given an implied significance: we assume that the second mate has degenerated into total selfishness and moral isolation.)

Unlike Smollett, Conrad is extremely interested in how these letters are read by their recipients, in whether or not correspondents manage successfully to communicate with one another. How written words are read was a subject of continued interest to Conrad, and his letters and essays are full of references to his concern with the reader of his fiction. In his Author's Note to *Typhoon and other Stories,* the volume in which *Typhoon* was collected, he noted that 'in everything I have written there is always one invariable intention, and that is to capture the reader's attention, by securing his interest and enlisting his sympathies for the matter in hand, whatever it may be'. Writers in *Typhoon* have very varying degrees of success in securing such interest on the part of their respective readers.

MacWhirr's letters elicit different levels of response and of understanding depending upon to whom they are addressed. His letters to his two parents are read carefully enough for them both to become acquainted with 'a good many names of ships, and with the names of the skippers who commanded them' (p. 5). But MacWhirr is apparently not fully in tune with his readers even in this instance, as it is made clear that his letters do not give the sort of information his parents would like to have.

> [His first letter home] was short, and contained the statement: 'We had very fine weather on our passage out.' But evidently, in the writer's mind, the only important intelligence was to the effect that his captain had, on the very day of writing, entered him regularly on the ship's articles as Ordinary Seaman. 'Because I can do the work,' he explained. The mother again wept copiously, while the remark, 'Tom's an ass,' expressed the emotions of the father. (*Typhoon,* p. 5)

It is palpable that MacWhirr does not have the imagination to put himself in his parents' position, and because of this he cannot imagine what sort of information they would like to receive from him.

In his correspondence with his wife, MacWhirr's lack of imagination is yet more crippling, compounded as it seems to be by a comparable want of the same faculty in her. The letter MacWhirr writes to her after the experience of the typhoon contains passages of 'absorbing interest' for his steward, so much so that he is twice nearly caught in the act of reading them. But MacWhirr's wife does not read with interest.

> She reclined in a plush-bottomed and gilt hammock-chair near a tiled fireplace, with Japanese fans on the mantel and a glow of coals in the grate. Lifting her hands, she glanced wearily here and there into the many pages. It was not her fault they were so prosy, so completely uninteresting – from 'My darling wife' at the beginning, to 'Your loving husband' at the end. She couldn't be really expected to understand all these ship affairs. (*Typhoon,* p. 93)

The last quoted sentence is unambiguously represented thought; the word 'these' makes this apparent. And the content of the penultimate sentence suggests that it also represents Mrs MacWhirr's opinion. The passage as a whole implies very strongly that the triviality of MacWhirr's wife makes her unfitted to read her husband's letters. There is no doubt that the description of her living room is replete with scorn; its furnishings and décor suggesting appallingly conventional petty-bourgeois taste and triviality of mind. Ironically, she is for once reading a letter worth reading, one written by a sadder and wiser MacWhirr. But his correspondent lacks the imagination with which his words must be read if they are to be properly understood.

In direct contrast to MacWhirr, Solomon Rout is presented as a letter-writer with imagination. With imagination comes communication.

> Mr Rout wrote likewise letters; only no one on board knew how chatty he could be pen in hand, because the chief engineer had enough imagination to keep his desk locked. His wife relished his style greatly.
> (*Typhoon*, p. 15)

And not just imagination, but also humour. Rout it is who smiles at Jukes's antics with MacWhirr's umbrella, and Mrs Rout laughs 'immoderately' when the visiting curate misunderstands her reference to 'Solomon'. Conrad is not noted for his humour, but *Typhoon* in particular has a number of wonderful little humorous touches, and the work as a whole leads the reader to associate a sense of humour with imagination and human sympathy.

In between MacWhirr and Rout as correspondents is Jukes, in many ways a more complex character.

> Mr Jukes, unable to generalize, unmarried, and unengaged, was in the habit of opening his heart after another fashion to an old chum and former shipmate, actually serving as second officer on board an Atlantic liner. (*Typhoon*, p. 16)

'Unable to generalize' strikes, I think, a somewhat unexpected note. What does this tell us about Jukes? Perhaps that he lives too much in particulars, that he has not learned to extract general lessons from his experience, that he responds to new experiences in isolation, rather than attempting to relate them to other aspects of his knowledge. 'Unmarried and unengaged' is perhaps also something of a surprise to the reader. Why should this information be considered relevant? I think that it has to be seen in the light of Jukes's discovery of the importance of human solidarity in the course of the typhoon, a discovery the implications of which (from the evidence of his final letter in the work) seem only imperfectly to have worked their way into his consciousness. The picture we get of Jukes is of a gregarious but nonetheless rather isolated man living too much in a world of his imagining, a world idealized to the point of falsification.

This impression is confirmed in part by seeing how Jukes's correspondence is received by its addressee. Whereas Solomon Rout's letters are relished by Mrs Rout, and MacWhirr's are ignored by his wife, Jukes's, although enjoyed by his friend, are seen to give a totally false picture of what has actually happened during the typhoon.

> But Mr Jukes' account was really animated and very full. His friend in the Western Ocean trade imparted it freely to the other officers of his liner. 'A chap I know writes to me about an extraordinary affair that happened on board his ship in that typhoon – you know – that we read of in the papers two months ago. It's the funniest thing! Just see for yourself what he says. I'll show you his letter.'
>
> There were phrases in it calculated to give the impression of light-hearted, indomitable resolution. Jukes had written them in good faith, for he felt thus when he wrote. (*Typhoon*, p. 97)

'Calculated' is revealing; Jukes aims at producing an effect upon his reader, not dishonestly, but one which is nonetheless misleading. It is misleading because Jukes lacks knowledge of himself and is unable to remember exactly how he felt during the typhoon; his Jim-like imagination has veneered over the reality of that experience with a romantic fiction, a fiction which in all good faith he proceeds to convey to his chum in the Western Ocean trade. This propensity should not come as too much of a surprise to the reader, for it has been hinted at in earlier descriptions of Jukes.

> First of all he would insist upon the advantages of the Eastern trade, hinting at its superiority to the Western ocean service. He extolled the sky, the seas, the ships, and the easy life of the Far East.
>
> (*Typhoon*, pp. 16-17)

To extol an easy life – especially of the Far East – is always a danger sign in Conrad's fiction, and Jukes bears no small resemblance to Jim at this point. Moreover, what he says is proved plainly to be untrue: the seas of the Eastern trade turn out to be far more dangerous than Mr Jukes has realized possible, and on the voyage in question his life is as far from easy as is imaginable. Such failures of insight on Jukes's part lead the reader to treat his ensuing account of MacWhirr with some circumspection. And after this account is finished, an authorial narrative comment reinforces the reader's sense that Jukes's view of MacWhirr is not necessarily to be relied upon.

Thus wrote Mr Jukes to his chum in the Western ocean trade, out of the fulness of his heart and the liveliness of his fancy.

He had expressed his honest opinion. It was not worth while trying to impress a man of that sort. If the world had been full of such men, life would have probably appeared to Jukes an unentertaining and unprofitable business. He was not alone in his opinion. The sea itself, as if sharing Mr Jukes's good-natured forbearance, had never put itself out to startle the silent man, who seldom looked up, and wandered innocently over the waters with the only visible purpose of getting food, raiment, and house-room for three people ashore. (*Typhoon*, p. 18)

What we are led to expect from this passage is that when it *does* put itself out, the sea may well discover depths in MacWhirr invisible to Jukes, perhaps, indeed, still only potentialities waiting to be called into existence by the typhoon. MacWhirr's lack of imagination is thus related to a lack of extreme experiences on his part.

he had never been given a glimpse of immeasurable strength and of immoderate wrath, the wrath that passes exhausted but never appeased – the wrath and fury of the passionate sea. He knew it existed, as we know that crime and abominations exist; he had heard of it as a peaceable citizen in a town hears of battles, famines, and floods, and yet knows nothing of what these things mean – though, indeed, he may have been mixed up in a street row, have gone without his dinner once, or been soaked to his skin in a shower. Captain MacWhirr had sailed over the surface of the oceans as some men go skimming over the years of existence to sink gently into a placid grave, ignorant of life to the last, without ever having been made to see all it may contain of perfidy, of violence, and of terror. There are on sea and land such men thus fortunate – or thus disdained by destiny or the sea. (*Typhoon*, pp. 18-19)

MacWhirr's lack of imagination, then, is not innate: it is at least in part the product of his not ever having been made aware of the extremes of experience life can hold. But there is more to be said about this passage, for here, surely, is the evidence that for Conrad MacWhirr's experiences in *Typhoon* are of crucial moral significance: they are related, directly, to our ability (or inability) to sympathize with and understand the sufferings of our fellow human beings. This passage, then, takes up an issue upon which Conrad touched in 'An Outpost of Progress' a lot more pessimistically.

Everybody shows a respectful deference to certain sounds that he and his fellows can make. But about feelings people really know nothing. We talk with indignation or enthusiasm; we talk about oppression, cruelty, crime, devotion, self-sacrifice, virtue, and we know nothing real beyond the words. Nobody knows what suffering or sacrifice mean – except, perhaps the victims of the mysterious purpose of these illusions. (OP, pp. 105-6)

MacWhirr's ability, finally, to achieve that fellow-feeling with and understanding of his fellow human beings which is lacking at the start of *Typhoon* – to know something 'real beyond the words' – is indicative of a more optimistic view of the resources of imaginative sympathy than we are given in 'An Outpost of Progress'. Imaginative projection into the situation of another is possible, but some people at least have to be schooled into such sympathetic ability by undergoing extreme experiences themselves. Referring to MacWhirr's being capable of assimilating the reliable information that the world was to end under the rubric of 'dirty weather', the authorial narrator comments that 'belief does not necessarily imply comprehension' (p. 20).

This concern with 'knowing' is related to the work's involvement in the issue of communication. 'Knowing' is a prerequisite for full and successful communication. If we do not know what the words we use really mean, then we cannot expect those who hear or read our words to make intimate contact with us by means of, or via, these words. But if certain words conjure up a sense or understanding of a specific reality to two people, then these words can unite them in a common knowledge, a common relationship to that reality. In our concern so far with the use of the written word in *Typhoon* we have seen that this is a good description of the way in which letters allow for real communication between Solomon Rout and his wife. But not in the case of Captain MacWhirr: because of his lack of imagination, signs do not bring a distant reality to his mind. His response to language is – at the start of the work at any rate – similar to his response to other signs. 'Omens were as nothing to him, and he was unable to discover the message of a prophecy till the fulfilment had brought it home to his very door' (p. 6). MacWhirr believes that 'facts can speak for themselves with overwhelming precision' (p. 9), and writes home

> from the coast of China twelve times every year, desiring quaintly to be 'remembered to the children,' and subscribing himself 'your loving husband,' as calmly as if the words so long used by so many men were, apart from their shape, worn-out things, and of a faded meaning.
> (*Typhoon*, p. 15)

But how can MacWhirr expect to be understood through his written words by his wife, when he himself cannot use words to conjure up an absent, not concretely experienced reality? The language MacWhirr understands is the language of facts, and in making this point, *Typhoon* draws attention to the differential manner in which MacWhirr treats facts and words.

The China seas north and south are narrow seas. They are seas full of every-day, eloquent facts, such as islands, sand-banks, reefs, swift and changeable currents – tangled facts that nevertheless speak to a seaman in clear and definite language. Their speech appealed to Captain MacWhirr's sense of realities so forcibly that he had given up his state-room below and practically lived all his days on the bridge of his ship, often having his meals sent up, and sleeping at night in the chart-room. And he indited there his home letters. Each of them, without exception, contained the phrase, 'The weather has been very fine this trip,' or some other form of a statement to that effect. And this statement, too, in its wonderful persistence, was of the same perfect accuracy as all the others they contained. (*Typhoon*, p. 15)

For MacWhirr facts, not words, are eloquent, speaking in the clear and definite language that MacWhirr does not find in books. And of course to have one's interest restricted to immediate facts inevitably entails a limited perception of possible future events.

A certain qualification is necessary at this point. MacWhirr's concern for the bad lock on the door is – whether he is conscious of this at the time or not – a concern for potential situations which might require an effective door-lock. At the moment when MacWhirr's eyes fall on the defective lock, we are told that to him, 'the view of a distant eventuality could appeal no more than the beauty of a wide landscape to a purblind tourist' (p. 8), and yet by concerning himself with the lock MacWhirr is in a sense concerning himself with possible distant eventualities. Perhaps the point here is that fidelity to standards and forms of behaviour laid down by a living tradition of service entails preparation for distant eventualities, even if the individual involved is unaware of this. MacWhirr's concern about the defective lock shows how the collective mind embodied in a tradition can plan for distant eventualities unforeseen by the individual.

But given his own relation to written language, MacWhirr should hardly be surprised that his wife fails to find his own letters eloquent, fails to perceive a clear and definite language in them which can convey human or natural facts to her. Mrs MacWhirr's attitude to an absent husband and to weather conditions thousands of miles away is very similar to Mac-Whirr's own attitude to the 'dirty weather' suggested by barometer and seamanship book: supposition only. Neither wife nor husband are possessed of the imagination necessary to put flesh on the bare bones of language – at least before the experience of the typhoon changes the husband.

So far *Typhoon* sounds very much like a *roman à thèse*, a work written to illustrate a set of ideas in which the characters are puppets subordinated to their task of exemplifying certain issues. That *Typhoon* is actually much more than this can be attributed to the fact that it is also a study of *change*, of human development attendant upon the extreme experiences recounted in the work. It is only comparatively recently that such a view of the work has gained acceptance among Conrad critics. In his book *Theories of Action in Conrad*, Francis Hubbard argues that the crucial experience for MacWhirr is that he foresees the possibility of losing his ship, and 'has thereby been forced to give up his belief that only present facts matter'.[5] Hubbard cites in particular the following passages:

> 'Can't have . . . fighting . . . board ship . . .' (p. 60)
> 'Had to do what's fair by them . . . (p. 81) Had to do what's fair
> . . . (p. 82) Had to do what's fair, for all – they are only Chinamen. Give them the same chance with ourselves – hang it all. She isn't lost yet. Bad enough to be shut up below in a gale . . . Couldn't let that go on in my ship *if I knew she hadn't five minutes to live.*'[6]

Forced by the typhoon to think forward to possible future eventualities, imagination is born in MacWhirr; he realizes that there is a world beyond immediate facts which can be apprehended only through signs, tokens, omens, or whatever.

> The hurricane, with its power to madden the seas, to sink ships, to uproot trees, to overturn strong walls and dash the very birds of the air to the ground, had found this taciturn man in its path, and, doing its utmost, had managed to wring out a few words. Before the renewed wrath of winds swooped on his ship, Captain MacWhirr was moved to declare, in a tone of vexation, as it were: 'I wouldn't like to lose her,'
>
> (*Typhoon*, p. 90)

Behind this passage lies a whole philosophy of language, a belief that it is from the demands the physical world makes on human beings that language springs, fulfilling the need human beings have to express possibilities glimpsed in extreme actualities.

As I pointed out in my earlier study of Conrad, MacWhirr's attitude towards books changes from frustrated dismissal to reluctant acceptance that they can tell us something about aspects of the real world hidden from us, separate from our personal experience. It is a sign of this change when MacWhirr says to Jukes that, 'According to the books the worst is not over yet' (p. 81).

Two other things testify to the fact that a significant change has taken place in MacWhirr during the typhoon: his insistence that Jukes go below to stop the Chinamen fighting, and his ability to inject resolve into the despairing Jukes – to communicate fully and effectively with him. MacWhirr has earlier dismissed with contempt Jukes's use of the word 'passengers' to describe the Chinamen, using the dismissive term 'coolies' about them (p. 31). And yet it is MacWhirr who worries about them during the typhoon, not Jukes, nor the boatswain who, after reporting on the situation below, 'gave no more thought to the coolies' (p. 59). MacWhirr is now able to *imagine* what the reported situation is like, and what it may become, and this makes him more fully human.

> He was glad the trouble in the 'tween-deck had been discovered in time. If the ship had to go after all, then, at least, she wouldn't be going to the bottom with a lot of people in her fighting teeth and claw. That would have been odious. And in that feeling there was a humane intention and a vague sense of the fitness of things. (*Typhoon*, p. 85)[7]

This passage precedes MacWhirr's thinking 'I shouldn't like to lose her' of the ship, and this suggests that his imagination has been brought into action as much by his human sympathy for the Chinamen as by his becoming aware of the possibility of losing his ship.

MacWhirr *forces* Jukes to go below to sort out the situation there. Jukes, it should be noted, is unwilling to do this because of his *excessive* imagination; he is convinced that the ship is lost. But once he has done this (and, by the way, given the crew some useful inspiration), he is in a position to receive MacWhirr's philosophy of life and to be given confidence by it.

> 'You are always meeting trouble half way, Jukes,' Captain MacWhirr remonstrated quaintly. 'Though it's a fact that the second mate is no good. D'ye hear, Mr Jukes? You would be left alone if. . . .'
> ....
> 'Don't you be put out by anything,' the Captain continued, mumbling rather fast. 'Keep her facing it. They may say what they like, but the heaviest seas run with the wind. Facing it – always facing it – that's the way to get through. You are a young sailor. Face it. That's enough for any man. Keep a cool head.'
> 'Yes, sir,' said Jukes, with a flutter of the heart.
>
> (*Typhoon*, pp. 88-9)

The passage has all the signs of having a meaning that is of much wider application than merely to certain questions of seamanship. Imagination is necessary; one needs to be able to interpret signs, to consider possible eventualities. But these should never leave one to forsake the sanity- and humanity-guaranteeing action of facing the immediate demands made upon one by physical and human reality. From this point on we note that all contact with MacWhirr during the typhoon serves to strengthen Jukes and to raise his spirits. Hearing the captain speak to the engine-room,

> For some reason Jukes experienced an access of confidence, a
> sensation that came from outside like a warm breath, and made him feel
> equal to every demand. The distant muttering of the darkness stole into
> his ears. He noted it unmoved, out of that sudden belief in himself, as
> a man safe in a shirt of mail would watch a point. (*Typhoon*, p. 89)

In case we should be in any doubt as to the source of Jukes's access of
confidence, in the subsequent paragraph we find Jukes's thoughts adopting
a phrase from MacWhirr: 'She rumbled in her depths, shaking a white
plummet of steam into the night, and Jukes' thought skimmed like a bird
through the engine-room, where Mr Rout - good man - was ready'. The
'good man' is MacWhirr's formulation, and it is indeed to Jukes's adoption
of the despised MacWhirr's outlook, his obedience to his commands, that
his access of confidence must be attributed. (We should also note that
MacWhirr had earlier talked of firing Rout out of the ship in protest
against the engineer's swearing; we presume that his later characterization
of Rout testifies to a maturing judgement on MacWhirr's part.)

If we are to compare Jukes with Jim we must also compare the circumstances of both men. Jim's captain abandoned his ship, Jukes's insists
upon 'facing it', on doing his duty and striving to make others do theirs.
The implication seems clear: the responsibility for individual actions cannot
simply be allotted to the individual in question. What we are, what we do,
are in part products of our circumstances - particularly our human
circumstances. Such a conclusion helps us to understand why a character
such as Brierly in *Lord Jim* should be so shocked and dismayed by Jim's
jump, for not only was Jim's action in part the product of the moral failure
of his fellow officers, but there is the additional danger that it will
generate further failures on the part of others. The feeling that one's
colleagues are absolutely solid in their commitment to the requirements of
a tradition of service helps to encourage one to conform to these same
requirements oneself. But when one senses or witnesses a breaking of
ranks, one's own commitment falters (which is the psychological basis on
which strict army discipline is founded).

We note, however, that whilst the lessons learned by MacWhirr
during the typhoon seem to have stuck, Jukes appears to revert to his old
self in his final letter to the Western Ocean trade chum. Some individuals,
Typhoon seems to suggest, can successfully internalize the requirements of
a tradition, while others need the permanent support and discipline
provided by a strong and living external tradition, by their fellows. In the
difference between Jukes and MacWhirr we can find what we can see as
Catholic and Protestant views of the road to salvation: through membership of a strong church which will provide the discipline the individual
lacks, or by means of the development of inner resources sufficient to cope
with unforeseen eventualities. As a whole, *Typhoon* opts for neither

extreme. Human beings are seen to be dependent both on their inner resources and also on example and encouragement from their fellows.

I have compared *Typhoon* to Smollett's novel *Humphry Clinker*, but in one respect this comparison does not hold at all. Because *Typhoon* is not a pure epistolary novel but has a narrator possessed of more than human knowledge, a consistency of narrative *tone* not to be found in Smollett's novel is a striking feature of *Typhoon*. The narrative voice we encounter is both pitying and sympathetic, fatalistic (even wearily so at times) and ironic.

I use the term 'possessed of more than human knowledge' rather than 'omniscient' because at times in *Typhoon* the narrator admits to ignorance.

> Yet the uninteresting lives of men so entirely given to the actuality of the bare existence have their mysterious side. It was impossible in Captain MacWhirr's case, for instance, to understand what under heaven could have induced that perfectly satisfactory son of a petty grocer in Belfast to run away to sea. And yet he had done that very thing at the age of fifteen. It was enough, when you thought it over, to give you the idea of an immense, potent, and invisible hand thrust into the ant-heaps of the earth, laying hold of shoulders, knocking heads together, and setting the unconscious faces of the multitude towards inconceivable goals and in undreamt-of directions. (*Typhoon*, pp. 4-5)

The tone generated by passages such as this is crucial to the overall effect of *Typhoon* upon the reader. 'It was enough, when you thought it over': the voice of the narrator is recognizably human – expressing quizzical bemusement at MacWhirr's unexpected action but appealing to a shared pool of human experience to which both narrator and reader have access. But it is also god-like in its distanced view of the human participants in the narrative – an impression strengthened by the ant-heap example, with its talk of 'inconceivable goals' and 'undreamt-of directions'. Human beings, in this view, are necessarily ignorant of what the future holds in store for them.

One particular characteristic of the narrative of *Typhoon* is its heavy reliance upon simile. The similes which we find in the work are, additionally, of a particular sort: presenting the reader with unexpected, often grotesque comparisons.

> A dense bank of cloud became visible to the northward; it had a sinister dark olive tint, and lay low and motionless upon the sea, resembling a solid obstacle in the path of the ship. She went floundering towards it like an exhausted creature driven to its death. (*Typhoon*, p. 26)

When she rolled she fell on her side headlong, and she would be righted back by such a demolishing blow that Jukes felt her reeling as a clubbed man reels before he collapses. (*Typhoon*, p. 43)

She was like a living creature thrown to the rage of a mob: hustled terribly, struck at, borne up, flung down, leaped upon. (*Typhoon*, p. 47)

The second mate was lying low, like a malignant little animal under a hedge. (*Typhoon*, p. 59)

They were keeping a full head of steam, and a profound rumbling, as of an empty furniture van trotting over a bridge, made a sustained bass to all the other noises of the place. (*Typhoon*, p. 71)

With a sound as of a hundred scoured saucepans, the orifice of a ventilator spat upon his shoulder a sudden gush of salt water ....
(*Typhoon*, p. 71)

The boatswain, with one leg and one arm embracing a stanchion, struggled with a lamp pressed to his breast, trying to get a light, and growling all the time like an industrious gorilla. (*Typhoon*, p. 79)

He noted it unmoved, out of that sudden belief in himself, as a man safe in a shirt of mail would watch a point. (*Typhoon*, p. 89)

Jukes' thought skimmed like a bird through the engine-room ....
(*Typhoon*, p. 89)

It is the narrator who sees these similarities, not the characters themselves, and this perception seems nearly always to have the effect of reducing the importance – or self-importance – of the situations or characters concerned. The characters are fighting heroically for their lives: the narrator thinks of saucepans, gorillas and furniture vans. By this means the limitations of the characters and their imaginations are underscored; from the perspective of the detached narrator the characters and their experiences seem as much ludicrous as heroic. The repeated use of bathetic similes forces *us* to use our imaginations much as the typhoon forces MacWhirr to use (or discover) his; we can no longer confine our outlook to that of the characters themselves, but have to set characters in the context of an indifferent and violent universe. Thus the very tone of *Typhoon* contributes to our sense of human limitations, of the absolute necessity for us to escape from our imprisonment by the demands of immediate experiences and to collaborate with our fellows to overcome the restrictions of our own puny intellects and foresight.

1 Stephen K. Land, *Conrad and the Paradox of Plot*, London, Macmillan, 1984, p. 92.
2 Land, p. 92
3 Land, p. 93.
4 'This is my first attempt at treating a subject jocularly so to speak'. Letter to J. B. Pinker, ?November 1900, CLJC 2, p. 304.
5 Francis A. Hubbard, *Theories of Action in Conrad*, Ann Arbor, UMI Press, 1984, p. 16.
6 Hubbard, p. 88, Hubbard's emphasis.
7 As is often the case in *Typhoon*, it is important to register the use of represented thought here; the penultimate and ante-penultimate sentences in the quoted extract give us MacWhirr's thoughts, not the comments of an authorial narrator.

9
Under Western Eyes and the Expressive Body

'What can the prejudice of the world reproach me with? Have I provoked his confidence? No! Have I by a single word, look, or gesture given him reason to suppose that I accepted his trust in me? No!'

(UWE, p. 38)

Arguing with himself immediately after having decided to betray Haldin, Razumov assesses the extent of his personal obligation to the fugitive assassin early on in *Under Western Eyes*. At this point in the novel Razumov's view of an individual's moral responsibility to others is clearly individualist, assuming that such responsibility can be contractually established only by means of the free assent of both parties. In this view of human relationships, individuals are like limited companies: their contractual obligations constitute the outer limits of their duties. And the means whereby these contracts are effected are carefully spelled out: words, looks, gestures. *Under Western Eyes* is reiteratively preoccupied with these three areas of human communication, with human word language, facial expression and eye-contact, and what we can call bodily communication. Conrad's concern with language and with 'seeing' in the novel has received considerable critical attention already, but it has not always been recognized that the communicative and expressive potentialities of the physical human body are also closely scrutinized in this work.

Writing in chapter 1 about Razumov's attempt to use language to deal with the enormous problems he has to face after Haldin's appearance in his room, I contrasted this reliance on language with the disillusioned view of language held by the teacher of languages. *Under Western Eyes* is a novel which examines the case for and against language in considerable detail. But it does not do so in a vacuum. Our use of language continually intermeshes with other forms of expressive and communicative behaviour – especially in direct interpersonal contact. The words that a character such as Peter Ivanovitch uses are received by Razumov alongside the evidence of other senses – especially that of sight. *Under Western Eyes* is full of references to eyes, to seeing (both real and hallucinatory), but it is also full of references to the expressive physical disposition of the human body: posture, gesture, movement, touch, expression. Moreover, such deep-rooted forms of communication (older by far than is human word language) are seen very often to have a force, subtlety and sophistication that goes way beyond the reaches of language. More specifically, while Razumov is able to use language to refer to human beings in a way that distances him from their humanity, this humanity and its moral implications force themselves upon him in a number of immediate personal confrontations.

An insight into this power of physical presence to evoke complex human truths comes to the teacher of languages towards the end of the novel, when he catches sight of the motionless figure of Mrs Haldin, inclined slightly forward, with a pale hand resting on the arm of the chair and with her white head bowed.

> The thought that the real drama of autocracy is not played on the great stage of politics came to me as, fated to be a spectator, I had this other glimpse behind the scenes, something more profound than the words and gestures of the public play. (UWE, pp. 338-9)

Mrs Haldin is wordless and motionless, and yet what she presents to the teacher of languages is more profound than the words and gestures of the public play; her posture is a window on the otherwise concealed world of private suffering, the backstage truth behind the publicly acted performance. The theatrical image used by Conrad is a revealing one: *Under Western Eyes* is a work much occupied with questions of concealment and openness, with the interlocking relationship between privacy and public performance. 'Acting a part' before a critical or unsympathetic audience is what many characters in the novel are forced to do; Razumov most of all. The backstage truth behind this acting is revealed on occasions by language, but it is often the eyes rather than the ears which pierce deception and falsity in *Under Western Eyes*. During Razumov's long discussions with Sophia Antonovna, as I will argue, what she sees, and the effect of her physical presence, are as crucial as what either character says to the other.

Soon after the passage I quoted above, immediately following Razumov's first confession, Nathalie Haldin points mournfully to the 'tragic immobility' of her mother. The teacher of languages comments:

> That gesture had an unequalled force of expression, so far-reaching in its human distress that one could not believe that it pointed out merely the ruthless working of political institutions. (UWE, p. 355)

As I commented in chapter 1, we should remember that Razumov's first confession is effected wordlessly: he presses 'a denunciatory finger to his breast with force'. Here, a few lines further on in the novel, another act of pointing is described as having 'an unequalled force of expression'. In this novel so overtly concerned with words, with language, a novel in which the main character talks (and writes) obsessively to himself, some of the most dramatic and expressive acts of communication are gestural. It is wholly appropriate that the epigraph to *Under Western Eyes*, taken (slightly changed) from the text of the work itself, should portray the obtaining of freedom as a physical action saturated with expressive force.

Razumov's confession to Nathalie seems to have a multiple motivation. It is in many ways the culminating point in his process of discovery, discovery of a range of responsibilities.[1] Immediately, it is his conversation with Nathalie which prompts the confession that is no longer forced upon him; Razumov is affected by the words they speak to each other. But reading the confession scene, and also Razumov's later account of it, it becomes clear that the physical presence of both Nathalie and her mother has a crucial determining effect, one which may be as important in bringing home his human responsibilities to Razumov as are the words he hears and utters.

> The convulsive, uncontrolled tone of the last words disclosed the precarious hold he had over himself. He was like a man defying his own dizziness in high places and tottering suddenly on the very edge of the precipice. Miss Haldin pressed her hand to her breast. The dropped black veil lay on the floor between them. Her movement steadied him. He looked intently on that hand till it descended slowly, and then raised again his eyes to her face. (UWE, pp. 349-50)

When Razumov comes to write of the confession, it is upon Nathalie's physical presence that he concentrates his attention.

> 'You were defenceless – and soon, very soon, you would be alone. . . . I thought of you. Defenceless. For days you have talked with me – opening your heart. I remembered the shadow of your eyelashes over your grey trustful eyes. And your pure forehead! It is low like the forehead of statues – calm, unstained. It was as if your pure brow bore a light which fell on me, searched my heart and saved me from ignominy, from ultimate undoing. And it saved you too. Pardon my presumption. But there was that in your glances which seemed to tell me that you . . . Your light! Your truth! I felt that I must tell you that I had ended by loving you. And to tell you that I must first confess. Confess, go out – and perish.
> 'Suddenly you stood before me! (UWE, p. 361)

It is necessary that Nathalie stand before Razumov. After his betrayal of Haldin, Razumov is shocked by the sudden thought 'that perhaps the superior authorities of police meant to confront him with Haldin in the flesh'.

This thought struck him like a bullet, and had he not clung with both hands to the banister he would have rolled down to the next landing most likely. His legs were of no use for a considerable time.

(UWE, p. 85)

What one can do to a person at a distance is not possible when they stand before us, 'in the flesh'. This is why Sophia Antonovna's questions are so difficult for Razumov, as they are accompanied by her physical person, and by her perception of his. And this is because our flesh is not just physical matter, but is expressive of our humanity in so many different ways. Razumov's confession, we are surely to understand, had to be exacted in part by Nathalie's physical presence.

Under Western Eyes does not treat words, looks and gestures as autonomous or closed systems. As we shall see, attempts to partition human experience and moral responsibility into discrete or self-contained sections are subjected to considerable scorn in the novel. We are left in no doubt that however much certain human beings may try to compartmentalize themselves or their lives, and to live in a world in which responsibilities and duties exist only in as much as they are voluntarily contracted for, the human individual and human society are – secrecy, fear and deception notwithstanding – indivisible. And on more than one occasion we see not just looks and gestures affecting language, but the reverse too. Take the following passage, which follows Razumov's thoughts during an interview with Councillor Mikulin.

'I must positively hold my tongue unless I am obliged to speak,' he admonished himself. And at once against his will the question, 'Hadn't I better tell him everything?' presented itself with such force that he had to bite his lower lip. (UWE, p. 91)

Not only do Razumov's words to himself have a physical effect on him, but it is one which he cannot control, a visible sign available to the sharp-eyed, displaying something not available in Razumov's public statements. In *Under Western Eyes* lips have much to say to those who look at them as well as listen to what they utter: it is the three most sympathetic female characters in the novel who are portrayed with quivering lips: Nathalie (p. 171), Tekla (p. 234), and Sophia Antonovna (p. 381).

Of course it is true that Razumov is shown to be unable fully to control the words he uses – either privately to himself, or publicly to others. He repeatedly rebukes himself for saying unwise things. And yet language is, in spite of this, shown to be more subject to personal control than are looks and gestures. This is most clearly so in the case of written language, a fact dramatically conveyed to the reader by means of Tekla's accounts of Peter Ivanovitch's behaviour during the writing of his great works. While his writing process is painful, frequently interrupted, and accompanied by bad temper and worse manners, his works read smoothly and present a far more attractive man to the world. As I have pointed out elsewhere,[2] many things are misread in the novel: Peter Ivanovitch's books, the newspaper report of Haldin's death, Haldin's letter to his sister – perhaps even Razumov's written account. Speech is also misinterpreted in *Under Western Eyes*, but perhaps less often and less radically. Involuntary statements or paralinguistic features cannot be edited out of speech; the originator's expressive presence cannot be so easily removed from speech as it can from writing. Nonetheless, there are many deceptive, misleading, and misunderstood speeches in *Under Western Eyes*.

People who are not accomplished actors have greater difficulty in controlling their physical movements and appearance than in controlling what they say, and to this extent such communicative and expressive behaviour may reveal things that the person concerned wishes to conceal – and would have concealed in his or her use of language. Even so, posture and gesture are also liable to be misinterpreted.

What *Under Western Eyes* illustrates is that we are *naturally* expressive, and especially so in our communicative physical movements – our gestures. However much our will may enjoin secrecy upon us, it is betrayed by a fifth column within us, a natural expressiveness that manifests itself wordlessly even if we are successful in disciplining our use of language. Various critics have pointed out that almost every character in the novel has his or her eyes and eye-movements described. But it is also the case that the same is true of hands and hand-movements. Throughout *Under Western Eyes* physical appearance, gesture, posture, and other forms of bodily communication are obsessively detailed. Such detailing is easy to miss, for it is rarely foregrounded, and often takes place in the context of fuller descriptions of human interaction which frequently fix the reader's attention on to things other than the described gestures. (As is the case in real life, when we are often quite unconsciously influenced by gestural behaviour while responding far more consciously to linguistic behaviour.) Gestural behaviour in *Under Western Eyes* is nearly always presented as part of a communicative and expressive complex which also includes words and looks. When Razumov first meets Councillor Mikulin he is simultaneously influenced by Mikulin's beard-stroking and by his tantalizingly unfinished sentences.

Life in a culture different from the one in which he was raised may well have made Conrad unusually aware of gestural behaviour, just as his adoption of a foreign language presumably sharpened his insight into aspects of language. It is when we are abroad that we recognize that the bodily communication of people in other cultures is governed by conventions different from those operative in our own culture. How near should one stand to another person? Does a shake of the head imply assent or dissent? What expressive hand gestures reinforce or qualify speech? We get different answers to such questions in different cultures, and this makes us more aware of the conventions operative in our native culture.[3] Conrad's son John has drawn attention to his father's un-British manners and gestures.

> I noticed that my father's rather foreign way of bringing his heels together, bowing from the hips and kissing the backs of their [women's] hands seemed to upset their equilibrium and some went so far as to snatch their hand away as though they had been stung.[4]

John Conrad adds a characteristic anecdote: when a padre and his wife visited the Conrads, and Conrad attempted to raise the lady's hand to his lips, her husband knocked it away saying, 'We do not do that sort of thing in this country!'

> JC looked surprised, then gazed at him for a short while and said, 'No, of course not. Now I come to look closely you have difficulty finding your mouth, to judge by your clothes! Good afternoon', turned on his heel and retired to his room, slamming the door.[5]

John Conrad also relates the confusion his father caused in a chemist's shop by raising his hat to a Gipsy woman who had been begging for old stock. The woman fled in incomprehension before this unfamiliar gesture.

In *Under Western Eyes* the reader's attention is drawn to the way in which Razumov, Peter Ivanovitch and the teacher of languages raise their hats. Tekla says to Razumov,

> 'Directly I saw you for the first time I was comforted. You took your hat off to me. You looked as if one could trust you. Oh!'
> She shrank before Razumov's savage snarl of, 'I have heard something like this before.' (UWE, p. 233)

Razumov's savage reaction is attributable to his recollection that a similar misinterpretation on the part of Haldin initiated his present troubles. Conventional politeness is just that: no more and no less. What it signifies has to be worked out just as carefully as has the meaning of the words spoken or written by a character. Peter Ivanovitch's ironic raising of his hat to Tekla prior to admonishing her for failing to prepare eggs for Madame de S— in the correct way is clearly deliberate in a way that Razumov's raising of his hat is not, whilst the teacher of languages seems merely to display his conventionality when he raises his own hat.

Before we look more closely at the text of *Under Western Eyes*, a warning is in order. We need to distinguish between the way in which characters appear, or behave *to one another in the novel*, and the way in which they are *presented to the reader*. Such presentation is itself a complex issue. Ostensibly we are reading the teacher of language's narrative, one which may adopt forms of presentation from Razumov's written account and attributable to him. But a ghostly authorial narrator[6] lurks in the pages of *Under Western Eyes*, a presence which is neither the teacher of languages nor Razumov – nor even the real Joseph Conrad. And it is to this ghostly presence that some character presentation must be attributed.

Take for example the way in which Prince K— is encountered both by Razumov and the reader as little more than a set of disembodied parts. Such a presentation indicates the lack of any moral coherence in the Prince. He is not an integrated person; he lacks cohesive and autonomous humanity. Razumov's first meeting with him is representative:

> To his intense surprise Razumov saw a white shapely hand extended to him. He took it in great confusion (it was soft and passive) and heard at the same time a condescending murmur in which he caught only the words 'Satisfactory' and 'Persevere'. But the most amazing thing of all was to feel suddenly a distinct pressure of the white shapely hand just before it was withdrawn: a light pressure like a secret sign.
>
> (UWE, p. 12)

The Prince's language and appearance are symmetrically balanced: asyntactical words and unfinished sentences, disembodied and discrete body-parts. It is never a person with whom Razumov feels in contact – merely a limb, a hand, a touch. When the Prince takes Razumov's arm after having requested, 'Your arm, young man', the younger man gasps, 'feeling unexpectedly in the dark a momentary pressure on his arm' (p. 42). At the start of their meeting with the General the Prince waves 'an impressive hand' (p. 44), and when the two part the Prince is still presented as an assemblage of disconnected body-parts.

> On getting out on the pavement Razumov saw an ungloved hand extended to him through the lowered window of the brougham. It detained his own in its grasp for a moment, while the light of a street lamp fell upon the Prince's long face and old-fashioned grey whiskers.
>
> 'I hope you are perfectly reassured now as to the consequences. . . .'
>
> 'After what your Excellency has condescended to do for me, I can only rely on my conscience.'
>
> '*Adieu*,' said the whiskered head with feeling. (UWE, p. 53)

Again we see the way in which a perception of the Prince's lack of physical integrity is echoed by his uttering of incomplete sentences. With the Prince, nothing hangs together. But *who* perceives this absence of cohesion? Razumov? The teacher of languages? Or that ghostly authorial presence in the text? Were we to be too literal-minded we would have to say that this information can only come to the teacher of languages through Razumov's written report, so that the perception must be Razumov's. But it is certainly not the perception of the Razumov who meets the Prince, for the passage signals clearly that at this stage he is less than fully conscious of the Prince's lack of moral or human integrity. Razumov is as much deluded victim as critical interpreter; it is surely central to a satisfactory reading of this passage that he does not perceive the Prince's inadequacies.

Nor is it likely that the Razumov who writes his report in Geneva, and who presumably composes the relevant part of it well prior to his first confession, is self-critical enough to see the Prince in this new light. He is faced with a set of incomplete clues to a person rather than a full human being and, assuming that such a human being must lie behind these clues, he seeks to interpret them so as to discover it. It is small surprise that, faced with such a task, his interpretations are no better than those of many others in the novel. Signs are taken for wonders: the pressure of Prince K—'s hand is responded to as to a secret sign, and Razumov begins to search for the code that will unlock its meaning. The signs of appearance and gesture, no less than the words of speech or writing, have to be interpreted. They are not unambiguous, nor do they convey meanings unmediated by conventions. *Under Western Eyes* contains innumerable misinterpretations, and these can as well involve gesture, posture, 'manners', physiognomy, as they can involve either written or spoken language.

Madame de S—, like Prince K—, is also presented to the reader in the form of a set of relatively discrete body-parts whose sum does not necessarily merit the privilege of a personal pronoun.

> Again Peter Ivanovitch tapped him slightly on the shoulder. Thereupon he bowed, and was about to turn away when he received the unexpected favour of a bony, inanimate hand extended to him, with the two words in hoarse French –
> '*Au revoir!*'
> He bowed over the skeleton hand .... (UWE, pp. 225-6)

'The skeleton hand' of Madame de S—, like 'the whiskered head' of Prince K—, is as insufficient in indicating full personhood as are the abbreviated names by which the two are known in the novel. We could contrast the description of Nathalie Haldin (who is known by three different versions of her first name in the novel), as she is seen sighing, and 'refastening a button of her glove which had come undone' (p. 177). Nathalie's moral integrity and coherence confer identity on to her clothes; if we contrast 'her glove' with 'the skeleton hand' or 'the whiskered head' the importance of such personal pronouns (or of their absence) is apparent.

The Prince's hand was ungloved when it was passed to Razumov through the lowered window of the brougham, and we are to presume that Razumov reads more into this detail than is actually warranted – that it implies intimacy, for example. The absence of certain items of clothing can be as meaningful as their presence. Gloves, veils and hats are scrupulously detailed in the course of the novel. A hat performs an important function in 'The Secret Sharer', written in a break from the writing of *Under Western Eyes*, and the significance of Mr Verloc's hat in *The Secret Agent*, worn among other places at the dinner table, hardly needs to be commented upon.

Nathalie Haldin's veil is referred to on a number of occasions in *Under Western Eyes*, and the reader is surely meant to have recourse to the familiar artillery of symbolic meanings that the word 'veil' is possessed of. Conrad comes near to semiotic cliché when Razumov carries off this veil after his confession to Nathalie.

Soon after this, Nathalie says good-bye to the teacher of languages.

> Her hand fell into mine.
> 'It's difficult to believe that it must be good-bye with us.'
> She returned my pressure and our hands separated.
> 'Yes. I am leaving here to-morrow. My eyes are open at last and my hands are free now.' (UWE, p. 376)

The force of Nathalie's comment can be explained only by reference to the recurrent and cumulative insistence on the importance of both eyes and hands in *Under Western Eyes*. The eyes and the hands are the two most communicatively significant parts of the human body, and Conrad's repeated references to the eyes and hands of all the characters who enter the world of *Under Western Eyes* plays a crucial rôle in focusing the reader's attention on to expressivity and communication in the work. We respond to these reiterated descriptions not just because eyes and hands are naturally expressive and communicative, but also because as a result of this fact the language is full of metaphors which refer to eyes or to hands. This makes it easier for Conrad to keep referring to eyes and hands without necessarily foregrounding the fact too crudely.

In some cases, of course, there is foregrounding. The reader's attention is drawn to the image of Haldin, in Razumov's room, lying on the bed with the backs of his hands over his eyes, perfectly motionless and silent (p. 23). The image is memorable not just because Razumov keeps recalling it, but also because it is naturally symbolic. Haldin's posture is expressive of his moral blindness and his resignation – and it prefigures his death (the eyes of the dead are covered). This last point is made explicit, when Razumov thinks back to Haldin's presence in his room.

> What was he doing now? Lying on the bed as if dead, with the back of his hands over his eyes? (UWE, p. 32)

But the posture is memorable for other reasons. It is seen again by Razumov in Nathalie's behaviour, and thus her presence serves to goad Razumov's conscience concerning his treatment of her brother. Indeed, when the teacher of languages sees Nathalie after her brother's death but before her first meeting with Razumov, she is described as sitting with 'her strong white hands lying inverted in the lap of her mourning dress' (p. 119). Even such a short description sets off complicated chains of association in the reader's mind, conscious or unconscious. For if her inverted hands remind us of her brother, the word 'strong' distinguishes her from such as Prince K– and also Peter Ivanovitch who, a few lines further on, we witness flourishing 'slightly a big soft hand'. We build up an estimation of different characters in a way comparable to the way in which we construct our opinion of people in everyday life – both by responding to what they say and do, and also by reacting (perhaps less consciously) to physical details such as the hardness or softness of their hands. And towards the end of the novel the intimations of death are again linked to this posture; after Razumov's confession to her, Nathalie is portrayed sitting,

> Her hands were lying lifelessly, palms upwards, on her lap. (UWE, p. 356)

Where Razumov's earlier betrayal of one Haldin leads to an actual death, his later, incomplete betrayal of the sister is followed by an existential death.

There is, too, a faint hint of the crucifixion in this recurrent posture, palms exposed. Haldin is the sacrificial victim, his betrayer is described as a Judas, and Ziemianitch is found in a stable.

The frequently *involuntary* nature of gestures is crucial to the importance they assume in *Under Western Eyes*. In an extreme situation a human being can always choose to say nothing (although this itself may have an eloquence of its own), but it is well-nigh impossible not to reveal one's inner turmoil in posture, gesture or movement. As a well-known study of human communication has it, one cannot not communicate.[7] Consider the following passage from early on in *Under Western Eyes*, in which Razumov is engaged in an uneasy conversation with the tall student.

The student turned his big hollow eyes upon Razumov, who said unguardedly –

'His people are abroad.'

He could have bitten his tongue out with vexation. The student pronounced in a tone of profound meaning –

'So! You alone were aware . . .' and stopped.

'They have sworn my ruin,' thought Razumov. 'Have you spoken of this to any one else?' he asked with bitter curiosity.

The other shook his head.

'No, only to you. Our circle thought that as Haldin had been often heard expressing a warm appreciation of your character . . .'

Razumov could not restrain a gesture of angry despair which the other must have misunderstood in some way .... (UWE, p. 74)

Razumov makes an 'unguarded' verbal comment, but 'could not restrain a gesture of angry despair'. The suggestion is that although one can unwillingly reveal what one would wish to keep secret both in speech and in gesture, the average person has somewhat more control over the former than the latter. Faced with the danger of saying the wrong thing one can bite one's tongue out – as Tekla declares herself capable of doing else-where in the novel – but certain gestures cannot be restrained.

To take another example. When Razumov is first interviewed by Mikulin, we are told that in the midst of his concealed fears concerning the interrogation – should he use the word 'mistrusted' or the word 'misunderstood'? – his concentration on the detail of his verbal behaviour is not matched by a comparable concern with his non-verbal performance.

And his head ached terribly. His passed his hand over his brow – an involuntary gesture of suffering, which he was too careless to restrain. (UWE, p. 87)

It is apparent that Councillor Mikulin is as aware of the significance of such involuntary gestures as he is of that of Razumov's carefully chosen words. Mikulin's own gestures are certainly far from involuntary.

Councillor Mikulin raised his hand and passed it down his face deliberately. (UWE, p. 96)

In such contrasts there lies an implied moral distinction. Razumov's inability convincingly to control his gestures bears testimony to a life in which he has not tried to school himself to the point of being able to control his non-verbal behaviour. It is a wonderful touch to have Razumov suddenly suspect Mikulin of wearing a wig during his interview with him: the reader is thus shown that at one level Razumov is aware that there is something false about Mikulin's appearance, that his surface is deceitful and not to be trusted. But this perception is not carried far enough into Razumov's overburdened consciousness for him to draw the correct conclusions from it.

A neutral exterior can be natural or contrived. We are told by the teacher of languages that his own physiognomy 'has never been expressive' (p. 143), and if we believe this (it accords well with his rôle as semi-neutral observer in the novel) we surely take this to imply something other than duplicity. Perhaps it suggests the poverty of his inner life. But when Madame de S— declares to Razumov that

> 'You haven't said twenty words altogether since you came in. You let nothing of your thoughts be seen in your face either.' (UWE, p. 220)

we recognize that Razumov's natural reticence, a reticence misinterpreted by Haldin, has been overlaid by a deliberate attempt to conceal and mislead. But the attempt, as we have seen, is not fully successful. Even the teacher of languages has earlier remarked that

> I caught in his physiognomy, in his whole bearing, an expression compounded of curiosity and scorn, tempered by alarm – as though he had been holding his breath while I was not looking. (UWE, p. 182)

A much more skilled and sensitive observer such as Sophia Antonovna is certainly proficient in the reading of silences[8] and expressive blankness, and gestures such as the following.

> He checked himself, passed his hand over his forehead, confused, like a man who has been dreaming aloud. (UWE, p. 257)

The fact that such movements and gestures are shared suggests a link between Razumov and Nathalie, his belief that he can steal her soul notwithstanding. After her first interview (that seems the right word) with Peter Ivanovitch, Nathalie asks the teacher of languages if he knows to whom she was talking. In response to his somewhat sardonic reply, 'Miss Haldin passed her hand over her forehead' (p. 131). Such reiterated gestures form patterns of connection between characters – in this instance, characters whose inability to control their expressive behaviour bespeaks an absence of practised guile.

There is one curious contradiction in the teacher of languages's description of Razumov's face which I should mention in passing. Very early on in *Under Western Eyes* the English narrator, describing Razumov's face, tells the reader that

> It was as if a face modelled vigorously in wax (with some approach even to a classical correctness of type) had been held close to a fire till all sharpness of line had been lost in the softening of the material.
>
> (UWE, p. 5)

This makes Razumov seem not so different from Peter Ivanovitch, of whom the teacher of languages says

> He had one of those bearded Russian faces without shape, a mere appearance of flesh and hair with not a single feature having any sort of character. (UWE, p. 120)

But much later on in his narrative the teacher of languages describes Razumov thus:

> His features were more decided than in the generality of Russian faces; he had a line of the jaw, a clean-shaven, sallow cheek; his nose was a ridge, and not a mere protuberance. (UWE, p. 179)

It is hard to explain this contrast in terms of a change in Razumov, as the teacher of languages has not seen the Russian before his arrival in Geneva. The change may well be in Conrad's conception of his character, a change of which he was insufficiently conscious to modify his earlier description.

Throughout *Under Western Eyes* Razumov is shown unable fully to control his bodily movements at moments of great pressure. Nathalie tells the teacher of languages that when first she uttered her brother's name to Razumov, 'He positively reeled' (p. 172). At other points in the narrative Razumov sways slightly (p. 182), totters a little (p. 184), and again shudders (p. 199). Given the novel's concern with truth and falsity, openness and concealment, language and silence, these are more than merely naturalistic touches. They provide evidence that moral isolation and emotional pressure can force give-away signs even from the person who is most dedicated to secrecy. They also, however, demonstrate that such evidence has still to be interpreted, and that it can be misinterpreted. Nathalie completely misunderstands the significance of Razumov's reeling upon hearing her utter her brother's name.

Under Western Eyes suggests that it is the more positive characters who have learned least well to restrain such potentially revealing reactions. It is the lips of Tekla, Nathalie and Sophia Antonovna which quiver – not those of Peter Ivanovitch or Councillor Mikulin. Peter Ivanovitch's urbane behaviour is as efficient at covering his hypocrisy and unpleasantness as is his laboured writing.

Our bodily movements are not just expressive. They can be consciously communicative (we can point at things), and they can involve direct contact through touching. To say that Peter Ivanovitch's hand is soft is not just to indicate its appearance, but to isolate potential tactile qualities. Given the emphasis on the eyes and hands of characters in the novel, then, handshakes are of great importance. The handshakes about which we read in *Under Western Eyes* are invariably of dramatic significance and revelatory of character. Thus when the teacher of languages leaves Miss Haldin early on in the novel he informs us that

> we parted with an expressive and warm handshake. The grip of her strong, shapely hand had a seductive frankness, a sort of exquisite virility.
> (UWE, p. 118)

This is a suggestively rich passage. 'Warm' 'expressive' and 'strong' are words which confer positive qualities on to Nathalie. 'Shapely' and 'seductive' give us a concealed warning of the undercurrent of sexual attraction present in the relationship between her and the teacher of languages. And 'grip' and 'virility' associate Miss Haldin with the slightly masculine Sophia Antonovna and her force and will. In contrast to this is the handshake between the teacher of languages and Razumov.

> Before Miss Haldin had ceased speaking I felt the grip of his hand on mine, a muscular, firm grip, but unexpectedly hot and dry. Not a word or even a mutter assisted this short and arid handshake.
> I intended to leave them to themselves, but Miss Haldin touched me lightly on the forearm with a significant contact, conveying a distinct wish. (UWE, p. 179)

Razumov's grip is at least 'firm', but it is also 'hot and dry' and 'arid'. It betokens a will devoted to a destructive and ill-fated purpose, one from which nothing good will develop. Again in contrast, Miss Haldin's light touch involves *significant* contact, and conveys a *distinct* wish: her body speaks in a precise and controlled manner. These are very limited signs, clues; but the text suggests that they are capable of being correctly interpreted.

Shortly after this scene Razumov takes Miss Haldin's hand which, prophetically, holds and retains his 'against a drawing-back movement' (p. 180). Razumov is to be 'held' by Nathalie in more profound ways – his drawing-back notwithstanding – before the close of the work.

Sophia Antonovna also has a 'manly hand-grasp' (p. 238), one which matches the 'exquisite virility' of Nathalie's. We are not surprised to read that Razumov returns 'the pressure of her hand with less force than she had put into it' (p. 238). In Conrad's manuscript of the novel we are told of Sophia Antonovna's greeting that it was, 'as though she had been a man, with a warm dry vigorous handgrasp'.[9] Here as elsewhere, Conrad's alterations between manuscript and published version (as between different published versions, especially periodical and book) clearly reveal a writer intent on producing an exact and appropriate description of the handshakes of his various characters. Sophia Antonovna's handshakes and use of bodily contact (as, for instance, when she slips her hand under Razumov's arm and impels him towards the gate) are typically accompanied by words such as 'firm' and 'decided' in the text; as Donne might have said of her, it is as if her body speaks, testifying to her intellectual decisiveness and moral solidity. It is entirely appropriate that Razumov should feel her scrutiny of him almost as physical contact.

> Razumov had felt that woman's observation of him like a physical contact, like a hand resting lightly on his shoulder. At that moment he received the mysterious impression of her having made up her mind for a closer grip. He stiffened himself inwardly to bear it without betraying himself. (UWE, p. 251)

Sophia Antonovna's handshakes are in stark contrast to those of less attractive revolutionaries – that of the thin conspirator he meets with Necator, for example.

> raising an arm that felt like lead [Razumov] dropped his hand into a largely outstretched palm, fleshless and hot as if dried up by fever, giving a bony pressure, expressive, seeming to say, 'Between us there's no need of words.' (UWE, p. 265)

Such descriptions have a cumulative effect, like the reiteration of a particular Shakespearian image cluster. The reader becomes more and more sensitized to what they reveal of characters and their interaction, and they have the additional important effect of charging many dead metaphors involving – to take one important example, hands – with new life. (The same is of course also true of many metaphorical expressions involving eyes and sight in the novel.)

Thus when Sophia Antonovna tells Razumov that what he wants 'is to be taken in hand by some woman' (p. 243), the statement, coming late in the novel, has a more powerful force than it would have in a more neutral context. It is, however, probably only on a second reading of the novel that the reader feels the full thrust of the early statement that 'All [Razumov's] strength was suddenly gone as if taken out by a hand' (p. 26). Razumov is shortly to meet General T–, whose hands are focused upon a number of times during the encounter, in such a way as to suggest the violence that is part of the man's character and power. It seems hard to believe that Conrad did not include so many metaphorical expressions involving hands by design. Razumov thanks Prince K— early on in *Under Western Eyes*, and 'expressed his gratitude for the helping hand' (p. 52): ironically, perhaps, as the hand is about the only bit of himself that the Prince has committed to Razumov's aid. During his first interview with Mikulin, 'Razumov remembered his intention of making [Mikulin] show his hand' (p. 96), and again the comment is replete with ironies. When Mikulin literally displays his hand and strokes his face, Razumov is puzzled by the gesture; 'to show one's hand' evokes card-playing, and the encounter between the two is like a game of poker in which Razumov is consistently outsmarted by Mikulin.

When the teacher of languages hears that Razumov grasped Nathalie's hands upon hearing the name of Haldin, he speaks of Razumov's 'welcoming your name, so to speak, with both hands' (p. 173). When Miss Haldin leaves the teacher of languages alone with Razumov the older man surmises that Miss Haldin's action was intentional, 'since, by a mere accident I had been found at hand' (p. 183). Sophia Antonovna describes herself as Peter Ivanovitch's 'right hand' (p. 253), and she is presented to the reader as 'the old revolutionary hand, the respected, trusted, and influential Sophia Antonovna', whose father, all the years of his life, 'had panted under the thumb of masters' whose rapacity extracted so much from him (pp. 261-2). Mikulin thinks that the revolutionaries have put Razumov into his hand (p. 307), while Razumov, alone in his room, feels that only there is he free from Haldin's phantom, for there 'it was [he] who had the upper hand, in a composed sense of his own superiority' (p. 300). A few pages further on, however, we learn of 'the precarious hold he had over himself' (p. 349), even though he believes that Haldin has actually delivered his sister 'into my hands' (p. 359). Such references to hands are paralleled by mention of trampling down, which seems to echo Razumov's experience of walking over the hallucinated image of Haldin.

Given such repetitive mention of hands in *Under Western Eyes* it is not surprising that hand gestures can assume an unusually dramatic importance in the novel. The act of pointing occurs in highly charged circumstances on more than one occasion; I have already referred to Nathalie's pointing at her immobile mother, and to perhaps the most dramatic moment of all - Razumov's wordless confession to Nathalie. But there is also Kostia's response to Razumov's forgetting to take the money he has stolen for him.

> Upright, with a stiffly extended arm, Kostia, his face set and white, was pointing an eloquent forefinger at the brown little packet lying forgotten in the circle of bright light on the table. (UWE, p. 315)

Conrad is highly suspicious of conventional eloquence, but when the word 'eloquence' is applied to non-linguistic communicative acts he seems normally to use it unpejoratively.

Symbolic hand gestures also play an important rôle in *Under Western Eyes*.

> 'Our three lives were like that!' Miss Haldin twined the fingers of both her hands together in demonstration, then separated them slowly, looking straight into my face. (UWE, p. 116)

The slow untwining seems to be as prophetic of the growing isolation of her mother as it is of the death of her brother, and Nathalie's gesture here is perhaps picked up at the end of the novel when she tells the teacher of languages that 'My eyes are open at last and my hands are free now' (p. 376). Her freedom is the freedom of loss as well as that of independence.

Razumov, in conversation with Tekla, makes use of a comparable symbolic gesture. Having informed her that he is engaged in dangerous work, she asks if this is under Peter Ivanovitch. When she learns that it is not, she responds

> 'Then – alone?'
> He held up his closed hand with the index raised.
> 'Like this finger,' he said. (UWE, p. 234)

Razumov's sign here, probably unbeknown to him, conveys his vulnerability and weakness as much as his isolation. All the way through this scene Tekla is nursing and caressing the cat, and her physical contact with the cat serves as an implied contrast to Razumov's raised finger. (In an earlier scene [p. 151], the detachment with which this same cat receives Tekla's caresses conveys something of the manner in which Tekla's kindness to others is generally received).

The word 'flourish' plays an important part in *Under Western Eyes*, and it is worth detailing some of the ways in which its gradual accretion of associations enriches the novel. The character to whom it is applied most of all is Peter Ivanovitch, and with him in particular it seems to imply theatrically insincere behaviour, behaviour on a par with his seeking after effect in his writing. When we first meet Peter Ivanovitch he is portrayed 'Flourishing slightly a big soft hand' (p. 119), a comment that, as I have already remarked, contrasts sharply with the earlier reference to Nathalie's 'strong white hands'. At the close of this scene Peter Ivanovitch, having heard that Nathalie may be expected to pay a visit to the Chateau Borel, snatched her right hand with such fervour that I thought he was going to press it to his lips or his breast. But he only held it by the fingertips in his great paw and shook it a little up and down while he delivered his last volley of words. (UWE, p. 130)

He relinquished her hand with a flourish, as if giving it to her for a gift, and remained still, his head bowed in dignified submission before her femininity. (UWE, p. 131)

There is heavy narrative irony in this description of course, and the use of 'paw' instead of hand (repeated a number of times elsewhere in the work) is presumably designed to remind us of the animal beneath the human veneer, an animal revealed openly during Peter Ivanovitch's prison escape. His flourishes are like his writing: calculated and insincere, a thin layer of refinement covering a crude brutality. Consider another example.

When he had finished a glass, he flourished his hand [in a beckoning manner] above his shoulder. At that signal the lady companion, esconced in her corner, with round eyes like a watchful animal, would dart out to the table and pour him another tumblerful. (UWE, p. 218; phrase in square brackets in Conrad's manuscript but deleted from the published version).

It is not just Peter Ivanovitch who flourishes his hand in *Under Western Eyes*, however. At the start of the novel it is Haldin, who, telling Razumov about the assassination, 'now and then .... flourished an arm, slowly, without excitement' (p. 16). Haldin's flourishes are, we presume, on a level with his rather glib use of revolutionary clichés. But Razumov is also associated with this telling word just after having beaten the insensible Ziemianitch.

When passing before the house he had just left he flourished his fist at the sombre refuge of misery and crime rearing its sinister bulk on the white ground. It had an air of brooding. He let his arm fall by his side – discouraged. (UWE, p. 31)

It is as if Razumov tries to play a rôle here, but is forced to recognize its inappropriateness and to drop it as he drops his arm. And, of course, we see here Razumov, unable to communicate with other people, communicating to an imagined audience. We witness this again after he has written his short 'manifesto' and has pinned it to the wall. This done,

he stepped back a pace and flourished his hand with a glance round the room [as if pointing it out to a crowd of silent and invisible witnesses of this act]. (UWE, p. 66; phrase in square brackets in Conrad's manuscript but deleted from the published version.)

If Razumov here imagines that he is in company, in another scene (p. 254) 'He almost forgot that he was not alone'. Conrad's manuscript includes an additional passage in which Razumov, 'half unconscious', makes 'a vague gesture'. Cut off from real people, Razumov invents imaginary ones before whom to act, just as his thought processes involve imaginary conversations with himself and with others. But at this stage of the novel his gestures are as indicative of self-deception and posturing as are his clichéd speeches to himself. His flourishes bespeak dishonesty and a concealment of his true motives.

Such flourishes are in sharp contrast to Razumov's actual bodily movements and gestures when in company. No longer self-assured and theatrical, we find repeated references to his 'stumbling', 'reeling', 'tottering', and so on. His bodily movements oscillate between two extremes: from sudden, violent, energetic movements and exertions, to excesses of lassitude and collapse.

Thus 'he struck a table with his clenched hand and shouted violently' (p. 27), he 'looked round wildly, seized the handle of a stablefork and rushing forward struck at the prostrate body with inarticulate cries' (p. 30), he 'stamped his foot' (p. 32), he 'shut up all the books and rammed all his papers into his pocket with convulsive movements' (p. 71), he 'threw himself back violently' (p. 192), and clasped his hands 'with great force' (p. 195). He also strikes his breast with his fist (pp. 32, 209).

In contrast we learn that all Razumov's strength 'was suddenly gone as if taken out by a hand' (p. 26), that he 'experienced a slight physical giddiness and made a movement as if to reach for something to steady himself with' (p. 77), and that when he hears the name Haldin from Nathalie he positively reels and, 'leaned against the wall of the terrace' (p. 172). With the teacher of languages 'He swayed slightly, leaning on his stick' (p. 182), and shortly afterwards 'tottered a little' (p. 184). The teacher of languages notices his 'unsteady footfalls' (p. 186), he quivers (p. 198), and in the garden of the Chateau Borel he stops on the first step and leans his back against the wall.

Many more examples could be quoted. These extremes and sudden alterations allow Conrad to suggest Razumov's inner conflict; they serve as signs of his moral struggle working its way out to the surface of his behaviour. And once Razumov has confessed, he achieves the self-control that has eluded him during the period of his duplicity.

Peter Ivanovitch is also associated with sudden and convulsive gestures. Words such as 'seize', 'stamp', 'flung' and 'flew' recur in descriptions of his movements; he may have a hand like a paw but his movements are not strikingly leonine. And the parallel between his and

Razumov's movements serves to underline the dangers of moral collapse involved in Razumov's acting as a secret agent for the Czarist authorities. Razumov is in danger of ending up like Peter Ivanovitch.

Often Conrad adds to an individual characterization by deft little references to physical appearance or gesture. Thus Necator is introduced as a character with 'lifeless, hanging hands' (p. 266), and a number of occasions in which the words 'hang' or 'hanging' are used may be the residue of Conrad's early plan to give Razumov the death actually given to Ziemianitch - suicide by hanging. Haldin was hanged, however, and three weeks after his meeting with Mikulin, Razumov, after watching the hands (!) of his watch, is also associated with the word 'hanging'.

> 'And, after all,' he thought suddenly, 'I might have been the chosen instrument of Providence. This is a manner of speaking, but there may be truth in every manner of speaking. What if that absurd saying were true in its essence?'
>
> He meditated for a while, then sat down, his legs stretched out, with stony eyes, and with his arms hanging down each side of the chair like a man totally abandoned by Providence - desolate. (UWE, p. 301)

The echoes of the crucifixion and of Judas's betrayal of Christ in this passage seem deliberate. Judas was in a sense the instrument of Providence but he was also totally abandoned by this same Providence, and in a novel so saturated with Biblical echoes and references such parallels seem unlikely to be accidental.

One of the most pregnant references to gesture and manner in *Under Western Eyes* comes towards the end of the novel, during the last meeting between Miss Haldin and the teacher of languages.

> Natalia Haldin looked matured by her open and secret experiences. With her arms folded she walked up and down the whole length of the room, talking slowly, smooth-browed, with a resolute profile. She gave me a new view of herself, and I marvelled at that something grave and measured in her voice, in her movements, in her manner. It was the perfection of collected independence. The strength of her nature had come to surface because the obscure depths had been stirred. (UWE, p. 373)

If Razumov moves from an imagined independence of others to a realization of his dependence on them during the course of the novel, Nathalie's development is in the opposite direction. From an excessive dependence on others (her brother in particular), she matures into 'the perfection of collected independence'. It is not that she now feels free of other people, but that she recognizes the autonomy of her own moral responsibility and the need for her self to be 'collected' if such moral responsibility is effectively to be exercised. But note that this new 'perfection' can be witnessed 'in her voice, in her movements, in her manner'. As I remarked of Sophia Antonovna, her body speaks her self; it is in her communicative behaviour, her bodily expression, as much as in her language, that her maturity is spoken forth. It would be hard to find clearer testimony to Conrad's belief that a person's total personality is revealed in 'word, look, [and] gesture'.

This belief is not inaccurately described as, among other things, aesthetic in its essence. Razumov's growing moral awareness comes not just from people, but from art as well. When Razumov waits with Prince K– to see General T–, the Prince comments upon a statue in the room in which they are waiting.

> Filling a corner, on a black pedestal, stood a quarter-life-size smooth-limbed bronze of an adolescent figure, running. The Prince observed in an undertone –
> 'Spontini's. "Flight of Youth." Exquisite.'
> 'Admirable,' assented Razumov faintly. (UWE, p. 43)

The Prince's response seems clearly meant as an object lesson in how not to benefit from the richness of art; it is 'aesthetic' in a negative sense. His comment is both that of the ivory-tower aesthete and also that of the bourgeois collector, starting with the name of the artist and ending with an 'Exquisite' which sees the statue as a thing in itself, cut off from any significant reference to the problems of living. His response is on a par with the disembodied nature of his whole existence. The reference cannot however escape Razumov, who is in the process of witnessing his own youth fly away. Razumov here is brought face to face with the regrettable fact that powerful existential meanings can either be read from the expressive body or can be reduced to triviality in the unperceptive gaze.

This at any rate seems to be implied later on in the text; some memory of the scene with the statue must, surely, be behind Razumov's response to Haldin as the latter leaves Razumov's room.

> Razumov started forward, but the sight of Haldin's raised hand checked him before he could get away from the table. .... Haldin, already at the door, tall and straight as an arrow, with his pale face and a hand raised attentively, might have posed for the statue of a daring youth listening to an inner voice. (UWE, p. 63)

At this point the connection is visual, and moral only in its aesthetic potentiality, but the seeds of later developments in Razumov's under-standing are already present. We must remember that from this point onwards Razumov has to listen hard to his own inner voice; he engages in constant argument with himself up to the point of his confession. So that there is a basis for identifying himself with Haldin through the half-consciously remembered statue, a basis which can contribute to Razumov's later realization that it was himself that he gave up to destruction when he betrayed Haldin.

In Razumov's final written message to Nathalie, what again appears to be a submerged memory of the statue surfaces.

> I remembered the shadow of your eyelashes over your grey trustful eyes. And your pure forehead! It is low like the forehead of statues – calm, unstained. (UWE, p. 361)

Haldin told Razumov of his sister's trusting eyes, and here it is as if a complex memory of Prince K–'s response to the Spontini statue has led him to identify himself with the woman he had thought of betraying in the way he betrayed her brother.

It is of course possible that it is Conrad the novelist rather than Razumov the character who is making these connections, and on a couple of occasions the teacher of languages makes comments which call the Spontini statue to the reader's mind. Responding to what he takes to be an indication from Nathalie that she wishes him to remain with her, he

> stayed, not as a youth would have stayed, uplifted, as it were poised in the air, but soberly, with my feet on the ground and my mind trying to penetrate her intention. (UWE, p. 180)

My own view is that there is an echo here, but it is difficult to say whether we are to assume that the teacher of languages remembers Razumov's account, or whether the intention behind the echo is to be attributed to the author's aesthetic purpose.

The same is true of a perhaps even fainter echo, when Nathalie is about to leave the teacher of languages Razumov later on in the novel.

> While speaking she raised her hands above her head to untie her veil, and that movement displayed for an instant the seductive grace of her youthful figure, clad in the simplest of mourning. (UWE, p. 347)

It seems to me apparent that on one level the reader is being warned that Nathalie's youth – like Haldin's and that of the boy in the statue – is about to fly away. The extract comes from a longer passage in which the 'timbre' of Nathalie's voice alongside a 'spasm of pain' affecting her features may all contribute to a complex effect on Razumov. But it is interesting to register that the teacher of languages

> perceived that with his downcast eyes [Razumov] had the air of a man
> who is listening to a strain of music rather than to articulated speech.
> (UWE, p. 348)

His response, in other words, is aesthetic to at least some degree.

I conclude that in many different ways *Under Western Eyes* traces a
development away from isolation towards solidarity with one's fellows,
and, paradoxically, away from moral subservience towards existential
independence. This is saying little new. But the extent to which these
movements are traced not just through language but through the aesthetics
of posture and gesture has not been fully recognized. Razumov's discovery
of himself and of his moral identity is accomplished perhaps mainly
through verbal striving. As the teacher of languages says of Razumov's
written record,

> In this queer pedantism of a man who had read, thought, lived, pen
> in hand, there is the sincerity of the attempt to grapple by the same
> means with another profounder knowledge. (UWE, p. 357)

But Razumov's moral maturing - like Nathalie's - is achieved not just by
means of words, written and spoken. It involves a network of sensuous and
expressive contacts with other people which are bodily as well as linguistic,
concrete as well as abstract, aesthetic as well as practical - and which are
available for interpretation by the right observer.

---

1 There is an extremely interesting discussion of Razumov's confession in the
   chapter on *Under Western Eyes* in Terence Cave's *Recognitions: A Study in
   Poetics* (Oxford, Clarendon Press, 1988).
2 See my Introduction to the World's Classics edition of the novel, Oxford,
   OUP, 1983, p. xii.
3 See, for example, Michael Argyle, *Bodily Communication*, London, Methuen,
   1975; D. Morris, P. Collett, P. Marsh & M. O'Shaughnessy, *Gestures: Their
   Origin and Distribution*, London, Cape, 1979; and David Efron, *Gesture,
   Race and Culture*, Paris & The Hague, Mouton, 1972 (first published as
   Gesture and Environment, New York, King's Crown Press, 1941).
4 John Conrad, *Joseph Conrad: Times Remembered*, London, CUP, p. 108.
5 John Conrad, p. 108
6 See my definition of this term earlier, chapter 1, note 8.
7 P. Watzlawick, J. Beavin & D. Jackson, *Pragmatics of Human Communication*, London, Faber, 1968, p. 48.
8 The importance of being able to 'read silences' is something that a number
   of Conrad's characters come to appreciate. In 'The Return' Alvan Hervey
   thinks back over the history of his relations with his wife.

He perceived in a flash that he could remember an infinity of enlightening occurrences. He could remember ever so many distinct occasions when he came upon [his wife and the poet]; he remembered the absurdly interrupted gesture of his fat, white hand, the rapt expression of her face, the glitter of unbelieving eyes; snatches of conversations not worth listening to, silences that had meant nothing at the time and seemed now illuminating like a burst of sunshine. (TOU, pp. 148-9)

There is also an interesting passage in Conrad's manuscript of *The Rescue* which does not appear in the published version. Mrs Travers tells Lingard:

It is good to be quiet some times – to be silent. There is often a closer communion in silence than in speech. ('The Rescuer', p. 284)

Of Charles Gould in *Nostromo* we learn that 'His silences, backed by the power of speech, had as many shades of significance as uttered words in the way of assent, of doubt, of negation – even of simple comment'. (p. 203). Conrad's interest in silences does not begin with *Under Western Eyes*. It is perhaps most fully explored in this novel however. During the silence at the beginning of Razumov's first meeting with Councillor Mikulin we are told that this lasted some time, 'and was characterized (for silences have their character) by a sort of sadness' (p. 86). As the teacher of languages tells us later on, when two Russians come together the shadow of autocracy, among other things, haunts 'the secret of their silences' (p. 107).

9   Joseph Conrad, holograph of *Under Western Eyes*, p. 238.

10
'The Tale': Conrad's Unreadable Work

Conrad's 'The Tale', which with one other short story comprised Conrad's total fictional output in 1916 (it was published in 1917), is a tantalizing piece. It is tantalizing in ways that call to mind Henry James's 'The Turn of the Screw', inasmuch as the problem of whether a narrator is reliable is intertwined with larger interpretative uncertainties and with problems relating to authorial intentions. Jocelyn Baines claims that the story is 'exceptionally ambiguous', (Baines, p. 488), and yet in his summary of it he seems to me to leave out a key constituent element of the ambiguity: the 'Chinese box' structure of the narrative. William W. Bonney argues that 'The Tale' actually contains four concentric tales, those of 'the non-human narrative voice of the story', the commanding officer's confession to the woman, the Northman's story as recounted to the commanding officer, and the 'inward voice, a grave murmur in the depth of [the commanding officer's] very own self, telling another tale' (TOH, p. 73).[1] Telling and believing are clearly central issues in this story, and the different examples of tale-telling have a cumulative force in the work, throwing light – and doubt – upon one another. If all that we had of 'The Tale' was the story of the commanding officer, it would certainly not be ambiguous in the way that the actual work is, in which local ambiguities connect and interact with larger ambiguities involving the larger theme or themes of the story, and authorial attitudes to these.

For all that there is a complicated patterning in 'The Tale', it seems to me that there is one worryingly incomplete set of parallels within the work which lies at the heart of its ambiguities: parallels involving the relationship between the commanding officer and the woman on the one hand, and the between the commanding officer and the Northman/neutral ship on the other. The story opens in a domestic setting with the commanding officer and a woman.

> It was a long room. The irresistible tide of the night ran into the most distant part of it, where the whispering of a man's voice, passionately interrupted and passionately renewed, seemed to plead against the answering murmurs of infinite sadness.
> At last no answering murmur came. His movement when he rose slowly from his knees by the side of the deep, shadowy couch holding the

shadowy suggestion of a reclining woman revealed him tall under the low ceiling ....

....

    The darkness hid his surprise and then his smile.

(TOH, pp. 59, 60)

The darkness and the word 'tide' are the first hints (appreciable, of course, only on a second reading) that there is a connection between this situation and the situation described in the commanding officer's story. The fact too that the commanding officer's second in command meets him 'with the breathlessly *whispered* information that there was another ship in the cove' (my emphasis) is important, as it echoes the whispers of the commanding officer at the start of the story. More hints follow. The woman replies to a later comment of the commanding officer's, 'in a *neutral* tone which concealed perfectly her relief – or her disappointment' (p. 62, my emphasis again). Moreover, the commanding officer's ship, according to him,

> was of a very ornamental sort once, with lots of grace and elegance and luxury about her. Yes, once! She was like a pretty woman who had suddenly put on a suit of sackcloth and stuck revolvers in her belt.

(TOH, p. 63)

So far, it would seem that we are faced with a neat parallel. The commanding officer does not know whether to believe the woman; he does not know whether to believe the Northman. Darkness and neutrality offer cover both to the neutral-toned woman and to the neutral ship. And at the end of the commanding officer's tale, when we return to the frame situation, the immobility of the woman parallels that of the neutral ship prior to its being sighted:

> The narrator bent forward towards the couch, where no movement betrayed the presence of a living person. (TOH, p. 80)

But there are other aspects of these two situations that do not parallel each other, and these divergent elements present the reader with certain puzzles of interpretation. It is as if the reader is being asked to put the last piece in the jig-saw, only to discover that it does not fit.

    To start with, it is strongly suggested that the woman is the commanding officer's mistress, that she is deceiving her husband with him. When the commanding officer reminds the woman that he has only five days' leave, she responds

> 'Yes. And I've also taken a five days' leave from – from my duties.'

(TOH, p. 61)

If we accept that the woman is the commanding officer's mistress, then in conventional terms, she is a 'guilty party', is (we presume) deceiving her husband, just as the Captain suspects the Northman of deceiving him. But the commanding officer is necessarily involved in the woman's guilt if this is the case. So that here there is a lack of fit between the two situations: were the commanding officer *married* to the woman, and suspicious that she was being unfaithful to him, then the domestic situation would mirror the larger situation.

If this were the case, 'The Tale' would be a simpler, but a less profound work, a story with a straightforward portrayal of an honest man whose professional and personal judgement is destroyed by suspicion. In neither case would we know whether his suspicions were justified, but given such a structure the strong suggestion would be that they were not.

There is one way to read 'The Tale' so that the parallel between commanding officer and woman, and commanding officer and Northman/neutral ship can be seen to be without contradictions or incoherences. The commanding officer's moral indignation is rather patriotically delimited. A present-day reader might assume that it is just as much a breach of neutrality for the Northman to take a cargo 'of a harmless and useful character .... to an English port' (p. 71), as it is for it to supply German U-boats. According to such a reading, we should register the fact that the commanding officer becomes enormously outraged at the thought that the Northman supplies German U-boats, while being morally complicit in the Northman's equally serious breach of neutrality in taking goods to an English port. This would parallel his double standard in conversation with the woman – arguing for sincerity and frankness while conducting an illicit liaison with her.

The trouble with this interpretation is that at the time the story was written it was not a breach of their neutrality for the ships of non-combatant nations to bring cargoes that did not contain specific goods defined as contraband to British ports.[2]

What alternative interpretations of the story are there? Do we have a fiction comparable to James's 'The Turn of the Screw', in which (according to many recent accounts of James's work) the reader is misled into accepting as reliable a personified narrator who may not be so – who may, indeed, be neurotic and unhinged?

First of all, I suggest that we must recognize that the relationship between commanding officer and woman is left ambiguous, that it is never confirmed that the duties from which the she has taken a five days' leave are her marital duties. Moreover, the commanding officer responds to her comment about her duties by saying that he likes the word 'duty', and by explaining that the woman thinks that it is horrible because, 'you think it's narrow. But it isn't. It contains infinities' (p. 61). He explains, in response to her scorn, that this could be an 'infinity of absolution, for instance' (p. 61). It seems pointless to attempt to deny that this exchange is ultimately ambiguous and opaque. It *could* mean that the woman thinks only of her conventional marital duties, whereas the commanding officer believes that some duties can supersede and override such conventional ones, and that it may even be one's duty to condone a technical breach of marital fidelity. But the truth is that for all the suggestiveness of the exchange, it is impossible to fix an unambiguous meaning to it - I mean on the literal level.

The commanding officer certainly believes himself committed to the virtues of openness and honesty:

> She interrupted, stirring a little.
> 'Oh, yes. Sincerity - frankness - passion - three words of your gospel. Don't I know them!'
> 'Think! Isn't it ours - believed in common?' he asked, anxiously, yet without expecting an answer, and went on at once .... (TOH, p. 64)

> 'But [the] commanding officer was in revolt against the murderous stealth-iness of methods and the atrocious callousness of complicities that seemed to taint the very source of men's deep emotions and noble activities; to corrupt their imagination which builds up the final conceptions of life and death. He suffered - '
> The voice from the sofa interrupted the narrator.
> 'How well I can understand that in him!'
> He bent forward slightly.
> 'Yes. I, too. Everything should be open in love and war. Open as the day, since both are the call of an ideal which it is so easy, so terribly easy, to degrade in the name of Victory.' (TOH, p. 67)

But *is* the commanding officer sincere and frank? *Is* he open in love and war? *Is* he in revolt against 'the murderous stealthiness of methods and the atrocious callousness of complicities . . .'? On the evidence of his own story he is not. First of all, he lies on two occasions. He tells the North-man, 'I've no suspicions' when we know from his own testimony to the woman that he is overflowing with them; furthermore, he tells his officers, 'I let him [the neutral ship] go' when we know that he has actually *ordered* the Northman to take the ship out into the open sea. (It is, I suppose, possible to claim that the commanding officer believes that he has no suspicions because he is *certain* of the Northman's guilt, but this seems a weak defence against the charge of dishonesty on his part.)

So that when the frame narrative reports of the woman that 'She knew his passion for truth, his horror of deceit, his humanity' (p. 81), the reader should surely perceive this statement to be deeply ironic, and at variance with what we know of the commanding officer.

There is more evidence to support the view that the commanding officer is less than fully sane. The test which he gives the Northman is the invention of a moral lunatic, on a par with that of the traditional way of testing whether a person was a witch by throwing them in a pool: if they sank and drowned they were innocent, if not they were guilty and were burned. If the Northman and his crew are innocent they will all perish – as they do.[3] Even so, the commanding officer's suspicions remain, he still is not convinced of their innocence. But if they are guilty they will survive – and will then be able further to evade justice either by denying the commanding officer's story, or by returning to a neutral country. It seems clear that when the commanding officer sets his trap, he is neurotically in the grip of his suspicions, rather than concerned to exercise justice or committed to sincerity and frankness. Indeed, it is almost as if he has decided that Northman and ship are guilty, and have to be sent to their fate.

But if the commanding officer seems morally crazy, so too does the woman. Having heard the commanding officer's story, she responds with sympathy only for him – none for the probably innocent men who have been drowned.

> He rose. The woman on the couch got up and threw her arms round his neck. Her eyes put two gleams in the deep shadow of the room. She knew his passion for truth, his horror of deceit, his humanity.
> 'Oh, my poor, poor – '
> 'I shall never know,' he repeated, sternly, disengaged himself, pressed her hands to his lips, and went out. (TOH, pp. 80-1)

This is, surely, an extraordinary response. At least the commanding officer shows some concern for the fate of possibly innocent men – although a concern lacking the appropriate level of self-reproach.

Does this give us a firm enough basis for claiming that the commanding officer is a supremely unreliable narrator, who imposes his own obsessions on to the world just as much as does the governess in James's 'The Turn of the Screw' according to certain interpretations of this work? Can we posit a deliberate, conscious attempt on Conrad's part to portray the workings of a diseased mind? Or can we, alternatively, posit what some recent critics have also attributed to the author of 'The Turn of the Screw': a deliberate attempt to produce an unresolvable ambiguity in the tale?

Some helpful clues may be found in a much earlier short story of Conrad's: 'The Return.' There is much in the earlier story that is reminiscent of the later: the social class of the man and woman, the melodramatic element perceivable in both works (the opening page of 'The Tale' almost parodies melodramatic clichés), the element of sexual jealousy and actual or potential adultery.[4] More particularly, the endings of both stories have much in common. 'The Return' ends with Alvan Hervey suffering agonies of incertitude and suspicion:

> He stood with uplifted hand . . . The years would pass – and he would have to live with that unfathomable candour where flit shadows of suspicions and hate . . . The years would pass – and he would never know – never trust . . . The years would pass without faith and love. . .
> 'Can you stand it?' he shouted, as though she could have heard all his thoughts. (TOU, p. 185)

She shouts back angrily, 'Yes!', but he replies, 'Well, I can't!', and strides out of the room and the house. The last sentence in the story is, 'He never returned'. It requires no forced reading of either story to detect clear parallels between them. What is important for our purposes, is that Alvan Hervey in 'The Return' is portrayed unambiguously as self-deceived, as imprisoned in a net of social conventions and threatened self-esteem which keeps him from communicating with his wife or from an accurate perception of reality. It thus seems worth considering whether we should view the commanding officer as more like Alvan Hervey than most readers of 'The Tale' have assumed him to be.

One problem should be admitted straight away. Alvan Harvey's wife is not an ambiguous or morally suspect character in the way that the woman of 'The Tale' is. She has been tempted to elope adulterously with the author of *Thorns and Arabesques*, but she has resisted this temptation. What is more, the marital problems which contributed to her temptation are seen to be very largely the responsibility of her husband.

But what we are still left with is two men each of whom is unwilling to accept incertitude as a condition of living, each of whom demands to be possessed of a certainty beyond doubt and suspicion. Is it not believable that Conrad was exploring a neurosis in 'The Tale' similar to that considered in 'The Return'? If so, it is quite appropriate that the Northman and his ship should present the commanding officer with evidence which is inconclusive. It is almost as if Conrad scatters contradictory evidence and clues in front of him. The Northman denies involvement in an immoral and illegal trade supplying German U-boats. He tells the commanding officer,

> 'Of course, nothing could induce me. I suffer from an internal disease. I would either go crazy from anxiety – or – or – take to drink or something. The risk is too great. Why – ruin!' (TOH, pp. 78-9)

But of course there is considerable evidence that the Northman *has* taken to drink: his drunkenness is confirmed by independent witnesses apart from the commanding officer. And yet this certainly does not *confirm* that he is guilty – any more than the eventual loss of his ship confirms his innocence.

The exchange between commanding officer and Northman which follows the commanding officer's order that the neutral ship must be taken out of the cove is also strikingly opaque.

> "'Must I? What could induce me? I haven't the nerve."
> "'And yet you must go. Unless you want to – "
> "'I don't want to," panted the Northman. "I've enough of it.'"
>
> (TOH, p. 80)

What exactly is the alternative to leaving the cove that the commanding officer hints at and the Northman pantingly refuses? Is the commanding officer giving the Northman the chance to continue supplying U-boats? I must confess that I find this exchange bafflingly opaque. Moreover, this passage provides us with the second occasion on which the Northman says that he lacks the nerve for something: the first was for supplying German U-boats, the second for leaving the cove. But the Northman *does* leave the cove; does this imply that he also supplied U-boats? There is no way of telling.

Then again there is the issue of the commanding officer's inward voice.

> 'The commanding officer listened to the tale. It struck him as more plausible than simple truth is in the habit of being. But that, perhaps, was prejudice. All the time the Northman was speaking the commanding officer had been aware of an inward voice, a grave murmur in the depth of his very own self, telling another tale, as if on purpose to keep alive in him his indignation and his anger with that baseness of greed or of mere outlook which lies often at the root of simple ideas.' (TOH, p. 73)

In general in Conrad the inward or inner voice is to be listened to, but with circumspection: in *A Personal Record* Conrad writes that, 'The inner voice may remain true enough in its secret counsel', and that 'may' expresses the central point. Writing to William Blackwood during the composition of *Lord Jim* Conrad stated despairingly,

> Scores of notions present themselves – expressions suggest themselves by the dozen, but the inward voice that decides: – this is well – this is right – is not heard sometimes for days together. (CLJC 2, p. 194)

But the opening of *An Outcast of the Islands* describes Willems's stepping off the 'straight and narrow path of his peculiar honesty .... with an inward assertion of unflinching resolve to fall back again into the monotonous and safe stride of virtue as soon as his little excursion into the wayside quagmires had produced the desired effect' (p. 3). Inner voices – like the voices of other narrators – may proffer good or bad advice; the commanding officer would perhaps have done well to have trusted his inner voice a little less, and the voice of the Northman a little more. It certainly seems to me that the words 'as if on purpose to keep alive in him his indignation and his anger' suggest a maliciousness in the inward voice which does not inspire one with confidence concerning its reliability or veracity. It is as if the commanding officer – or that part of him represented or constituted by his inward voice – is more concerned to luxuriate in his indignation and anger than he is to discover the truth (or to accept the impossibility of determining the truth).

What is for me the most striking parallel between 'The Tale' and James's 'The Turn of the Screw' is also perhaps the most difficult to establish: the way in which the reader is yoked into moral complicity with the main personified narrator. For just as James's governess and Conrad's commanding officer are unable to accept that full knowledge is sometimes impossible, just as both of them extract what they believe or claim to be certainties from essentially ambiguous evidence, so too the reader strives continually to find out truths which cannot be detected behind the opacity of the text. The reader of 'The Turn of the Screw' cannot finally establish whether the governess reports actual events or the projection of her own neuroses; the reader of 'The Tale' cannot determine whether the woman is the commanding officer's mistress, whether the Northman and his crew are guilty of supplying U-boats, whether the captain's narrative is that of a near-insane individual. And yet we try: we do just what the Northman does, we try to establish certainties on the basis of evidence which is insufficient to achieve this end. During his inspection of the Northman's ship the commanding officer perceives this:

> And the Englishman felt himself with astonishing conviction faced by an enormous lie, solid like a wall, with no way round to get at the truth, whose ugly murderous face he seemed to see peeping over at him with a cynical grin. (TOH, p. 76)

But he cannot accept this powerlessness, must risk murder in the attempt to break down this wall.

Jakob Lothe has drawn attention to the importance of the verbs 'to see' and 'to seem' in 'The Tale'.[5] Both recur several times in the course of the work, in the frame narrative and the commanding officer's story. There are also references to seeing in the Northman's tale. 'The Tale', then, dramatizes what was a central problem for Conrad: the elusiveness and inaccessibility of the truth behind the surface appearances of the world. And by presenting the reader with tantalizingly opaque and ambiguous surface appearances and 'seemings' in the work itself it forces us to become aware of the potentiality in us for the same sort of neurotic reaching after certainty that we witness in the commanding officer. On the penultimate page of the story the Northman admits to the woman that he will never know whether

> I have done stern retribution – or murder; whether I have added to the corpses that litter the bed of the unreadable sea the bodies of men completely innocent or basely guilty. (TOH, p. 80)

Some things, Conrad knew, are like the sea: unreadable. 'The Tale' is not just about such unreadability, it is itself in several crucial respects a work that is unreadable.

---

1   William W. Bonney, *Thorns and Arabesques: Contexts for Conrad's Fiction*, Baltimore, Johns Hopkins UP, 1980, p. 208. Jakob Lothe, who brought Bonney's argument to my attention, has a useful discussion of it in *Conrad's Narrative Method*, pp. 73-4.

2   The Declaration of London was not formally binding on combatants when war broke out as although all the principal powers had signed it they had not deposited their ratifications. The Americans asked the belligerent nations whether they would abide by the conditions of the Declaration; Germany stated that it would do so without qualification; Britain that it would do so 'subject to certain modifications and additions'. Under the terms of the Declaration neutral ships were permitted to carry cargoes not including a range of specified goods, so long as these were not destined for a fortified place belonging to the enemy or 'other place serving as a base for the armed forces of the enemy'. Britain announced that it would cease to abide by the terms of the Declaration in July 1916. Thus the information that 'It was in the early days of the war' (p. 63), and that 'The cargo of the ship was of a harmless and useful character. She was bound to an English port' (p. 71) is very important. See J. M. Kenworthy & George Young, *Freedom of the Seas*, London, Hutchinson, 1928; R. H. Gibson & M. Prendergast, *The German Submarine War 1914-1918*, London, Constable, 1931.

3   I am indebted to Bjørn Tysdahl for this point.

4   After writing this chapter I discovered that a number of similar points had been made by Gaetano D'Elia in an article with a somewhat different focus: 'Let Us Make Tales, not Love: Conrad's "The Tale"' (*The Conradian* 12(1), May 1984, pp. 50-58).

5   See his chapter on 'The Tale' in *Conrad's Narrative Method*.

Index